INDEPENDENT
MONTHLY
LITERARY
MAGAZINE

REVISTA
LITERÁRIA
INDEPENDENTE
MENSAL

ADELAIDE

Independent Monthly Literary Magazine
Revista Literária Independente Mensal
Year IV, Number 33, January 2019
Ano IV, Número 33, Janeiro 2019

ISBN-13: 978-1-952570-07-0

Adelaide Literary Magazine is an independent international monthly publication, based in New York and Lisbon. Founded by Stevan V. Nikolic and Adelaide Franco Nikolic in 2015, the magazine's aim is to publish quality poetry, fiction, nonfiction, artwork, and photography, as well as interviews, articles, and book reviews, written in English and Portuguese. We seek to publish outstanding literary fiction, nonfic-tion, and poetry, and to promote the writers we publish, helping both new, emerging, and established authors reach a wider literary audience.

A Revista Literária Adelaide é uma publicação mensal internacional e independente, localizada em Nova Iorque e Lisboa. Fundada por Stevan V. Nikolic e Adelaide Franco Nikolic em 2015, o objectivo da revista é publicar poesia, ficção, não-ficção, arte e fotografia de qualidade assim como entrevistas, artigos e críticas literárias, escritas em inglês e por-tuguês. Pretendemos publicar ficção, não-ficção e poesia excepcionais assim como promover os escritores que publicamos, ajudando os autores novos e emergentes a atingir uma audiência literária mais vasta.

(http://adelaidemagazine.org)

Published by: Adelaide Books, New York
244 Fifth Avenue, Suite D27
New York NY, 10001
e-mail: info@adelaidemagazine.org
phone: (917) 477 8984
http://adelaidebooks.org

CONTRIBUTING AUTHORS IN THIS ISSUE

Lisa Lebduska, John Riebow, Chrissie Molitor, Vivek Nath Mishra, Colin Gallagher, Taylor Martin, Alexandre Henrique Ferreira Campos de Souza, Nathaniel Zebley, Charlie Turner, Noelle Florio, Uko Tyrawn Okon, Ryan James Lamb, Daniel Davis, Bonita LeFlore, Taylor G Mauck, Susie Gharib, Anna Schaeffer, Marcia Eppich-Harris, Alan Berger, Ruth Deming, Ibrahim N. Al-Huraiyes, Essam M. Al-Jassim, Beth Burgmeyer, Iggy J. Louis, Nate Tulay, Matthew Conte, Kurt G. Schmidt, Mellody Hayes, Jennifer Nelson, Sara Wetmore, Timothy Robbins, Mettamodernist, Susan Ayres, George Eklund, Rikki Santer, Susan Sonde, Debasis Tripathy, Ken W. Simpson, Benjamin Biesek, Katherine Carlman, Daniel Senser, Ian Ganassi

CONTENTS / CONTEÚDOS

POETRY

FICTION

JIMINEY

by Lisa Lebduska

On a blistering July morning in 1979, Connie and Maria entered the smooth, moneyed chill of The Plaza Hotel, trailing after Connie's father Tom, who crossed its gleaming marble with the long, confident strides of a Marine. "You're only an imposter if you act like one," he had told Connie, and she tried to practice what he preached. But once they arrived, his advice vanished like cigarette ash wiped away by the maids. Though Connie had visited The Plaza with him before, she still faltered under the crystal scrutiny of the chandeliers. While Maria winked at the crewcut bellboys pushing golden carts loaded with paisley luggage, Connie fought to ignore the loose buckles on her gum-soled sandals, chirping like crickets with every sticky step she took. Against the noise, she could hear her mother's dark fable.

When I was sixteen, a man groped me on the subway. And that was when the trains had wicker seats and it didn't stink of pee.

What did you do?

I drove my pearl hatpin into his leg as far as it would go.

What did he do?

Didn't make a peep. I wiped the blood on his trousers.

Each time her mother had told the story, Connie knew which questions were safe to ask and which were not. What she wanted to ask but could not, was why, out of all the women riding the subway, had the man picked on her? Was it because she was so petite and delicate looking, he thought she would never fight back? Or was it because she was so pretty, he could not resist the temptation to possess her? If her face had been a plain oval and not a petulant heart; if her nose had had a bump instead of a slope, if her smile had not been so white and even, would the man have approached her? Connie could not ask; she understood that she had to take a single message from the story, as if it had been a bullet: men are dangerous. But she also knew that her mother's dark beauty gave her the courage to demand that the world treat her as she wished. Connie had watched her getting ready for work, stretching her lashes long with coal mascara, pressing a deep ruby onto her full lips that matched a perfect manicure and looking back at herself with quiet satisfaction. "You take after your father's side of the family," she told Connie, who, ever aware of her farmer features--a squarish face and wide nose--had no reason to doubt her. And so at fourteen, she had buttoned herself into her plainness, a protective cardigan she wore year-round, punctuated only by the moments with Maria when she was persuaded to unravel it into an unruly heap and set it alight.

A trip to The Plaza with her best friend promised an entire box of matches and a flask of kerosene.

Unlike Connie, Maria wore her looks as a striped blue bolero. Connie had discovered Maria in Accelerated Geometry, a class filled with pale doughy boys who giggled every time Mr. Kagan said "intersection of sets." They bonded solving proofs and blowing light pink bubbles that they popped with muffling, sticky fingers, under their desks, as Mr. Kagan covered the board in chalky glyphs. Maria cracked wise against a world of lust that both terrified and beckoned Connie, and Connie laughed when no one else dared. The sister of four brothers, Maria served as self-appointed Sex Expert, answering Connie's questions about penises, because Connie had never seen one in person. Maria knew things but as important she also knew how to say "please" and "thank you" and look adults straight in the eye, and so Connie's mother never objected to their spending time together.

By tacit agreement the girls rejected the chronic competition of appraisal that hobbled the friendships of other girls, and they guarded each other's secrets, including the panty girdle that Connie's mother insisted she wear, the closest she came to talking with her big-busted, blonde daughter about dating: *Jiggling gives boys the wrong idea. Besides, it's not a corset; you get used to it, in time.* Connie had not protested.

"Take them off," Maria said. "Unless you're getting ready for a shoot-out at the O.K. Corral. Bare feet are sexy."

"Not in the lobby of the most famous hotel in the world," Connie said, in between sandal jangles.

Tom led the girls towards the elevators, past the shop that sold the Cointreau-filled chocolates that he brought home every Friday along with morsels about the hotel's jeweled clientele. He told his family he'd hit the jackpot when the Plaza agreed to rent him office space on its deteriorating fourteenth floor: "Too dilapidated for movie stars, but perfect for me." His wife bought him expensive jackets on markdown at Lohman's and kept his hair trimmed close, taking care to cover the bald patch that had emerged on the back of his head like a pink baby.

Since coming to The Plaza, Tom had transformed from an engineer who worried about the stability of concrete into a celebrity authority who knew who wore wigs and who cheated on their spouses. He talked about movie stars as if they all rode the bus together. Connie could feel the fame rubbing off on her, a small, glittering gem she hoped would someday captivate the man who looked at her the right way. She wanted Maria to catch some of it, too.

"Mr. Basso, who's the best person you've ever seen?" Maria asked.

"You tell me." Tom hummed a few bars of "I Think I Love You."

"You *saw* David Cassidy. What was he like?"

"Skinny. He's no Gregory Peck." Tom winked at Connie.

"We're going to hang around here before we come up to the office, O.K?" Connie asked.

Tom ran his fingers through distinguished greying temples but sounded like an East Side kid as he said, "Buy yourselves some treats and don't get me kicked out," and pressed ten dollars into Connie's hand before he stepped on to the elevator. He had given them half of his weekly allowance, doled out by her mother. *Your father spends two dollars for every one he earns. If I didn't watch every penny we'd be bankrupt.*

Connie and Maria headed back to the lobby. Maria asked, "Was your Dad serious about getting kicked out?"

"The Plaza rented him office space when they were running out of money. Then rich owners bought it. Now they want to terminate commercial leases and renovate."

"They can't *throw* him out," Maria said.

"No, but management can get really picky about whether they're abiding by their lease."

"Screw them."

"It would kill him. Nothing's like The Plaza. The Beatles and Elizabeth Taylor stayed here. My dad's part of it, just by going to work. It's fairy dust."

The girls strolled to two brocade lounge chairs and plopped down, watching guests.

A gray-haired woman wearing a stiff persimmon mini-dress and white pantyhose approached the marbled registration counter. She looked like a lollipop.

Maria pointed at the woman. "Don't see any fairy dust there. Bet her chauffeur hates her."

"The rich don't care. They don't have to care."

"Sounds dull as dirt. Who'd want to join that club?"

"My father. Dad grew up in a boys' home—his mother ran away to be the next Lana Turner; his father was a drunk."

"I didn't know. Geez." Maria bit her lip.

"Maybe I want to join that club, too," Connie confessed.

"Why don't we ride the elevator until a famous person comes on? You can snap my picture with them, quick, before their bodyguard kills you."

Connie smiled. Maria always knew when to help her run away. Still she had to say, "It might be against the rules."

"What rules? This isn't school." Maria headed for the elevator, and Connie followed, despite the dread that prompted her to blurt out, "If they catch us, they'll evict my dad."

"No one's going to catch us doing anything." As soon as they entered, Maria pressed random floor buttons.

"We could get into trouble."

"We're just taking a ride. What would Dylan Thomas say?"

"He didn't know about elevators."

"Do not go gently, Connie!" Maria wagged her finger. "And don't act like you're forty!"

"I don't remember that last part," Connie teased back.

"Potential trick SAT question."

Fur Elise drifted through the speakers as Maria pinched her nose and danced the Swim, wriggling down into a crouch. "Mystery Date. Who will you meet when the doors open?" she asked nasally.

"A Kennedy, maybe. A big tipper. Someone with a helicopter."

"Anything else?"

"Smart, so I'm not lonely."

"You can't kiss a brain, Connie." Maria studied her cleavage in the mirror, pushing her breasts together.

Connie's panic returned. "What if there's a security camera?"

"Gives the cops something to watch."

"If my father loses his lease because of us, they'll ground me until I'm old enough to wear dentures."

"They'll still let you go to college."

"It's Good-bye, David Cassidy! No more Palm Court. No more waiters unfolding my napkin." Harder to explain, even to Maria, was that she wanted to keep seeing the triumphant look on her father's face when he told people where he worked.

"What are you--a poodle?"

Chastened, Connie admitted, "I'm the upside-down kettle sitting on a branch in a *Highlights* picture: find the thing that doesn't belong."

Maria declared, "O.K., Teapot. Take my picture!" She tossed her long, dark curls and pouted. Connie pulled out her Instamatic and snapped pictures, saying in a deep voice, "Work with me! Work with me!" until they were both laughing and out of breath.

Maria grew restless. "Let's go to the gift shop. This elevator's going to make too many stops." As soon as they stepped off, a tall man with a blonde crewcut intercepted them. He looked about twenty-five. Sharp pleats divided each long leg of his navy trousers. He had lapis eyes and a faint trace of Midwest drawing out his words.

"Hotel Security," he said, flashing an ID. All Connie could read was the name "Arnold." He closed the wallet.

Maria muttered, "Marshall Dillon, at your service, Ma'am," but Connie did not laugh.

"Where are you girls going?"

"The buttons were already pushed," Connie stammered. Maria rolled her eyes and asked if he knew Peggy Lipton.

"Come with me, girls." Arnold towered over them, putting one hand on Maria's shoulder and the other on Connie's as he ushered them to the elevator. Maria quietly mouthed to her, *He's a hunk*. Connie tried not to cry. How could she have been so reckless?

They descended to the basement, a dingy warren of rooms stacked with claw-footed dressers and worn velvet chairs, a garage sale for the rich. Arnold led them into an office drenched in fluorescence. Cigarette-filled Styrofoam cups littered the linoleum and a few brown metal folding chairs, which were scattered as if their occupants had jumped up and run away.

"Animals," Arnold muttered. He closed the door, which had a yellowed poster of Connie Francis that Connie recognized. She had been named after the singer, whose story was used by her mother as another cautionary tale: A woman earning a living on her own, singing in revealing dresses was easy prey for the lunatics who roamed the world. It was a miracle she hadn't been murdered.

Arnold grabbed a chair, spun it around and sat on it backward, leaning over the top, stretching his legs out in front of him. He looked at Connie with a sleepy half-smile, but she did not forget that he was her judge and jury. She wondered if he smiled because he was thinking that the two of them were idiots. This trouble that had landed on her felt so different from the one time she came home fifteen minutes late, which got her grounded for a weekend and disappeared over pancakes and the Sunday paper. For this trouble, her father could not plead her case between requests for the more maple syrup and quips about Charlie Brown's latest heartache. This trouble would reach beyond her to slap her father. Its sting would never fade.

"Please have a seat." Arnold gestured to the chairs in a courtly manner. He reminded Connie of the maître-de in the Oak Room who had ushered her and her father to a lunch of grilled salmon and asparagus.

The girls obeyed.

Arnold turned toward Connie and surprised her with the gentleness of his appraisal. "I think I've seen you here before."

She shifted against the clammy metal. "I come to work with my Dad sometimes."

"Well that explains it," he said, widening his smile to reveal a small dimple on the left side of his face. "I always remember the pretty ones."

Out of the corner of her eye, Connie saw Maria smirk, but she didn't care. She returned the smile and studied his face. His bright eyes suggested playfulness, that he wasn't half as serious as his job made him be. He was not as old or as serious as he was pretending to be, and as he continued talking, she convinced herself that someone else must have written it, maybe even forced him to memorize it.

"Our guests expect a certain level of decorum here, as you might imagine. It is my job to give them what they want, which includes ensuring that The Plaza maintains its ambience," he explained. It was a script spoken by an actor, just like the people who called on the phone insisting that a subscription to *Redbook* magazine would change their lives.

Maria nodded. "Yes, Sir. We understand. We're very sorry." She crossed her long legs, pointing her painted toes in his direction, but Arnold didn't seem to pay attention.

"I appreciate your apology," he said politely, then turned back to Connie, who noticed, for the first time, that his pinky finger bore a class ring with a yellow stone. His fingers looked strong and neat, with white rounded nails and smooth skin.

"You look like an actress. Has anyone ever told you that?"

Connie brushed a lock of hair from her eyes. "No Sir," she said, feeling that she had been pulled into the middle of a board game that someone else had made up. No boy had ever complimented Connie like that. He was looking at her in a way that made her feel pretty, made her feel seen, even in the middle of all the trouble they were in. She had to stay focused. Arnold was still in charge, and he had the power to get her father thrown out of The Plaza.

Maria broke the spell. "How old are you?"

"Twenty-four. Got this job right out of the army. How old are you?"

"Eighteen." Only Maria could lie so quickly.

Connie's heart sped up. Aronold was not that much older than they were; her Aunt Trudy and Uncle Rob were ten years apart, and they had four kids.

"Wow," Maria said. "This is a very prestigious position, watching out for all of these important guests. Will you let us go so you can get back to work?"

"Not so fast, Miss. Some of the most famous people in the world stay here. They don't want to wait for their elevators. Even when they're being ridden by a blonde cutie." He looked at Connie as if she had enchanted him.

Connie felt a flash of power as she gazed at Arnold. This must have been what Maria and her mother knew. She wanted to wield it, the way they did, to see if, when she needed it the most, she could get what she wanted. She tilted her head and looked deep into his eyes. "We really are so very sorry. We never meant to cause trouble for you or the hotel."

"I'll bet. But I'm in a difficult position." He offered a sad half smile as he held her gaze.

Connie leaned toward him, and touched his hand lightly. "Can't you forget it?"

Arnold sat up, expanding his chest as if to reveal something written on it. "I get paid to remember. I'm the one who sees what others can't. Or won't. I keep folks safe so they can relax, so they don't have to worry about the underground."

"What?" Maria demanded.

"The Plaza is just like Disney World. You ride Space Mountain, eat candied apples and walk around thinking it's the friendliest, cleanest place in the world. Then you take their underground tour and find out that there's all this garbage getting whisked away, below, so the tourists never have to think about stinking diapers and crushed ice cream cones. The Plaza is like that. I manage their underground." Arnold doffed an invisible hat. "Welcome, Princess."

Connie laughed. "Please let us go. We won't do this again. It was just a crazy idea."

"Don't you like your magic kingdom?"

"I *love* The Plaza. It has so much excitement, so much fame and elegance." She wondered if he lived at the hotel somewhere, in payment for his work. He probably dined at the Oak Room every day.

"Oh brother," Maria groaned.

"We need to get back to my father," Connie added. "He's going to worry." She rose, as elegantly as she could, smoothing out the wrinkles in her linen shorts.

Arnold stood up with her. "Oh, Princess, not yet." He grabbed her wrist.

Shocked, Connie twisted in his grasp. Arnold clenched his jaw. His eyes narrowed, his face hardened. Whatever power she thought she had had melted like a tear.

"Please," she said.

"Come on, Princess. If I just let you go, I could get fired. That's a lot to ask of me, isn't it?"

Connie felt herself detaching as she fought against the chaos of her thoughts. She wondered, for a moment, what it would feel like to be him. She wondered if he could see terror in her eyes, could feel the frantic pulse racing under his fingertips. Only the words of regret, of apology and contrition had power enough to form and she hated herself for that. "I'm sorry. We need to go. My dad is waiting."

He released her wrist. "You are so sweet. Those eyes of yours--intense! Maybe we could let your girlfriend go back upstairs and we could talk? Go upstairs to Palm Court later for some ice cream?"

Maria erupted. "What's the matter? Can't get a date?" Connie felt like a tiger cub being defended by its mother.

Arnold gripped the back of his chair, so that his ring rattled against the metal. "Mind your own business, or you'll be in more trouble than you've bargained for."

"We'll tell her father," Maria threatened.

"You'll get him evicted. He's not a real tenant." Arnold raised his eyebrows in victory. He had said what Connie had always suspected her father felt. Arnold had unearthed it and pressed it against her face.

Connie stammered, "He pays rent like everybody else."

Arnold stated flatly, "He's not the same and Management knows it. He's not ordering room service and spa treatments. He's not giving the doorman twenty-dollar tips or sending bouquets of gardenias to Jackson Hole. He's a working stiff, like the rest of us."

Maria stood up. "We'll tell everyone."

Arnold's face reddened, but his voice remained calm and even. "Go ahead. Your word against mine. Who's more believable? A security officer who served his country or a couple of giggling girls?"

"You can't do this," Maria said.

"I can do what I please. Today, for example, I feel like telling Management that her father," he said, pointing at Connie, "lets his daughter run wild, that she's disturbing the other guests, vandalizing hotel property, and putting them at risk."

"Please. It was such a tiny mistake." Connie choked against the whine escaping from her throat.

"You sound like the politicians that parade through here every October." His face had reddened; his lips had thinned in anger.

Maria took a deep breath and exhaled, never taking her gaze away Arnold. "Look you don't need to get angry. Let's think about this," she said, carefully. "I could use some spending money. I waitress and sometimes customers are looking for a little extra. I know way more than Connie does."

Arnold tipped his head back, narrowed his eyes and inhaled as if to catch Maria's exhalations. He appraised the two girls. "Connie. Constance. Beautiful name." He looked back at the poster on the door, then to Maria he said, "Maybe we can work something out. I like your hair." He reached up, and Maria bent down, her brown curls falling into his hands as he wound the ringlets around his fingers.

Connie's stomach heaved.

"Twenty dollars and no report to management, right?" Maria said, straightening. She beamed at Arnold, then caught Connie's gaze and glanced at her macramé bag.

"Agreed. A fair exchange of services between two consenting adults."

Connie's head pounded so hard that the room began to hum. The tiny freckles on Maria's nose--pale pinpoints that Maria hated because she said they made her look like a kid-- stood out in the harsh light. They reminded Connie of a trip they took to Point Pleasant, where Maria had taught her how to body surf against the cold, churning ocean: "Don't be afraid. Plunge in and ride!" Connie had winced and shivered at the salty chill and then, with her friend, stood in the sun against the gritty waves and laughed.

Maria sat down again next to Arnold and began murmuring in a low voice. He closed his eyes and laced his hands behind his head in a relaxed cradle. "You can watch if you'd like, Princess," Arnold said languidly.

Connie's mind wandered to the proud look on her father's face whenever he told someone he had an office in the Plaza, and the Munch painting that he pointed out to visitors, and the silent maids in their dark uniforms and flat rubber shoes who were forever wiping ash from burnished metal cigarette trays with their rags. She recalled the flowered Palm Court teacups, with eggshell porcelain so delicate she barely touched her lips to them. She wondered what would happen if she went there one day and, instead of sipping her chamomile tea, bit down on the edge until it shattered.

Reaching into her bag, Connie withdrew the camera, and aimed it at Arnold's square jaw.

She pressed the shutter release. Each click fell clear as a shot.

As she ran with Maria, she thought her sandals sounded like spurs.

About the Author

Lisa Lebduska directs the College Writing program at Wheaton College in Massachusetts. Her work has appeared in such journals as Writing on the Edge, The Tishman Review, Lunch Ticket and Narrative, among others. She lives in Salem, Connecticut, just off Witch Meadow Road.

AN INSTANT OF EVERYTHING

by John Riebow

The night air was crisp as he emerged from the heat of the crowded club. It was just after midnight and, thanks to a three quarter moon and a cloudless September sky, it was brighter outside than it had been inside the shadowy venue. He was soaked, scalp damp, underarms and back of his neck dripping with perspiration, a half round stain on the front of his favorite CLASH shirt. A breeze snaked between the tall buildings, down the flag-lined street, tossing leaves into a whirling vortex. He felt a sudden chill and the immediate need for a cigarette. Pulling the crumpled pack from his shirt pocket, he rummaged his pants for the lighter.

The smoke crawled down his throat, soothing and burning at the same time, adding to the powerful solution that was flowing through his veins. Despite the warning on the pack, he never thought about the dangers of smoking. Just like the beer he drank, everything these days came with a dire message from the do-gooders that did nothing to halt production or consumption of the offending products. The ciggies gave him a shot of something only a smoker could appreciate, like a cup of strong coffee that helped get him through the day, the benefits far outweighing the inevitable and injurious side effects.

People were still emerging from the club doors, mere outlines as the house lights blazed inside, while bartenders collected glasses and threw away cups, and roadies packed up the gear to be carried out to the waiting van. He was in orbit around the venue, a satellite caught by the powerful gravity of the gig, smoking as he lingered, not wanting to break free just yet.

What a show! The music had been so fucking good: a Paul Weller cover band, a quartet of guitar, bass, keyboard, and drums. They even did Jam, Who and Kinks songs to boot. They really killed it. And the audience was so down with everything, singing and clapping, bouncing, and chanting, "We are the Mods. We are the Mods. We are, we are, we are the Mods" between songs, while guitars were tuned or beers guzzled from the stage. For a time, it all seemed a bit like Pete Townshend's Lifehouse concept, where everyone in the entire world, the entire universe, was connected via a musical umbilical cord, one great, massive consciousness, melting into one another, a collective heartbeat. The connectivity now severed, his mind was still racing.

People passed him on the way to their cars or homes, laughing, screaming, singing. They pushed one another, hugged one another, pulled one another, playful and aggressive. Women giggled and men roared. One rather husky woman with thick thighs had a petite friend with wild hair on her shoulders, staggered across the road as the upper torso flapped its arms like a disorientated bird. He watched some of the hot legs and nice round asses in mini skirts recede into the night, wishing they might be going where he was going. But it was not to be. He looked for the cute blonde who was next to him for most of the night. She had been so drunk and so free, dismissing her disinterested boyfriend, or whatever he was, as she danced close and sang into his face, her hand fleetingly brushing against his cock. It was all he could do to resist the urge to kiss her. He thought about her regretfully, knowing the mystical and departed creature probably wouldn't even remember him, not doubting that the lovely spirit had to be a blast in the sack. "Bastard!" he spat, cursing his luck, cursing the universe, cursing himself.

The crowd was thinning as he finished and flicked away the diminished smoke. There wasn't much to see any longer; the gravity was ebbing, reality intruding. He supposed he had better get walking to his car, four or so blocks away. As his sneakered feet slapped the concrete pavement, the back of his ears were still ringing and his eyes were dry, but he hadn't felt this good in weeks and was so glad he decided to head out, even after Paul canceled at the last minute. Paul was always having some crisis or another. This time it was the psychotic woman with the ex in jail that caused him to have to unload his ticket on Stubhub. The poor guy couldn't seem to get his shit together but was a good friend nonetheless. It was a shame he couldn't be there to share this moment. It was weird to have been so connected to everything, strangers nonetheless, and now to find himself alone.

It had been a wicked night. And he so needed it. The summer had been a bit of a bust; all he did was work his ass off, and didn't get to do any of the things he had expected the season to hold: weekends at the beach, the three-day music festival in the mountains, or the week he was going to spend hiking the Appalachian trail. The show had been a startling high in a summer of relative lows.

He hadn't expect to break up with Carole either. Like his prospects for the summer, things were pretty much shot to hell that night, when, as she fell asleep in his arms during the French movie she promised was going to be so good but turned out to be excruciatingly dull (he was so bored he didn't even care when the chicks got naked), he picked up her vibrating phone from the floor and accidentally read the text. Seeing the first sentence had been purely unintentional, but once the evidence presented itself, he doggedly dug for more. To his immediate disgust, her phone was full of playfulness and sexual innuendo, something they no longer shared, so it should not have been a surprise that Carole was seeing someone else named Ted. But how could he not have known?

He shook the phone at her in absolute fury. Her face turned sad but he could not see any trace of remorse. If anything, she seemed almost defiant, perhaps pleased to have been caught out. "I'm sorry Jared," she sighed. "I really am."

"Sorry for who, you or me?" he almost spat. His pulse was racing and he couldn't decide whether to cry or vomit.

"For us."

"Us!" he said with a mocking laugh. "You're sorry you've been caught."

Carole shook her head. "I didn't want it to be like this. I wanted to tell you myself."

"Were you going to tell me before you left on the honeymoon, or were you just waiting to see if this other guy didn't work out?"

"It's not easy to tell someone you care about that you have met someone else."

He continued to be dismayed by her lack of tears, what he took as a total disregard for what they had. "But it's easier to let the person you care about find the texts that say you have the best tasting pussy in the world?"

The defiance on her face turned to sudden anger. "That was private! You shouldn't have been reading my texts."

Now it was his turn to be defiant. "Well, Ted whoever the fuck's text invaded MY privacy."

"I really didn't mean for you to find out this way, but things happened so quickly. This wasn't expected."

"Is that supposed to make me feel better, Carole?"

"No. Of course not."

"So that's it?"

"I am truly sad it came out like this. It just evolved."

"Like a fungus." He could not believe the expression on her face. She didn't look sad at all and seemed almost relieved that the truth was now out in the open.

"As things do. As we did. This was just faster. I wasn't looking for it."

"That makes everything so much easier," he scoffed. "Your conscience is clear because you were not looking for someone else to get into your pants. So, where does that leave us?"

"Is there still an us?" She asked the question as if she knew the answer.

"I don't think so. I don't know. Right now, no." He was angry, hurt, confused, wanting to lash out at something. He wanted to smash her phone on the floor and punch Texting Ted right in his face.

Carole seemed resigned, almost content as she nodded her head. "That's fair enough. I would feel the same."

"Would you? Well, la de dah." As much as he wanted to, he knew he couldn't physically hurt her, and even his words were failing him.

"I expect I would be pretty pissed if I found out you were with someone else."

"But it's ok for you?"

"No. Yes. Well, it was obvious we weren't going anywhere."

Her last statement was like she had picked him up and pile-driven him right into the ground.

"It was? I tell ya, it wasn't fucking obvious to me, Carole. I thought we were serious. Two years is pretty damned serious, right? But not serious enough, I guess."

That had been the end of May, just two weeks before his 28th birthday, a drunken night with his brother Nick, best forgotten, bar hopping for half the evening and puking his guts out until dawn. He was sick of her and missing her and wishing they had never met, but had somehow resisted the urge to call or text her. She left his apartment that night, not long after the fight, with her purse and her favorite pair of boots from the closet but never came back for the rest of her stuff. The books, music and trinkets they shared apparently held less value to her than their relationship. Aside from spotting a car that looked like hers at the Chick Fil-A drive thru window a few weeks later, he never saw her again. In a complete and tear-filled rage, he tore clothes from the drawers, scooped makeup off the bureau, emptied her prescriptions from the medicine cabinet, and stuffed everything with the faintest link to her into black trash bags that still lay in the bottom of his bedroom closet.

"One day, I'll toss that shit," he mouthed. "One day."

"Hey brother, got a light?" A voice came from the shadows, startling. Suddenly, the last night with Carole was a million years ago and he was back on the dark city streets, alone, as he had been since she walked out the door.

The question was from a tall black kid, not much older than maybe sixteen, in a dark hoodie and black jeans that hung low, wearing a backpack, leaning casually against a building, offering a pleading smile.

"Uh, sure."

He stopped, pulled the lighter from his pants, tossed it to the kid. The youth slowly lit his cigarette, warily watching as he brought the flame to his face, hesitating before he handed the lighter back.

"Cool. Cool. Cool." The youth mouthed, blowing smoke into the air.

"No problem."

He watched the smoke dissipate and moved to go but found a hand on his arm, not tight but menacing, certainly surprising. He realized the conversation was heading into confrontation, and like the girl in the club who danced in his face, he struggled to keep his urges in check, like his grandfather had taught him. If he had been anything like his worthless old man, he would have decked the kid and kicked him in the balls to boot. No matter how this boy tried to play the hard villain, he was just a kid, and after the amazing night he had just had, Jared tried not to think that the shadowy figure could have a knife or even a gun; he was just a kid.

"Now how about some cash?"

The voice was trying sound weighty but came out rather mousey. Jared pulled away from the grip and started to walk, not too fast; he was not about to give the kid the satisfaction of seeing him run. "I'm all tapped out, friend." He just wanted to get away. Wherever it was heading, the night had been too good for it to end like this.

The youth pursued, a few paces behind. "Just a little. You know, help a guy out."

"I'm sorry, but no." He tried to be firm, solid, perhaps he could scare the kid off. Maybe he should use his Christian Bale Batman voice.

"No?" the youth cried in disbelief, stopping his feet on a metal basement door. The sound echoed into the night, menacing.

"Yes, no." He stopped as the echo died, then moved away again.

The youth was alongside him, shuffling in a weird sideways gait. "That's not cool."

"I don't have anything," he insisted.

"Come on. Not even some change?" The voice was almost breathless. Was the kid panting?

"No. Nothing."

"You don't look like you got nothing," the kid accused. "Your clothes is alright. I bet you got a nice phone."

He stopped and turned to face the kid, who seemed momentarily relieved that the chase had halted. "Seriously? Shorts and a sweaty tee shirt make me look like I have money? Well, I don't. And you would laugh your ass off if I showed you my flip phone."

The kid was briefly startled but quickly regained his composure. He loomed close, almost eye-to-eye. "I bet you got plastic," he squinted. Jared wondered, did he need glasses? "You can just go to the machine in that store over there and get out a few greenbacks for your buddy."

His plea was almost like a joke, or a child nagging a parent, holding little menace.

"I can't do that," Jared said with a mocking laugh that turned the kid's face sour.

"Why not?"

"Look man, I work in a warehouse, putting spools of wire up on racks and taking them down again, over and fucking over. I had a long day and just want to go home."

"And get something to eat? Crawl into your warm bed? Have a smoke before you drift off to sleep and dream your sweet dreams. Don't I deserve the same?"

"I'm not stopping you."

He stormed off, a little faster. His pursuer did not follow.

"I'm hungry, man!" the kid called into the night. "Help a brother out."

The kid played a good game, he had to give him that. But Jared wasn't buying. The pleas were no better than a round of three-card Monte, designed to pull at his heartstrings and elicit some sympathy that would undoubtedly be played to his disadvantage. Maybe he was being softened up for the kill. Maybe there was a silent helper lurking in the shadows, ready to beat him to a pulp with a baseball bat. Not matter how good he felt, he had to remember that this was still the city with the second highest murder rate in the entire country. He was smart enough to know that the house always won and the player was a sucker, so he was not about to place a bet.

He stopped and turned. "You're doing a good job of trying to make me feel sorry for you. But I don't have anything, least of all a heart. That was ripped out a few months ago. Not that you would understand, or care."

"I'm not asking for much, bro. You think I am unworthy of bare necessities?"

"Not at all, Baloo."

The kid stared for a long moment then smiled as he fathomed the reference.

"Then just share a little green. It's Friday, man. You've been out having a good time. I know you had a good time, I can see it on your face. You probably been drinking, staring at titties, and getting lap dances all night, so how about you share some of that love in your heart."

The kid was grinning now, all trace of menace evaporated after the Jungle Book reference.

"Little man, I already told you that I don't have any money. I'm not kidding. Look, how about I give you my cigarettes? And my lighter? You can have that too."

He handed the pack and lighter across to the kid, who scooped the offerings with outstretched hands, as if trying to collect drops of rain in a storm. No more words were spoken as Jared moved away.

Maybe because he expected the worst as he turned his back, Jared suddenly thought of his older brother. If he could see him now, he knew Nick would have called him a fool for tolerating such harassment, or taking his eyes off a potentially armed assailant. "Never engage with those crack heads, J. Think of yourself, your safety first. Knock em down and get the hell out of there."

He could have knocked the kid down, or pushed him aside and ran, but for all his inflated bravado, it was just a young man trying to make his way in the world, and that was something he could hardly fault the kid.

His car was just a block ahead. He could see it under the street lamp and knew that if he were in a Hollywood horror flick, he would reach his door but then the knife or gun would suddenly hit him in the back as suspenseful music blared and the audience was startled, spilling their popcorn. He fumbled in his pocket for the keys, trying to get the door key into his fingers, wondering how quickly he could open the door and dash inside.

As he opened the door, Carole's voice suddenly came into his head, the words she said before walking out the door that he didn't understand until that very minute.

"You never seem to be in the present, to appreciate the moment; a little piece of you always has to be questioning every decision you make, like you are unsure if you are even happy or not. One day Jared, I hope you find peace with yourself."

She didn't even offer a friendly kiss, let alone a passionate farewell, before she stepped out into the darkness, presumably into the waiting arms of Texting Ted. She may as well have slapped his face.

He was relieved to fall into the seat unharmed and surprised himself when he locked the doors. He started the car. Paul Weller blared from the speakers. For a brief moment, he was back in that hot, dark room, feeling connected to the entire universe, like he had finally found his proper place in the world. That instance seemed a lifetime ago and no time at all, a place where Jared Richards was a mere idea and Carole Poole a figment of someone's fevered imagination. But the song ended and the sensation was fleeting. He began to experience something new creep over him (fear? anger?). It gripped his chest like a fist clenched around his heart. He was breathless as he put the car into gear and drove off into the night, thinking maybe it was time he heeded the warnings on the packet and gave up smoking.

About the Author

John Riebow was born and raised in Philadelphia, where he attended the W. B. School High School of Agriculture Sciences, majoring in Horticulture. He holds a Bachelor of Science degree in Landscape Architecture from Temple University, is a LEED-Accredited Professional, and serves as Director of Design for a design-build-development general contractor.

WE ARE WAITING

by Chrissie Molitor

I'm on break when I get the call from Gram. I listen and nod along, pretending my heart isn't seizing in my chest. "Keep me posted," I tell her, and she sighs in exasperation.

It's the middle of the night, and Liv is staying at a friend's house. She texts me to say she's coming home. It's unsettling how comfortable my sister and I have gotten with this routine, how we know better than to run directly to the hospital as soon as we get the call. How instead we just...go about our day the best we can. Then again, it's not like we don't have time to kill. We won't be allowed in the room until after eight.

At a quarter to six, my cell phone again buzzes in the pocket of my jeans. I'm not supposed to have it on me, but it's practically impossible to enforce such a rule these days. I finish punching in the order of the family at the counter. The woman has an aggressively blonde dye job and too much foundation, and her GQ husband tries to corral the three children currently shrieking as they run through the Burger House lobby. It's a controlled, unfamiliar sort of chaos, and the sight of it makes my chest ache.

The couple herds their rambunctious pack toward a booth and I catch Marty's eye, mime smoking a cigarette. He shrugs, which isn't so much a sign of permission as it is surrender. I drag the visor from my head as I push through the back door to relieve some of the literal pressure, since there isn't much to do about the figurative. The sun, fiercely orange, is just cresting the horizon. I lean against the painted cinder-block and suck in a deep breath before I call Liv back.

"I don't want to be here alone," she announces.

I sigh and knead at the back of my neck, resisting the urge to tell her that she should have thought of that before. "I can bring you back here, but I have to finish my shift." I'm hardly a ripple in the water here. They don't me, but we need the money. And it beats the alternative.

"Okay," Liv agrees, too easily.

"I'll be there in ten." I disconnect the call and knock my head lightly against the wall, wishing I had two minutes to spare for that pretend cigarette.

During my interview, I'd bluntly told the hiring manager that an inflexible schedule was a deal breaker, and I would have an abnormal number of emergencies arise. They hired me anyway, probably out of desperation, probably underestimating my situation. There's a lot of guilt now over getting pissed when it happens. Having a terminally ill parent gets you a pass on a lot of things but even so, holding down a job is tough for someone in my position. But place like this? I'm here more than I'm not, and they can't afford to lose me. It works both ways, because I can't afford to not work.

I rap my knuckles against the door so the pimply-faced kid manning the drive-thru booth will let me back in the building and make a beeline for Marty. "I've gotta get my sister."

I should probably ask but, let's face it; the guy's running the graveyard shift at a third-rate burger joint, so how much say does he really have in anything? He raises his eyebrows.

"I'll be right back," I relent.

Rohrman 2

"Okay."

"Okay."

***

Dad is on the road. It happens more often than not, that I'm the one left to manage the aftermath. Far as I know he'll head back as soon as he's able, but it will still be tomorrow night before we see him. It's just as well. Even when he's here, it's like he's not. He hit the wall when I was seventeen, around the time I lost the inclination to care about schoolwork. It's a miracle I graduated.

I wait in the driveway, engine running. I prop my elbow on the door and palm my forehead and think about all the things I *should* be doing right now. Like college. Dating. Friends. Mom has told me – has *begged* me – not to give up my own life in exchange for hers, but it's easier said than done. And there's so much I have to do, taking care of her, it's doubtful she notices everything I'm not.

Liv emerges from the house, locks the door behind her. She drops into the car with a huff, and I immediately wrinkle my nose.

"What's that smell?"

"I made a cake."

"How?" I ask, shifting the car into reverse. Even if we never eat it, I understand *why*. Liv made a cake for the same reason I'm hauling her scrawny Betty Crocker ass back to Burger House with me. To delay the inevitable.

She quirks an eyebrow, but I stand by my question. No way in hell could I hope to make a cake now at nearly twenty, let alone at thirteen.

It's another way in which we are achingly different and growing apart more by the day. We might live in the same house, but I don't really know her. Mom first got sick when Liv was just seven, hardly even a person. We'd been closer then, even acted like sisters. We're practically strangers now, affected and changed. Something inside shuts down in a life like this; it's just easier that way. Our sisterhood was collateral damage of Mom's illness. If I really try, I think I can imagine the woman Liv will eventually be, and I wonder if this fantasy woman is the kind of person I would be friends with, let alone stand to be around.

Probably not, I settle on, and the realization barely even stings. I've known for a while now that once *it* finally happens, we won't fit into each other's lives anymore. This prolonged limbo is the glue keeping us together.

Liv crosses her arms and slouches in the passenger seat, looking put-upon. Like she didn't call begging for my company.

We've been through this song and dance so many times I've lost count. The worry and fear that follow the call look and sound different on each of us. For Liv, it's perpetual annoyance. For Dad, it's avoidance. And me? I'm just going through the motions.

Each time the phone rings, it could be *the call*, and I suppose I'm already steeling myself for it, solidifying the wall around my heart. Today, the panic, the fear, the worry – they've all been experienced in a rapid succession of brief but intense sensations, quickly replaced by the bleak, emotionless void I've been crafting inside.

I pull into a space at the back of the restaurant. Employees are supposed to park in the lot across the street, but I don't give a shit, and no one here can be bothered to make me.

In the harsh fluorescent lighting, I can see now that Liv has been crying, and I'm forced to remind myself that, for all my jaded outlook on what I laughingly call my life, she's just a kid. Too young still to train herself not to feel. And this is all the support I have to offer her: a break room the size of a closet with a dusty television that hasn't worked in months.

She surveys the small space, which admittedly reeks of fryer oil and BO. "What am I supposed to do?"

Marty knocks on the door behind me, a quick rap that tells me my grace period is up. "I don't know. Color or something."

She blinks at me, and I roll my eyes. I check the time on the clock, its plastic cover fogged with atmospheric grease stains. There's almost an hour left of my shift, and I don't know what Liv wants from me. She has one of those child-lock phones that won't let her do more than call and text and won't keep her occupied. I tug my own cell free of my pocket, hand it over. "If you tweet from my account, I'll shave your head in your sleep."

***

Every time I walk through these sliding glass doors, I think, *this is it*. This is the day I will have finally grown immune to the smell. And every time, I'm wrong. There's no hope of developing an immunity to this scent. This stinging, sterile odor.

Liv finally exhibits the adolescent clinginess that had her calling me at work, presses close to me as we move wordlessly through the lobby toward the bank of elevators. I punch the button, and it's a silent ride to the fifth floor.

My gaze reflexively goes to the first clock we pass; twenty minutes before visiting hours resume. I steer Liv into the family waiting room around the corner. Gram is already here – or here still, since she's the one who got Mom to the hospital at the first warning sign. She's perched stiffly in an armchair, purse on her lap. A Styrofoam cup of coffee is on the table next to her elbow, and it looks full despite the lack of visible steam.

She clucks her tongue as we settle into a pair of uncomfortable chairs. "I wish you wouldn't wear your hair like that, Kara," she says by way of greeting. Gram wears her stress like a judgmental bitch.

I cut her some slack and don't rise to the bait, just tuck a loose strand behind my ear.

This is the worst part; the waiting. But, really, that's all we do. All *I* do. Wait. I turn to Liv, frown. "Do you have homework to do?"

"It's July."

Somehow, this surprises me. I chew my thumbnail, which is already gnawed down to a jagged stub, and I think, *how the hell do I not even know what month it is? How is this my life?*

The past six years, I've had to be selfless and practical, all the things a teenager isn't meant to be. I'm over it. I'm not supposed to be, I'm not *allowed* to be, but I am. Sometimes I get caught up daydreaming of what life will be like when this is all over. And I feel...good. Calm.

And then, inevitably, I feel awful.

So, I push the daydreams aside, and remain hopeful. I have to, not just for Mom and Dad and Liv but for me, too. Without hope all I have is the sickening realization that my life won't truly begin until hers ends.

At eight o'clock on the dot, Gram gives us a meaningful look before leaving the room, coffee forgotten. The silence left in her wake is deafening.

"We should go in," I finally say, probably too loudly.

"Yeah."

But neither of us moves. Something on Food Network drones low in the background as we relish these last few moments of freedom, before we enter the next stage of our cyclical routine.

What will I do, if this is it? If the doctor doesn't have good news for us this time, and this is really it?

The nervous anticipation turns my stomach, and I swallow with difficulty. "Come on." I stand, and Liv follows my lead.

Mom smiles when we enter the room, the sort of full-face grin that chips away at the carefully constructed wall around my heart, because she's the strongest person I've ever known. She's been waiting too, for us, knowing we'd be here as soon as we were permitted. She's had a scare, but she's stable, in good spirits, and should be released by tomorrow afternoon. It's a relief and a burden at the same time. Dad will likely work out the remainder of his route now, leaving me to solo caretaking duties until the weekend.

She's going to be fine. This time. But we all know we'll be right back here in two weeks. A month. Three months.

And in the meantime, we'll all strengthen our internal defense mechanisms, and we'll all turn down the emotional dials another notch, and we'll all retreat a little further into ourselves. And we'll pretend that when we finally get *the call*, there won't be a little bit of relief mingled in with the hurt.

SMELL OF LEATHER

by Vivek Nath Mishra

After a long day, Subba walked down a narrow alley passing several sleeping, ruminating cows in the middle of the street, perturbing the sleep of stray dogs curled up in the betrayed corners. He reached his house in the dark and took out the key from his pocket. He kept wiping the beads of perspiration oozing on his forehead with the end of his shirt. His whole body had a tremor and it ran from his feet up to his hands and the keys fumbled in his hands as he took it out from his pocket. The key didn't turn easily in the lock, perhaps, it needed oiling, some lubrication to unlock. He struggled with it for a while, drenched completely in sweat and looked like as if he had come out straight from a shower. Suddenly, he observed that he was using the wrong key. He fumbled and took out the right key. The lock opened after much difficulty. Sometimes we just don't use the right key and keep forcing it the wrong way and eventually break the lock, Subba reflected. Subba unlatched the door and went in shutting the door behind him. An ear-splitting silence pervaded the room. It was pitch dark everywhere and he stepped forward gingerly, reaching out his hands to the wall for the switchboard. He turned on the light. The yellow sodium light lit all the corners of the room except the one place, his heart that remained dark, gloomy and hopeless.

He took his Kurta off and wiped his face, chest and armpits with it raising his hands above his head. His dark skinned torso shined in the dim sodium light. Subba threw the kurta in a corner, slithered out of his pyjamas and wrapped a lungi round his waist. He then dropped himself on the small bed in the corner of his room which was crammed with clothes, utensils and his son's books. He had planned to sell all those books as it was all needless to collect now but it was more difficult to part with it than he had thought. Sight of those books was associated with the memory of his son reading in this very corner and he wanted this memory to stay there- untouched and safe.

His body smelled of blood, flesh and leather. It never disturbed him before but now it was the smell and sight which was quite impossible for him to stand, although, he had no way to escape. He knew only this work like his ancestors. It had been his daily routine since he was thirteen years old when he had chopped a live stock for the first time. And it became a routine after that as mechanical as brushing teeth in the morning. He had a flat porous rock in the shop and he would wet it with water, then he would rub the edge of his knife on the rock for several minutes. He would sharpen his knife daily. Then he would grab a chicken by its leg and pull it out from a dirty, dingy cage which smelled of urine and chicken poop. Chicken would keep cackling as he grabbed it out. Customers would stand there covering their noses and mouths with a handkerchief. The stench of the place remained unbearable but all these never affected Subba. He remained oblivious of all that.

He would put the chicken on the piece of rock and then would slit its throat without giving it a second thought. He would let the blood pour down in a bucket as the chicken fluttered helplessly in pain. He would wait for the last drop of blood to trickle down. Then he would pull the feathers off its skin and begin chopping its legs and wings one by one. It all remained mechanical for him. He would slice the meat into the smallest possible pieces and then would pack it all in a plastic bag and hand it over to the customers. But now his hands shivered as he tried grabbing a chicken; his whole body trembled like a child suffering from malaria. He couldn't imagine himself doing that. How come it remained so mechanical for him for so many years! How come he never heard those cries before! How come he never noticed the terror in a chicken's eyes! Now he witnessed the horror. Every time he killed a life, image of his own son bleeding to death began dancing in front of his eyes.

Subba picked up a bucket and headed to the backyard where there was a small dilapidated well and a huge Peepul tree stood still just next to it. A small Banyan shoot had taken roots on the surrounding walls of the well. It would become gigantic in a few years and might bring down the entire well. The small shoot could do that. He must eradicate it by its root in time, Subba thought.

There was not even a hint of breeze that day and humidity was unbearable. He was sweating all the time and his eyes were burning. Subba drew a bucket of water from the well and poured it over, mumbling something to himself. He went inside all drenched and dripping with water. He then changed to another lungi, combed his hair neatly in front of a mirror but still the smell of blood and meat remained adhered to his body odour. He felt like asking someone if he still smelled like blood, if it's not just his imagination, but there was no one to answer.

Subba went in to his small dingy kitchen. He saw the dirty utensils piled up in a corner, flies buzzing around it. He sat on a low stool and began scrubbing a few pots and plates, rest he would do tomorrow morning, he thought. He felt too tired and was reluctant to cook but he also felt a fire of hunger burning inside him. Subba always felt more hungry when he was sad and depressed. He kept a pot full of rice on the boiler and began recalling his past few years.

Subba's wife had died during the delivery of her first son. Subba's sister had assisted him when he was completely broken and alone. In the most difficult phase of his life Subba counted on his sister. She was the first to come there on the news of her sister-in-law's death but didn't leave immediately as all the rites were over after thirteen days. She looked after the infant for several months but then for how long somebody is going to struggle for somebody else. How long his sister could stay with him? As the child began walking and was almost one and a half year old his sister went back to her husband. Her father-in-law was not very happy with her staying at Subba's for long. He kept persisting his son to bring back his daughter-in-law soon. After Subba's sister left, Subba would take Kooku, his son, to the shop with him but tied the child's legs with a rope as the child ran after the sharp knife and would play with meat and blood all day. The child fell to sleep daily after crying his heart out. Raising this child was Subba's biggest dream. He didn't even know if he had any other desire. He was completely occupied. His son was his only dream, his only aspiration. The child grew anyhow and began going to school. It gave Subba more space and relaxation. The child would return home on a rickshaw from school and Subba would roll down the shutters in the afternoon to return home before Kooku reached there. He fed Kooku and took him to the shop with him for the rest of the day. Kooku would keep playing in the street with little children and Subba kept an eye over him while going through his daily course.

Soon, Kooku had a thin layer of moustache and Subba's hair on the temple had begun greying when Kooku started assisting him at the shop. He was growing up well. Now he returned home from school on his own bicycle and helped himself to lunch. Now Subba didn't have to shut the shop in the afternoon. Subba dreamt of his son working in an office far from this dirty meat shop. He would always stop Kooku from coming to the shop.

This much was Subba's life, this much he aspired to live.

The world looked a satisfactory place then. Seeing his own child playing with other children in the street filled his heart. But everything said about heart and its tenderness is rubbish. Killing is as casual as breathing at the present times. Perhaps, the world has everything but a heart. There's too much concrete for a heart to thrive, perhaps.

Subba's train of thought broke as he heard the water bubbling. After the rice was cooked, Subba sliced an onion and a tomato and poured a few drops of mustard oil in it and mixed it all. He did only perfunctory cooking after his son's death; he lost all his interest in cooking. He used to cook so many varieties of dishes for his son and it contented him to see his child relishing it all. The curry plant was still there in the pot outside in the veranda. Subba had planted it so that he could put some curry leaves in sambhar and chutney that Kooku devoured greedily. But the plant was drooping now, the leaves looked withered and the earth parched. He must water it today, Subba decided. Now his cooking was limited to filling up his vile stomach. He observed that not much of the mustard oil was left in the jar. He would buy a packet from the grocery shop tomorrow while returning from the shop on his way home. Subba scooped some water in his hands, sprinkled it on the floor and swept it with a broom. He then rolled out a mat with frayed corners on the floor. He had barely sat to eat when he heard a persistent knock on the door. It was Kalawati on the door. An old widow who lived with her only son and his wife. She lived next door and was very fond of Kooku. She had a corpulent built and walked limping. She came in struggling to catch her breath and sat on the floor with great effort.

"What a lovely child he was! This world has gone to dogs. There's no sanity. I couldn't come earlier. You see I'm always sick. This old age is a sin, Subba. Everyone seems insanely inclined to cultivating hatred, Subba. Just yesterday, Bhola was telling me that somebody has thrown some acid on the bull who roamed about here. What is its fault? Why are they making it a victim of their retaliation? They keep killing one another in the name of religion. I fed that Nandi everyday. Now he's burned so badly that his bones are exposed."

Subba sat on the stool and began eating with his fingers. His eyes were brimmed with tears. He remembered how Kalawati kept calling Kooku from the street as he went to the school. She would call him out, "Oh Rajkumar! Wouldn't you take me with you to the school today?

"Wouldn't you tell me what your teachers taught you today? She would say in a loving manner as Kooku returned from school.

It all reminded him more of his son and he hung his head low unable to look into the eyes of Kalawati.

"I'll be leaving now. I'm on a fast today. I'm fasting every Tuesday, you know. If you need anything please let us know. We are your family just round the corner. Don't stress yourself out. God is watching," said Kalawati rising on her feet.

"Wouldn't you take tea? I was just going to make for myself," said Subba with quivering lips, still trying to stop his tears.

"O poor child, don't bother please. You already looked drained."

Subba latched the door as Kalawati left and went to his bed. He kept twisting and twirling in the bed but the cruel sleep kept eluding him till late past the midnight. No matter how much he tried to think of other things, the image of his son's throat getting slashed swiftly in one go kept coming to him. He would throw his arms in the air with anxiety and sit up. His dreams were more cruel than reality.

There was a rumour in the city that Subba, after pulling down the shutters of his shop, went to a slaughter house and slaughtered beefs secretly to make some extra money. The hostility towards him was afire in the mob. A group of barbarians, brandishing flags, had besieged him many times at his shop but he begged and convinced them of his honesty that he couldn't even dream of doing that. But the mob never trusted him fully.

"He's a liar. How many times we have found the carcasses of the cows on the outskirts of the city. Who else could do that if not you? We warn you one last time or we'll be compelled to take the law in our hands. Better you save your life," a young man had hollered from the crowd that day.

"Pull his beard, that bastard will learn no other way," other one screamed.

"Burn his skull cap," a raised voice came from the crowd.

His son was there and his young blood boiled as he witnessed his father's insult. His eyes were bloodshot. He couldn't bear all the humiliations piled on his father.

"Yes, we killed a cow. What will you do? Don't try to scare us. We are not some cowards," he had said jumping on his feet.

Subba pounced on him, grabbed him by his arm and threw him away in the corner, "don't say a word, Kooku. Have you gone mad? Just shut up, not a word anymore."

"He's a child. Please forgive him. He's a fool, complete idiot," Subba begged.

"Subba, keep your child under control. Better don't try our patience or test our tolerance. He wouldn't be young for long otherwise," threatened someone from the mob.

They had a hot talk that evening. Kooku told Subba that he was ashamed of his cowardice. One has to shed all the cowardice to live peacefully in this world. Had he let him handle the matter all the threats would have turned into a farce, Kooku had shouted. Subba had thrown him out of the gate snarling.

This was now a daily affair. Subba had thought it out several times to switch his worl but what else he could do! What else did he know? Like his ancestors he knew only chopping meat and slaughtering chickens and goats. There had always been clashes between different religions but this propaganda had come into existence very recently. Nobody had even the faintest idea of how to handle it.

One evening when Subba returned home he found the doors of his room wide open. He thought his son might have gone to the field to play cricket and forgot to latch the door. He was very indignant. How could Kooku be so careless? But as he approached near he saw a river of blood coursing down the floor. He ran in shouting and trembling. It was his son bleeding profusely on the floor, his clothes soaked in blood. A stream of blood was gushing out. After seeing his son fluttering in pain he ran everywhere, stumbling, shivering with fear but lost his voice and had fainted down right there. Next day the newspaper was fully covered with the news of lynching. A police complaint was lodged and a few suspicious molesters were put behind the bars but Subba had lost his ability to speak. He knew that his son was not coming back. From that day the sight of blood made him shiver terribly, however, life goes on with its cruel intent. Subba knew no other work. He had a knife with which he could commit suicide but his hands trembled as he held the knife. Perhaps, he didn't have enough strength to suicide. Perhaps, this was enough bloodshed.

In a moment, Subba's life was turned upside down. There was no ray of hope through which he could lead his life. He spent his days like a dead man sitting at the shop, following the daily routine.

The only thing that gave Subba some air was the field where his son used to play football. Each day as he went past this field he felt like he saw his own son playing. He noticed some shadow. He would stand there still for several minutes just to see the game. The laughter of children running about the field gave him some ephemeral sympathy.

That day it was raining heavily when Subba was going round the field. Like any other day he saw children playing football. He could see his own son's shadow in the field. But that day it was a different scene there. Children were laughing uncontrollably as a cow had sieged the ball and was not letting it go. A boy ran behind the cow and tried to shoo it away but the cow guarded the ball as if it was its calf. Subba didn't find any humour in it. In fact, the whole scene reminded him of something else. He couldn't comprehend it the other way. The ball was of leather, he observed. Did the smell of leather remind the cow of its calf, he reasoned. Suddenly a boy ran towards the ball and hit it in a direction of other boy and they began passing the ball to one another and the cow ran behind it in all the directions like a lunatic. The group broke out in a ruckus. Subba couldn't see all that and he ran behind the boys shouting at them, at the top of his voice, to stop but his voice drowned in the uproar of laughter. Subba kept running hither and thither after the boys, pleading them to stop this humiliation. The whole incidence was choking him. He ran in all the directions similarly like the cow did. Perhaps, both were in the same whirl of emotions. The whole scene was filled with mad commotion. Suddenly, Subba's slippers got stuck in the mud and he fell down on the ground as the laughter kept roaring. It was a deafening sound for him. He felt it piercing through his ears. Subba kept lying down there, enveloped in a layer of mud, breathing heavily. He had no strength even to rise on his feet. He felt drained. He kept staring at the dark clouds which rained down ruthlessly. He closed his eyes and dreaded that his voice would probably go unnoticed like the smell of leather.

About the Author

Vivek Nath Mishra is a writer and photographer residing in Varanasi, India. His short stories have appeared on many platforms including The Hindu, Muse India, The Punch magazine and Queen mob's teahouse. His photographs have appeared in several magazines including The Guardian and Sahapedia. His debut book is 'Birdsongs of Love and Despair'.

TELL A FRIEND

by Colin Gallagher

While walking up Sunset Street in Seattle, Washington, I pass office buildings, parking lots, restaurants and other businesses. I believe I had seen it all, yet to my surprise, I come across an outdoor flying saucer sales and lease service center. I know that technology is advancing in the USA but this is truly amazing.

It is 2035 and I will be retiring from ownership of a CPA firm where I spent the last thirty years consulting and hunching over my desk juggling figures and accounts on income statements, balance sheets, inventory sales and profit margins from my company's customer base. I am done with the stress.

Standing outside on the sidewalk in front of the saucer dealership before heading back to my hotel, a salesman is approaching me. "Hi, how ya doin' today! Can I interest you in this little run-about? It is the perfect vehicle for a hop, skip and jump to anyplace in the solar system?" he said, pointing to one of his smaller saucers. "The X87 turbo cruiser gets up to Mach 5 in the earth's atmosphere and has an automated re-entry system second to none. Four travelers fit comfortably and everyone gets his own window to observe the show out in the realm of the sun. Just perfect for that solar system cruise. Take the family out to Jupiter, look at that big red spot then come back for the grandkid's birthday party. What do ya say?"

I was dumbfounded. Could this really be happening? After catching my breath, "An X87 Turbo cruiser huh. Well, sure. I'll check it out!"

"Great! This little model is fresh off the production line. Came in first place at the inter-planetary race earlier this month. It kicked the crap out of the Chinese Dong-Fu model. This little baby was built to last and will keep you traveling for years and years to come."

"What's next? A test flight?" I ask.

"Sure, we can do that. Follow me!"

"We'll just need to run a quick credit check." he said as we walked toward his office. "It's company policy before we take a test flight. What's your social security number?"

He left the office and came back in about two minutes with a big smile.

"Great number you have a credit score of 789. Let's do that test flight!"

Walking to the sporty little model that he was promoting, the salesman put a key card into the anti-radiance security sleeve.

"This is just a formality as your card will open the sleeve as you approach."

"This sounds so fantastic. Is it very complicated?"

"I have this model and my little grandson does a lot of these preliminary chores. It is so easy a monkey could do it. You'll see!"

LED bulbs light-up all over the fuselage, a titanium drawer slides to one side revealing a set of steps. With a welcoming gesture, he leads me on board the model X87 turbo cruiser.

"Wow! This is spectacular! We could actually travel to the moon in this baby?"

"Sure, buckle yourself into the seat by the left window and we'll start. It operates by voice command to the control panel. Start X87 turbo."

I could hear the engine humming while a cloud of dust breezes past the window.

"Okay, you comfortable? Ready to take it for a little spin?"

"Sure! Let's go!"

"Rise to fifty-thousand feet X87!" he commanded.

The saucer rose like a fast elevator above the sales lot; higher than the office buildings; the space needle; higher than the clouds. As I look out the window, I can see the ocean, forest and the city of Seattle.

"Hang on to the handles on your seat, we're heading to hyper-drive."

"Yeah sure."

Feeling the g-forces push me back into my seat and looking through the window as we continue, I see all of North America then the earth and beyond. We pass into vacant stellar space.

"We are reaching cruising speed. The g-forces will be less apparent and we'll have a smooth ride."

After twenty seconds, "You can unfasten your seat belt now and relax. Would you like a cocktail?"

"Sure!"

"What's your pleasure?"

"Bourbon, please. On the rocks."

"Two bourbon on the rocks X87."

Immediately, two glasses with alcohol and ice rise out of the center console. The salesman gives me one and I sip it, "Very good."

"So, what do you think about this little doozey? The transporter engine is guaranteed for thirty million miles. The body is made by Boeing and the hyper-link engine is made by Northrop. I've sold dozens of these to happy travel-oriented customers. Have a large backyard? Land one of these next to the bar-b-que or jacuzzi!"

"Yeah! Sounds great."

"What would it take to get you into one of these little gems today?"

"How much does this model's cost?"

"This clean new model starts at two million, I mention a thirty-million-mile guarantee on the transporter will last years and years. Just fly it to the service lot and we'll take care of everything and shine it up. Got to have a good wax job – impress the neighbors."

"Would you want financing or prefer a cash payment?"

"I would take advantage of financing. But is there a manual or something where I would learn to fly one of these?"

"We have a three DVD set that explains everything you need to know so you can travel in style. Also, included with the leasing is four flight lessons. You'll be cruising to Mars in no time!"

"Terrific!"

"After the test flight we'll get your info and set you up in this baby!"

"Hey, there's the moon!" I said, looking out the window.

"Yeah, we'll just circle around it."

"Oh, there's a base right there."

"Yes, take the wife out for a flight to the lunar base. Experience the latest in comfort and speed. Spend the night in the Lunar hotel. Then travel to Mars in the morning."

"That sounds fantastic!"

"Put your seatbelt back on and hold onto that drink were headed back at hyper-speed. 'Return to Seattle launch base X87!'"

"We will be back shortly. I can start on the paperwork so when we get back, you'll be ready to sign the lease."

"We have your SSN. What about your work?"

"I'm am retiring. I own a chain of accounting offices with fifteen CPA's."

"Good, a solid steady profession there won't be any delay when we run the paperwork."

"Oh, there's earth again."

"Yes, we can travel extremely fast in this turbo-charged number. You'll love it."

I could see the North American Continent and a few seconds later I see the city of Seattle and the Space Needle.

"There's the sales lot!"

Touch down is very smooth and the seatbelts automatically unbuckle. The door opens and we walk the steps to a service attendant waiting outside.

"How was it?"

"Clean it up Johnny this one is a lease."

"Yes sir!"

Walking into the sales office, he confirmed the final paperwork.

"Okay. Ready for your signature."

"Great! Got a pen?"

"It's all done." He said after signing. "Here is your key card with access' to voice command. We're signing you up for our flight class' and here is your three DVD set to understand the advanced voice control system. Classes start tomorrow well see you then."

"Great! I hope my wife likes it!"

"Perhaps she would like one of her own?"

"Yeah maybe. Thanks for all your help. I can't wait to see Saturn's rings close up."

"As a token of our appreciation here is a gift certificate for a five-star weekend at the lunar base. You and your wife will love it. See you tomorrow at three o'clock."

"Great, bye!"

"Wait! Where ya headed too?"

"Oh, the Somerset Regency Hotel."

"They have a saucer pad. Would you like a lift?"

"Sure!"

Walking onto the lot, "This is my saucer lets go in it."

The salesman took out his key card to open the door. Walking up the steps, we sit inside.

"Would you like to fly this time?"

"Excellent!"

"Just tell it where you want to go."

"Somerset Regency Hotel X87"

I felt the smooth start of the engine and the rise of the saucer.

"This craft will get us there quick."

"It is so unbelievable what I've experienced today. I feel like I'm living five hundred years in the future."

"We're touching down."

With door opening, I walk down the steps.

"Thank you and you will see me tomorrow."

"Great."

I turned to walk away. But then I stumble though I quickly catch myself at the overlook wall.

"You know I went to the moon today and here I nearly lost it all by tripping over my own shoelace."

"You're doing fine."

"Okay! See you tomorrow."

"Tell a friend."

About the Author

Colin Gallagher has recently retired and has started writing one of his joys in life. He has joined the California Writers Club and has been published twice.

PEQUENA

by Taylor Martin

Pequena rustled in my arms, I tussled to calm her down. The looks from my schoolmates spelled disgust, dirty gazes at her dirt covered feathers. I ignored them all. In the midst of all them lied a murderer. I knew it. Pequena knew it. She let out a faint cluck, her big eyes targeting a ginger kid with a stack of books. I veered right to him, so close I could've counted his freckles. He stared at Pequena.

"Um..." his plump body jiggled like Jell-O as we focused on his every move. "Hey there little... chicken..."

"Pequena."

The boy jumped as I snapped at him, freckles turning pale.

"You address her as Pequena."

Pequena made no noise, but jerked her head back towards me. I stepped back, allowing the boy to continue down the hallway, which he did with haste. The bell rang, marking the end of this round of investigations.

I ducked into class, scanning the room. My classmates were settling in their seats when they noticed Pequena, giving her looks. Pequena spazzed every so often, but never clucked. A smack of a ruler from the front of the room interrupted the walk to my desk.

"Excuse me, Manny?" Mrs. Kindley held the ruler like a whip, pointing it straight at Pequena. "But that creature will not be tolerated in my-"

I slammed Pequena onto the teachers desk, her claws scuffing up the old wood. My classmates all stared in shock. I ignored them. Mrs. Kindley snapped her ruler towards the door. "Office."

A muffled landline rang against principal Nimoy's ear, practically pressed into the fat of his cheek. Between rings, the three of us sat in total silence, exchanging glances.

"Hello, Mrs. Manilla, this is Principal Nimoy from school..." He turned to me, blinking a couple of times through his big, square glasses as if he were taking mental photographs. "Yes I have your son, uh, Manny here with me... as well as a chicken."

"Pequena." I quickly corrected him. "You address her as Pequena."

Principal Nimoy slowly turned back to the call. "It's name is... Pequena." After Principal Nimoy carefully explained the situation, as not to get it mistaken, he hung up the phone. He tried to read me, scanning his eyes up and down from me to Pequena.

"Usually," he leaned back, having given up trying to figure me out for the moment, "I can get a pretty good sense of a student's behavior just by looking at them." His eyes squinted momentarily. "But I'm gonna need an explanation for this one."

I sat silently, staring at Pequena as she studied Principal Nimoy studying her.

"For better understanding."

"Pequena laid an egg yesterday." My head didn't move, only my jaw. "She hadn't laid one before."

"Well, that's... that's normal. Chickens do that."

"This morning it was gone."

Pequena squirmed a little bit when I said this.

"I see... well... oh how do I put this... what'd you have for breakfast?"

"Eggs." My eyes remained laser focused on his. "We have a chicken farm, why wouldn't we eat eggs?"

Principal Nimoy looked upon my stone cold stature and listened to my straight forward response as if I were speaking in another language. "And you don't think little... Pequena's egg got mixed up with the rest of them?"

"The chicken farm belongs to my family, but Pequena is *mine*. Noone in the house had the right to that egg."

Pequena, now quivering, looked to me for what I can only assume was comfort. "The loss of your kin is not normal Principal, and it never will be." I tried to soothe Pequena, who had curled up as much as she could. "I need to find out who." We both shifted our focus to Pequena. "For her sake."

A look of compassion crossed Principal Nimoy's face. "Well then, let me be the first to apologize to you both for your loss."

Pequena lifted her head up in a slightly twitchy manner.

"I do hope you find your culprit, but I can't let you investigate here." There was a soft knock at the door, Principal Nimoy lifted the large amount of himself from his desk to let them in. Mother silently walked in the door.

"Sweetie, I know you're upset, but Pequena needs to come home."

Principal Nimoy gave me a gentle nod. I stood from my chair and presented Pequena to her. She was snug in my arms, still as a statue, until the moment her twitching eyes landed on Mother's. She flapped and flailed her wings, attempting an escape. I pulled her away from Mother, wrestling to keep her calm. When Mother reached to help, Pequena let out an ear piercing crow.

About the Author

Taylor Martin grew up smack in the middle of Baltimore and DC. In his free time Taylor writes stories, both for paper and for film, and unwinds by playing video games and going on long drives. You can follow him on Twitter: @t_mart_17.

CURSED CHRISTMAS DINNER

by Alexandre Henrique Ferreira Campos de Souza

The cold wind howls through the city, the snow slowly falling and gathering on the roofs of houses. A normal Christmas Eve, families gathering, and presents being given and received. And that was how Gabrielle, and her family's night went until the nightmare began. Now she is running desperately down the hall on the first floor of her house trying to meet her family while portraits fly over her head. Her heart beating at the same pace as the portraits hit the walls, a devilish symphony on Christmas Eve.

"Oh God! Why did he have to buy that damn necklace?!" she yells. "I told him it was cursed. I felt the spirit presence in it."

Gabrielle is a 12 years old girl that, besides no one believe her, is a medium capable to see and talk with spirits.

Finally, she reaches the Master Room and finds her mother, Megan, sitting in the corner embracing her legs, and facing the door, her eyes glazed with fear. As he gets closer, he notices the marks of the night on her body: various bruises on her arms, legs and face; a cut in the head, the blood still dripping, impairing the vision of the right eye. He grits his teeth in anger and thinks worriedly about how his children are.

"Are you ok, mommy? Let's get out of here and find daddy and Michael," she says, trying to sound as gentle as possible.

"Stay away from me!" her mother yells.

"It's me, mommy. Please, calm down," she answers, even more gentle.

"Behind you!"

As Gabrielle turns, she sees a raid of flying objects of all kinds coming in their direction. She freezes, not capable to react. Her mother grabs her and her body in front of Gabrielle's. Then suddenly her father, Frank, and her brother, Michael, break the door and storm into the room, hitting the flying objects with their baseball bats.

"Stop it!" Gabrielle suddenly screams, and then all objects falls down, giving them time to take a breath. They stare each other, trying to find a way out of this situation.

"I have a plan, but you won't like," Gabriele finally says.

***

They are standing before the dining room; the smell of turkey still impregnates the air mixing with the smell of wine coming from a broken bottle laying next to the table. And the table is the only thing that still untouched in the house, with plates, glasses, forks and knives staying right where they're supposed to be; an island of peace among a sea of chaos and destruction destroyed furniture and all kind of objects all over the place, as if a tornado had passed leaving only the walls and ceiling in place .

"I'm going," Gabrielle finally says, staring with conviction to dining room.

As she gets closer, the air gets heavier and moving becomes more difficult like she was walking against a strong wind. The objects on the table starts to tremble and she feels the spirit's angry intention.

"I know you can hear me. Please, I just want to talk with you, help you." She says to the spirit, that still not visible to her. "I know you've been suffering for a long time, and I know you want to be free. But you won't be able to do so if you don't let us help you."

However, the spirit got angrier and started throwing objects in her direction. And so, a knife hits her thigh, sticking there firmly; she groans in pain, falling on her knee, tears falling over her face.

"Gabrielle!! I will destroy you, spirit!! No one hurts my little girl!!" Frank screams, going to where her daughter is. But Michael stops him, holding him and taking him to the ground.

"Stop it, dad! We need to trust her! She's the only one who can do this!" he says.

"I'm okay, daddy. I can do this," Gabrielle says, standing up again. Her father still not accepting this, trying to free himself from Michael. She looks to her mother that, with a sad smile, nods her head.

"I trust you, honey," she says, "even hurting me so much."

Gabrielle takes a deep breath, nods and turn back to the spirit that is now visible to her.

"I won't give up. I will help you and save my family. Tell me why you're doing this," she says looking directly to the spirit. The rain of objects got heavy again.

"I understand you're angry. You were a little girl just like me, but your father did horrible things to you in the middle of Christmas Eve. He broke you in every aspect possible, and then threw your body in the river. And your soul got trapped inside the necklace you were wearing," Gabrielle says.

"But this is not an excuse to hurt other people, innocent people. They're not at fault." She continues. The spirit seems to calm down a little.

"Is there anything we could do for you? Anything you wish?" she asks gently.

"We can do this," she suddenly says, then turns to her family and affirms "We will have a Christmas dinner with her, the one she couldn't enjoy in life. This will free her soul."

At this moment, nothing shocks them anymore and they accept without questioning.

***

A normal Christmas dinner except for the one empty chair where supposedly the spirit girl was sitting. Everyone except Gabrielle was nervous about having a dinner with a spirit that almost killed them and destroyed their house, but they tried to act as normal as possible to not upset the spirit again. After a while, the spirit got satisfied, and after thanking them through Gabrielle transcended to the other side, finally achieving the peace she longed for.

"You know, little girl," Frank says with a tired smile, "you were right from the very beginning. Next time, I will throw the gift as far as I can before opening it."

About the Author

Alexandre Souza was born and grown up in Recife, Brazil, and on his free time he watches animations and reads books. He loves dark and supernatural stories. Follow him on Twitter @AlexandreH98.

NO VACANCY

by Nathaniel Zebley

Rachel stood up, walked over to the smudged window in the small room, and looked out at the parking lot with only a few cars in it. The "No Vacancy" sign was blinking rapidly, and the neon "Motel" sign had the 'M' burned out.

"It's easy for you to say, you're not the one that has to think about this day in, and day out. You'll never understand how hard this is," she said.

Thomas walked over to the nightstand and picked up a bottle of the amber liquid. He finished off his glass before opening the large bottle and taking a swig from it.

"Can we at least talk about this tomorrow when you're not like this?" Rachel said.

"I'm fine."

Thomas took the bottle over to a loose chair in the corner of the room and sat down, taking another drink.

"I'm over this," Thomas said, in-between hiccups.

"Well that's not surprising, whenever anything gets too hard or doesn't go your way, you just give up."

"I don't give up, I'm just letting you make the decision without me.

Thomas took another swig from the bottle.

"Sometimes I just wish that I listened to my parents and never stayed with you," Rachel said, choking back tears. "Now I'm far away from home and the only thing I have to show for it is this shitty motel room and a boyfriend who spends our little bit of money on booze."

"Well that was one decision that didn't take you long to make," Thomas said, slurring his words.

Rachel sat down on the storage trunk and put hand on her stomach, ignoring Thomas' question.

He finished off the rest of the bottle and was now slumped in the chair, fading in and out of consciousness.

"I'm tired of dealing with a child," he said, before drifting into an unconscious state.

Rachel looked back at Thomas who was now passed out with an empty bottle of Jack Daniels slipping out of his limp hand. She put her hand on her stomach and walked over to her dresser. She packed what little of the belongings that she had in her suitcase, and all of the cash that she could scavenge. Rachel opened the door, before stopping halfway out.

"I'm going to keep it," she said, as she closed the door to the motel room.

About the Author

Nathaniel Zebley loved movies and any storytelling media containing horror. You can follow him on Twitter: @n_zebley."

A GROCER'S LIST

by Charlie Turner

Three dozen eggs. Ollie stands in the middle of the mess with a cigarette behind his ear. Our father, the deli manager, is across the store flirting with some young woman with dirty blonde hair. A regular customer. I guess they didn't hear the crash. "Move fast," I tell Ollie. He grabs an old floor mop and begins pushing the goop into a dustpan. It sticks to the tiled floor, so he uses his boot to kick it, then he picks it up by the handful. He makes five, maybe six trips to the waste bin behind the counter while I watch. When he steps in front of me, I snag the coffin nail. "You'll be here awhile. I'll smoke this for you."

Six pounds of honey ham. The package is from Peppy Pigs Farms, and our customers prefer it over every other meat that we sell. My father slices it thinly. He orders me to carve into the giant cylinder of provolone that has just arrived. In my arms, it weighs as much as a newborn, maybe more. I cradle it to the slicing station. The man who ordered the cheese is wearing a denim jacket and has a belly that droops over a bull horn belt buckle. He asks if he can try a piece, and I say no. My father looks at me, his jaw tight, his eyes wide. The muscles in his cheeks puff in and out, in and out. And during this moment of distraction, I hear his machine begin to grind. It's shrill, brain-rattling. The audible equivalent of a snake bite. It's the noise the slicer makes when liquid hits the blade, and this liquid is dark red.

Nine stitches. Ollie drives us home from the ER, and I sit in the back and watch the elms fly by. We had to close the deli early, and I think my father is more upset about that than he is about the tip of his thumb no longer being attached to his hand. For a moment, our eyes meet in the rearview. He stares at me, not blinking, not crying, not anything. He doesn't have to speak because his anger is strong enough to turn the August air cold. He's angry at me for not caring about the business, angry at Ollie for dropping a total of forty-eight eggs on the ground over the past week, angry at himself for believing that one day his sons would take over the deli. When his hands become too arthritic to run the machines, to cut the meat, he wants us to eagerly welcome the business into our lives and allow it to live on for another twenty, thirty, or forty years. "That's a dream," Ollie once told him. "You *know* we don't want this place." But the old man keeps trying. Tonight, instead of taking the easy way out and firing us, he'll sit us down and say the same thing that he always has. "Something's gotta change, boys. I don't know what, but something."

About the Author

Charlie Turner is an MFA candidate studying fiction at Emerson College in Boston. In 2017, he won Best in Competition during the Michael S. Roif Awards at UMass Amherst for his original screenplay, Paper Faces. Besides fiction, Charlie has had several film reviews published and is the owner of CharliesCut.com, an entertainment criticism website.

FERTILITY

by Noelle Florio

"It comes in waves, Miss. Loakey. Some days will be better than others sweetie, but the results of your spirometry test show your lungs have increased inflammation since your last visit," Doc said in a huff with a look of desperation on his face while Lana sat in the bubblegum recliner, her skeletal hand held over her chest. Doc reached into the worn out file cabinet to retrieve a tightly packed envelope labeled, "Loakey, Lana." He shuffled through the stack of papers then pulled out the desired collection he was searching for.

"Looking back on your test from last July, your inflammation was at an all-time high as well," Doc said, the papers shielding his doughy blue eyes and cleanly shaven face. A pause. More thumbing through papers. "You're not taking up that peach business again, right dear?"

"You mean the "Blue Ridge Ripest Peach" contest? Lana asked.

"I'll take that as a yes, dear." Doc's eyes popped up from the top of the pages and locked with Lana's rolling ones. While she was quite sick of Doc's 'dears' and 'sweeties,' he's been her pulmonologist ever since she was diagnosed with asthma and heart palpitations twenty years ago. She couldn't change now. Back then, it was just an occasional huff at the top of the stairs more often her condition turned into a looming huff just upon getting out of bed.

"Well, Doc, you know how much it means to me." A deep breath. "You really thought I'd listen to your orders?" Lana said, chuckling a little. "When do I ever do that?"

"You should do it more often to be honest with you." A pause. Lana was weary of what Doc would say next, for he didn't tag a pet name on the end of his sentence. When he did this she knew he was actually trying to be serious.

"You're pushing it Lana. While I know you want to pretend you are in your mid-50's, sooner or late you need to accept the fact that you are pushing your late 80's." A pause and a wheeze from Lana. "90 to be exact," Doc said as he put Lana's stack of files back into the cabinet. Lana's breathe was at a constant wheeze.

"Dear, you know I hate saying this, but I cannot guarantee that your lungs are strong enough to take on this contest," Doc said. "It's a risk I don't want you to take."

"Got it, Doc." Lana couldn't face listening to those orders.

The sunsets always looked like the painting palette of an artist's in the mountainside of Blue Ridge, Georgia; much like it was when she arrived at her house that evening. Pulling her wiry blonde hair back into a thin pony tail, Lana knelt down with one knee at a time and a deep breath to look at her tree. While she gripped for balance on the damp earth she gazed up at the cotton candy swirls of the sky until she gained a steady pace. Deep breathes. In and out, she thought. After a minute or two, Lana eventually got close enough to view the progress of her peaches only to find them browned and rotting.

"Damnit." Reaching for the hose, she thought she could salvage whatever bit of life was left within it. Every year that Lana entered the annual "Blue Ridge Ripest Peach" contest she failed terribly. Her peaches were either of the brown, mushy texture as they were now or they were bitter, leaving her with nothing but a sigh and a dim hope for the next year. The contest had a special place in her heart though, for she has been trying to grow a successful peach tree since she was a little girl.

"But why, Ma? How come the Mayfields and the Forrests always have these full, orange peaches and I got nothing but shriveled and moldy balls of mush?" twelve year-old Lana asked her mom as she sat with the hose snaked between her chalky legs. She sat next to her tree, day after day, as the sweat from the Georgia sun dripped down her face and stung her eyes.

"I'm sure your peaches will grow, honey. You just got to give it some time," Lana's mother would tell her. More than fifty years later and Lana was still giving it some time. She asked herself what had she done wrong all these years that prevented her from growing the fruit that her state loved and cherished so much? Perhaps it was the way she took care of the tree. Did she water it too much? Too much sunlight? Or maybe it was the geographic makeup of the land; it was simply not fertile enough to grow such a tree.

Lana always had to drive past the was the Maywells and the Forrests' plantations before she got to her own. Even though the Forrests' moved out once their kids grew up and began lives of their own, Lana still regarded the plantation as theirs. Maya Maywell was still there though, and because it was summertime, her grandkids were visiting. Lana knew this because as she pulled over to look at her peach tree, bikes with trainers on them and beat up hoola hoops were strewn all over the front lawn. She shut off her husband's Chevy Malibu that she just couldn't seem to part with and felt the cool breeze refresh her face that already began to sweat in the Georgia heat. The wind whistled through the small trees that swayed before her as the sweet scent of peaches filled her with a melancholy happiness. One foot out of the car and a deep breath with the other one, Lana was on her feet, staring at Maya's vegetation. She leaned over on the side of the road and just stared at the mixture of ruby red and orange that seemed so impossible for her to obtain. As she turned the peach in her delicate hands, feeling its soft and fuzzy texture, she was taken back to the days of her childhood. The days when she would run down the very road that she staggered on now.

"They have more than enough to go around, just don't let anyone see you when you do it, okay?" Lana's mother would say as she instructed her to go down to the Maywells' late on a Saturday night to steal peaches for breakfast on Sunday mornings. Lana would always hesitate for she despised taking something that was not hers, but always end up on giving in for the Maywells had the best peaches in town. Even better than the supermarket. The adrenaline would be pumping through her system, full well knowing that she could get caught at any second. Little puffs of dirt would follow in her tracks as each foot tapped off the ground, one step closer to the forbidden fruit. She'd kneel down on the side of the road, stuff two or three peaches in her shirt and take off in the night. She never took more than three peaches for only her and her mother lived on the plantation and Lana hated wasting food. In all the years that she stole peaches, her classmate Maya never found out. Even if she did, she never confronted Lana about it. Deep down, Lana always thought Maya secretly felt bad for her because in all the years they joined the contest together, Maya was always one of the top three contestants. Meanwhile, Lana was given a sticker that read, "I love peaches!"

It was the sound of sneakers scuffing against the ground that took Lana's head out of the clouds as she turned around to see Maya's grandkids quickly approaching her. They shot her a look that read, 'what are your doing next to our peach trees?' She stood up slowly and watched the kids' legs run at speeds she wished she could reach.

"We're going to win first place this year!" one of the boys said as he darted up to Lana then past her, leaving a trail of dirt to dissipate in the air. The other one, much shorter and younger, trailed behind as his short and stubby legs tried to catch up to his more agile brother. He had to have been around seven or eight years old as he stopped in front of Lana to catch his breath. For a second both of them stood there, looked and one another and took deep gasps before saying a word. Lana smiled as she watched him push the sweaty clumps of chocolate brown hair from his eyes.

"Is your grandma around at all?" she asked. The boy turned around and with a finger the size of those baby carrots you buy in the supermarket, pointed toward a woman awkwardly jogging down the dirt road. She held her white sunhat against the wind and tried to hold onto her dress before it got caught in the breeze, too.

"Lana!" She heard Maya scream as her arm arched over her head to wave at Lana. Lana hasn't seen her in over six months for her heart palpitations restricted her to only the food market and the doctor. Lana was surprised when she noticed the definite creases in the outer corners of Maya's eyes and forehead as she reached in to give her childhood best friend a hug. Despite the wrinkles, Maya had that same infectious beauty that had all the boys in school melting over her.

"What are you doing down here? I feel like I haven't seen you in ages! How you been?" Although Lana has known Maya since Kindergarten, one thing she never got used to was the rambling questions she would spew out at lightning speed.

"I'm still hanging in there, you know," Lana answered as she counted in her head to hold onto the pace of her breath. One-two-three, deep breath in. One-two-three, deep breath out.

"How's the good old heart? Still pumping?" she asked. In mid conversation, Maya shot her head over to the older brother, "Hey! Johnny, you put that rock down and stop pushing your brother!" Her head turned back to Lana. "I know you were having some heart trouble. I've been meaning to stop by but you know how it is with kids, ha!" she said. Right away, Maya must have seen the look on Lana's face for she quickly followed up with, "Oh! I'm so sorry, I forgot." She was visibly nervous for she began to twirl the ends of her hair. Lana's breath started to lose its steady pace again.

"Don't worry about it." A pause. "I should get going anyway," Lana said as started to turn toward her car.

"You're still entering the contest this year, right?" Maya asked.

"Um, I don't know if I have enough time for it this year," Lana turned around and answered. Although she tried to play it off as if she was too busy to grow the peaches, she didn't want to admit how horrible they were turning out.

"Well, there's still two weeks until the contest. You need any help? I can send one of the boys over to make sure you're doing everything right. I gotta teach 'em young, you know? They have to carry on the tradition. Right boys?!" Maya turned around to the boys, who were now wrestling in the grass. "Hey! Stop that!"

"No," Lana said without hesitation. Realizing that her tone gave off an irritable impression, "I'm fine, really," she followed with a smile. "My peaches are turning out quite good, actually." She turned back around to face her car, put the key in the door and unlocked it.

"But, I thought you didn't have time–" Maya asked but the sound of Lana's car door overpowered her question.

Lana cranked the window down and leaned her head out the window before pulling away.

"Tell the kids I said goodbye," she said. Lana drove off into the sunset as the two boys chased each other into Maya's home with handfuls of leaves they found in the yard.

By the time Lana made it back to her house, the sun was laying over the horizon, casting magenta hues onto the colonial styled windows of her house. She knelt down on the front lawn and stared at the yellowing leaves that piled at the base of her peach tree. She reached for the hose to wash away the dead leaves and then proceeded to water the root of the tree that was still damp from when she watered it earlier this morning. Letting out a sigh, she brushed the dirt off her pants and slowly headed for the house.

Surrounded by cascading hills, Lana's washed-out yellow house with cream colored shutters sat far back from the road which allowed for much privacy. Over the years, she painted it a variety of different colors from blood red to plum purple. She always came back to yellow though, for she thought it would attract more light into her house. She stood on the soggy lawn for a moment before entering and looked at each desolate window that faced in her direction. She imagined a home full of children. A set of twins playing cards in the top left window. A teenager brushing out her younger sister's hair in the right. She glanced down towards the dining room on the first floor and imagined a family gathered around the great big mahogany table that she and Robert bought at an auction right after their marriage.

"If we're going to have a family of our own one day then we need a place of meeting. A place where we can all be together to talk about our day; to ask how each other is doing," she said to him right before she placed the highest bid on the table. Robert gave her a hesitating glance, seeing that the table was five hundred dollars over their budget.

"Can't you just picture it, Robert? All of the kids around the table, passing around the mashed potatoes? Then coming back for a slice of that peach pie that your mother always used to make?" she said, with a great big smile on her face. Reaching into her back pocket, Lana pulled out a damp tissue and wiped off the corners of her eyes with it.

"Come on in Lana, it's time to eat!" a voice yelled, directing her focus from the dining room window to the front door where her nurse, Mary, waved a hand at her. Mary was a middle aged woman with a heavy-set build who came in to look after Lana for a few hours each day. When Mary first started coming around, she would stay for hours at a time. They would drink tea together and talk about all sorts of things from Lana's senior prom with Robert to Mary's favorite books of the month. But ever since she became a grandmother two months ago, Mary would leave right after cooking Lana's dinner to spend time with her *own* family. "I have to run now Lana; the baby is waiting for me!" she would always say.

"Feeling okay today? Dinner's all ready for you. How's the peach tree doing? Good? I know that contest is coming up soon. You have to submit the peach in a couple days right?" Mary said with a whirlwind of energy.

"Two weeks. The deadlines' in two weeks," Lana said, still trying to process the babbling thoughts that Mary spewed out in one breath.

"Well how do the peaches look? Any good ones?" Mary asked as she placed a spoonful of corn onto her plate.

"Bruised. Browned. Yellow leaves gathering around the root." She took a breath between each sentence.

"It's not your fault that the soil isn't fertile. It's just the way it is. Are the Maywells having the same problem?" Mary placed a few pieces of fried chicken on Lana's plate.

"I'm not very hungry," Lana said, ignoring further acknowledgement of the peach tree.

"Sometimes people's soil is more fertile than others', that's all," Mary followed, sliding Lana's dinner plate in front of her.

"But why?" Lana asked. She tapped her fork against the ceramic plate, poking at bits of chicken. She placed the fork down then slid the plate back toward Mary.

"That's just how God made the land, my dear! There's nothing you or me can do about it. Now finish that chicken for me." Mary said.

"How is the little one?" Lana asked after a short silence at the table. She knew exactly how to work Mary for if she asked her about her kids, Mary would forget all responsibilities and talk about them until she was forced to stop. She sat down at the little table for two, put a heap of chicken and corn on her plate and then went off on a tangent.

"Oh, they're just wonderful! You know how kids are during the 'terrible twos.' Tommy's just a bundle of energy. Every time he comes over I make sure to have all his toys set up for him you know," Mary said. Lana nodded. She regretted asking her about Tommy for although it diverged Mary, it forced Lana to wonder what her children would be like if she had one of her own.

"Once he gets tired of being inside all day he usually watches me out in the garden..." Mary babbled on. "But anyways, how can I help you with your peach tree? The sun hasn't gone completely down yet. Why don't we go out there to see what we can do?"

"No, I don't think that's a good idea." Lana said "I'd rather just go lay down."

Mary rose from her seat and made her way over to Lana. She put her arm on her shoulder to guide her up from the table.

"Now, don't speak like that. What better time to fix it then right now? Let's go. What's the worst that could happen?" Mary asked.

There must not have been worst that could happen for it was pitch black outside while Mary was hunched over the wilted peach tree with a shovel and pale in hand. She dug the shovel into the ground, removing vital roots of Lana's tree while Lana's chest rose and sunk with every dig of the ground. It was Mary's idea that she try to dig out the "dead" roots of the tree for it was a "family secret" that supposedly preserved all their fruits and vegetables. While it may have sounded like a good idea, Mary's stubby fingers were not nimble enough because she dug out whatever life was left in Lana's peach tree.

With a yellow bucket full of arm-like roots in her hand, "I'm so sorry, Lana dear! You know I wouldn't do this on purpose right? I thought I was good at this," Mary said with tears welling up in the ducts of her eyes.

"It's probably best if you just head home," Lana said as she grabbed the bucket from Mary and knelt down. She stared at the gaping hole that surrounded the now diminished bunch of branches and leaves that she called a peach tree. "There's no way. There's no way I can produce a peach from this. This mess. In two weeks."

"Why don't we go down to the Maywells' trees! All we need is one peach! She won't even notice," Mary chimed in.

"No, I made a vow to never take anything that wasn't mine ever again," Lana said. "Please, I just want to go to sleep. I need to take my medicine." Lana slowly leaned up from the ground that sloshed under her feet and turned for the house. She sent Mary home, told her not to worry and assured her that she would clean up dinner.

It was almost 10:00 pm when Lana finished with the dishes and was ready to go to sleep. When her breathing became too heavy to climb the stairs, Mary moved Lana's mattress to the guestroom on the first floor. She shuffled into the bedroom that wasn't truly hers but instead, was made for an outsider. The walls were bare white. No pictures or memories. Lana couldn't stand to take everything out from her real bedroom for she thought her lungs would be strong enough to tackle the stairs again one day. She opened a little wooden nightstand and changed into a pair of worn out cotton pajamas. Just as her head hit the pillow, a loud pounding off mahogany wood echoed into her room. Lana's heart started to race because she never had visited at this time of night. There was no one *to* visit her. Lana slipped out from the cool satin sheets on her bed and glided her fragile feet across the floor that creaked with every step. She scraped the door open just to get a good enough look of who was outside. All she saw in the dimness of the moonlight were two chubby hands holding one of the ripest peaches Lana had ever seen. She swung the door open to see that she who it was that possessed such a beautiful fruit.

"I know you didn't want to do it, so I did. The offer was too good to pass up!" Mary said as she stepped into the reflection of the moonlight. She was dripping in sweat and gasping for breath. Mary looked down to see that her slacks had dirt marks all over the knees.

"What happened?! Get inside, will you?" Lana said as she motioned Mary into the house.

"Oh, I'm fine," Mary said as she helped to walk Lana into the kitchen. She put water on the stove for a cup of tea while Lana opened the cabinet under the sink to get out a rag. Again, Mary waddled over to help her.

"Don't worry about me. Let me tell you what happened," Mary said. She went over to the cupboard and took out a sleeve of chocolate chip cookies. "I was driving home and I was just thinking, because I really felt upset about earlier." She shoved a cookie in her mouth. "And as I was passing the Maywells, it was staring at me right in the face," she continued through muffled chewing. "Anyways, long story short, I pulled over and scurried like a solder across the ground to get this peach." Mary stared at Lana with great big eyes; eyes that resembled Doc's doughy ones. "I knew how upset you were and I just swooped in and made it worse by practically destroying all your work."

Lana looked at Mary then down at the beautiful peach and then back at Mary, who's smile became wider with each passing second. Tears began to flow from Lana's eyes much like the hose she drowned the peach tree in every day. Lana sat hunched over the kitchen table as the water on the stove began to boil over in the pot.

"Oh now what's wrong? I thought you would love it! Stop crying dear, please. Talk to me," Mary said as she put the peach on the table and began to caress Lana's frail shoulders. The warmth of Mary's hands on her boney shoulder blades brought her back to the very day her husband was doing the same thing.

"We're going to figure something out, just like we always do," Robert, Lana's husband said to her fifty years ago as she was hunched over the kitchen table of her parents' home.

"Who am I going to care for? Who's going to care for us, Robert? In our old age?" Lana said through sobs. Her tears left a stream down her bare face, washing away the fresh concealer and blush that was on her cheeks. Her peachy colored tears traveled down the length of her chin and onto the letter that told her she was diagnosed with Endometriosis.

"Let's not think that far ahead. We gotta take it day by day. Were just gonna keep trying, you see?" Robert assured. At the age of 21, Robert had no idea how to handle such a heavy situation, especially as a newlywed. He was still trying to adjust to being married for it was only six months after the wedding that they found out Lana was unable to have children.

"But look what it says here: 'although not impossible, genetics show that *my* particular case shows greater struggle,'" Lana read the fine print on the letter.

"Wait a minute! I got it. Adoption, Lana. What if we look to adopt?" Robert said as he bounced up from behind the chair and sat down at the table.

"Adopt? But I want our child to be *ours*. I want to carry them in my *own* belly and want them to have our *own* features," Lana said as she looked at Robert through the clumps of hair that clung to her tears.

No matter how much Robert tried to convince Lana into adoption, it amounted to no avail for she felt too much guilt in taking ownership for something that was not hers.

"It doesn't feel genuine. I want my very own or I don't want one at all," Lana would remind Robert whenever he tried to convince her. Her stubbornness began to aggravate him to the point that her was no longer able to handle her. Robert left one Lana six month after the night they found out about Lana's diagnosis.

"I need to reproduce somehow," were the last words Lana heard from his mouth before he took a bus to his mother's home in New Jersey. She always wondered why he took the bus instead of the Malibu. Perhaps, he secretly wanted her to chase after him although she never did.

As Lana relived this painful memory that shaped who she became for the last fifty years of her life, she looked up from the table to see Mary staring at her with the peach in her hands. Lana took it from Mary with her lanky hand that still had her wedding band wrapped around it and stared at the peach.

"Just two more weeks." A pause and a deep breath. "I need you to hold out for two more weeks," Lana said as she looked down at the peach.

About the Author

Soon to be college graduate of English, **Noelle Florio** is an aspiring fiction writer. While she loved to read when she was younger, Noelle began to truly appreciate literature after her English teacher showed the film, "Dead Poets Society" during one of her last classes of high school. Throughout the years as an undergraduate student, she sharpened her skills both as a reader and a writer. Fertility will be her first published piece of work to which she hopes to begin her career.

ORGANIC FOOD

by Uko Tyrawn Okon

When Selena left me, I learned that the world is a trick and it starts with what you consume. The word vitamin is on everything now. All nuts are organic, all yogurt is fat free, and all bread is wheat. An early grave awaits those who think they eat healthy. Food is an ancient oppressor that oppresses uniquely. Labels give a false sense of security. They might say ten grams of sugar, but the servings are half the normal size. That is the new religion. That is the trick.

The trick is obsession and how bad it can burn. It puts you on a mission to feel the insides of an ex who left you because you had no religion, a topic my ex-wife Selena once took to heart even though she abandoned religion soon after I was out of the picture. It is impossible to have faith after working in a store like this for too long. I told her that peanut butter is the great dietary messiah, a religion of artificial sugar that colonizes every aisle like manifest destiny. Oreos have peanut butter, pop tarts have peanut butter, Snickers have peanut butter, peanuts even have peanut butter.

A peanut butter protein cookie stand is next to the Slim Fast at the veggie side of the grocery store. Behind the protein cookie stand is a door. In front of the door is a red rope with a sign that says "Meat Eaters Only."

It is dim in the meat eater section and the meat hangs on hooks from the ceiling with the sunken shoulders of prisoners. Most of the heads have been severed deeply at the neck and they flap on the backs of the bodies like maternal breasts. A middle aged man walks among the bodies and picks the heads like giant fruit from a tree and places them like stones in a fortification that faces the wall.

I peak inside the meat eater section every time I come to the grocery store. They only give access if your teeth grow more than an inch beyond their natural length. The teeth must be sharp enough to lacerate deep veins, which induces shock in victims and mollifies the pain. To kindle screams in food is medieval, so I sharpen my teeth routinely, anxious for the day my teeth start to grow.

The peanut butter protein cookies are in three different locations strategically organized like a zone defense, noticeable from minute angles. 15 grams of protein and 5 grams of sugar per cookie, but a serving is a quarter of the cookie (another trick). People buy this cookie all the time and eat it after they work out, then they get stomach fat. Every meat eater knows that meat marinated in fat is the sweetest. Sweetness makes you a target (A trick).

I look at all the products on the cereal aisle and notice the one thing that does not belong: the chocolate bars injected with vitamins that sport the word "organic" printed in Gadugi font. When did organic become healthy?

"Excuse me," a lady says from behind her cart. She moves toward the food and places her hand on my shoulder. I can tell she was once a tom boy. Her grasp is firm, her stature is straight, and her hair is short and whipped. She grabs a box of the organic peanut butter bars. The package is green, a false sense of hope. The color green has become a commandment in the grocery store corporate office. Make something light green and suddenly it becomes perfect. There are green Doritos and green Monster cans with the word vitamin spelled out in silver on the lid. Energy drinks taste like amalgamated sugar metal and people still drink it with a clean conscience.

The green box is in her basket and her hand slides to my lower back before she smiles and moves on. To touch my lower back is to bring me to a vibrant shiver, my sacred spot that cherishes labor. Selena discovered that spot after sacrificing a labor that could find diamonds at the center of a mountain. For that, she will always be my favorite ex. Ex, I love the sound of the world even though I hate the concept.

The wheels of the lady's cart squeak as she moves and it irks me, but I smile because she is gorgeous. She feels good about herself because she is organic today, falsely organic. Perhaps it works because there is not a single mark on her skin. My mind still transcribes the trail her hand took from my shoulder to my lower back, the hair on my body stands at attention and I imagine a warm rose glow of electricity that gives me the power to turn her heart from where I stand. I am not sure what she intended, but I am conscious of its contagious effect which pulses its way through my fortress of emotions. I don't know her fragrance because I forgot to smell her, but I imagine it as a color in the air that I devour until I am full. They say that before your teeth grow you develop an emptiness beyond what faith can fill.

I follow her to the end of the aisle. Her fingernails are newly rounded and painted red, less hippie than the average veggie eater. She passes the white bread and the first selection of Nature Owl's whole wheat bread. She picks up the 21 grain bread, a selection that has become popular because every ingredient inside is organic from the wheat flour to the dried cane syrup. I look back at her and she catches my glance. An older lady walks to her cart and they speak to each other in a foreign language. The old lady drops a bottle of orange juice inside the cart and it is heavy with pulp, which means she ingests fructose syrup, a natural ingredient that will make her kidneys sweet. If my teeth ever grow the first thing I will buy are a half dozen sweet kidneys in the meat eater section. The meat eaters love this grocery store because they do not wash the blood off of the meat before they sell it, a method considered to be organic by those with mature teeth. Fangs are the ones we all watch out for because they like their meat to still have a pulse.

It looks like both women have middle eastern roots from their dark almond skin. I assume the older lady is her mother because their black hair share the same grandiloquent sheen. Her lips have a pugnacious curl that remind me of a dog's canines and serve as a red line in the dirt between Fangs and her daughter. Her daughter's narrow features are of a less pessimistic season and she is the happy cadence of her mother's seasoned eyes.

"There are a few of them outside," her mother says and looks in my direction. "I think we better hurry up and leave."

"Oh don't worry," her daughter says. "There are rules they have to follow. We will be fine as long as they know that."

My eyes were lost in her hair until her mother said this and pushed their cart in the opposite direction. Fangs used to loiter outside of grocery stores in the middle of the day without shame. I saw one sitting Indian style with both of his elbows deep in a man's split gut, deranged eyes stuck on black as a mess of cars drove by. Men have little to worry about because a Fang's teeth will crack if you have the strength to fight back. Women protested until laws were passed, now they travel in groups at night just in case.

The lady and her mother explore the flavored drinks as I look at the 20 different brands of water. Her mother grabs Snapple and she grabs American Clear. The artificial flavors and sugar in Snapple will put her in an early grave, but I am not bold enough to verbally criticize their diet, a scoff should do. I scoff at the selection of Snapple and her mother looks back at me, her eyes furtive and dissembled. It is the second time we have made eye contact and I know she thinks I am a Fang.

I hear a chainsaw's motor in the meat section beyond the red rope. An armed guard paces back and forth by the entrance to the room where they prepare the meat. He is chubby and has the recognizable twitch Fangs get when they overfeed. They only hire Fangs that they deem trustworthy and have proven good behavior to guard the meat section, even though I am sure I have the strength to do the job.

Moments later, as I peruse the tofu wings, the lady's mother glances at me for a third time from the tempeh section. Her eyes follow me because she thinks I will attack even though my teeth have not grown in. Her daughter is oblivious to everything and is nose deep in her phone. She wears black spandex that detail curves graciously inherited from her mother. I know if I look below her waist her mother will throw moral castigations at me like knives.

The truth is that she has nothing to worry about because the emptiness and melancholy is not there. That is what a Fang gets, absolute emptiness that can only be fulfilled by meat.

The thirst.

The thirst is when someone feels that feeling. It is like all of your emotions are clogged in your throat forming a desiccated cotton substance that forces you to spit and cough. I have told people that I feel the thirst in my mouth on many occasions. I even managed to cough up a white mucus once, but it was a lie. If I ever get the thirst I promise to be civilized with the power. I will not trick the veggie eaters and cook them in a cauldron of boiling water. Instead I will put them in ice boxes. They say to freeze is the most preferred death because the body goes numb before the lights go out.

A man walks to the girl and embraces her. He is an inch or two taller than me, has thick dark hair that is a little unkempt and short orange mesh shorts. This is when I notice the wedding ring, a diamond I would normally notice from my peripheral vision through a forest. Of course she is taken. They are all taken by that age and they all have kids too. If the kids are not with them they are somewhere being watched by family. I wish desperately to have her kids. I wish all men could have kids the way women do, but I guess that is their gift.

He leans over the girl's shoulder and checks whatever is on her phone. The mother speaks to them in a broken and blocky English and glances in my direction for the fourth time. I try to get out of their sight, but the store is too small. They turn around and look at me as I go to the wine section and something in me snaps for a second. I'm not sure what it is at first, perhaps the lady and her spandex, perhaps the man who has her. It comes to me and it is not a surprise. It is loneliness, but I hope it is the emptiness. I have the urge to drink all this wine right her in the middle of the store. I could break the bottle and slit my wrist, drink until I piss toward the ceiling, and watch the bitter wine run on my clean wrist like blood. The feeling boils for a moment and I imagine scenes of terror, then it dissipates.

The wine section is its own little paradise, dark red next to fifty shades of gold. I push my cart through two rows and end up at the berries. Berries are more expensive than anything else in the grocery store in terms of what you actually get. Blackberries are the sweetest, but not as healthy as they pretend to be. They stand next to the raspberries and the blueberries. Blueberries are a bit of an outcast, healthier than the other fruits, but the ugliest of the bunch. A better aesthetic approach would be to place them next to the mundane grapes, particularly the firm and oval green grapes. I grab the blueberries and head to the checkout line.

I see the girl with the chocolate lips and her man with the mesh shorts in line. Her mother is at the rear looking around like security, perhaps looking out for me. I go to a line a few cashiers down so she does not have a reason to cause a scene. The cashier is old, but she is fast and has strong hands. It is her bagger that I am really after. It is Selena, my ex. We had a violent falling out and I was pleasantly surprised she did not call the cops the last time I was here. I would not have blamed her if she did.

She looks at me with a smile and I hope she has forgotten the holes I punched in her apartment walls a decade ago. She was a narcissist who treated the rest of the world like a disease. Things changed while I was locked away. The contagion didn't just humble pretty girls, it brought the entire west coast to its knees. Now she is a bagger.

I met her as I walked by a beauty salon years ago. The trick is to talk to them before they see you. She did everything in her power to stiff arm my advances, but I still managed to break through her walls. Part of me knows I can break through again. The only thing I remember from our relationship is her quiet morning yawns and the constant echo of disfunction, sounds that always left me speechless.

Her skin looks soft this evening, almost delicate and slightly more vibrant than glowing maple wood.

"Hi Selena," I say.

"Hello," she says with a wave that is more flirtatious than I expected. I am disappointed that she does not say my name. She never pronounced it right when we were together and a part of me wants her to stumble through it for old time's sake. We argued over it once when we were together. I told her I preferred the full pronunciation and the confrontation ended with a half dozen glass dishes shattered on the floor. The relationship drove me crazy for a little while and it was worse for me after it ended. I was barely able to crawl out of bed due to the weight of depression and she filed a restraining order on me after I broke a few windows. I cannot believe it has already been a decade. Time flies. I would love for her to say I'm sorry or I forgive you.

I lay my groceries out with pride: brown rice, two bags of kale salad, 2 percent milk, unsalted cashews, blueberries, nonfat plain Greek yogurt, frozen tofu wings, broccoli florets, unsweetened white corn, seven gallons of water each in their own individual jug. There is so much green and white in my groceries it looks angelic, almost innocent. Nothing can be judged. It is a perfect afternoon at the grocery store, a no hitter, a hole in one, an indication of a man living his best life. I see Selena pick up the brown rice.

"You even got the healthy kind," she says.

"Is there such a thing as unhealthy brown rice?" I ask.

"I don't know," she says.

She smiles and her dimples are sculpted deep into her cheeks.

"Miss, you can't bring that in here if it's unshaved," the cashier says.

An elderly lady with a poodle walks in the store and she freezes when she is yelled at. I get nervous when she walks by. She is obviously a Fang and sometimes they become violent and attack veggie eaters. Kidnappings were a problem a year ago when automatic weapons couldn't even keep a person safe, but authorities seem to have attacks under control now.

The old lady looks at me and I cannot help but admire the way the sharp tips of her teeth reach from her lips to her chin. She has the jitters, but they are not constant. They pulsate from her chest every few seconds like a heartbeat.

"They no longer shave the dogs in the meat section?" the lady asks.

The cashier shakes her head. The lady turns around and walks out. She carries the dog by the head, its motionless body a captured prize hung from the lady's clutch.

I look down at Selena's name tag and the urge to say her name is deep, but I refrain. I am not sure what I would gain from the sound of it, but I am drawn in her direction like repressed art. I want to make music with her. I want to have knowledge of her for the rest of my life in the same way she once wiped the sweat from my nude body. We could make knowledge together if she gave me the opportunity.

"I love dogs," Selena says and places her hand on my shoulder.

'Then let's have kids,' I want to say.

I think she squeezes my arm a little, but I am not sure. If she did squeeze it she did it in a way that only I would know. She squeezed it in a way that would send my mind in temporary turmoil so that I cannot think straight. Her hand is at the counter now and has forgotten about my shoulder that it once squeezed. I hate when women do that. That was the story of our relationship, temporary turmoil and a forgotten touch.

The lady with the chocolate lips walks out of the grocery store with her mother and husband. A part of me is angry that they are happy and the other part is angry that Selena doesn't love me, somehow these two things connect in my mind. We could feed together if we tried again, perhaps a little harder this time. I want to grab Selena's hand, follow them outside and hunt down the entire family.

"I love the obedience of dogs," Selena says. "Where else can I get such beautiful obedience as a single girl?"

I take that as a beautiful sign.

"I'll pay in cash," I say.

The cashier pushes buttons on the register and it opens like the mouth of a slot machine.

"Would you like help out?" Selena asks.

She leans in so much that I can smell her. Her smell is undefined, just like we left each other a decade ago. There is a weathered wind about her, a cruel philosophy of love that exist in our cloud of memories. The best part is that she does not wear perfume. I am not sure what she smells like. Atmosphere? Eyes a little weary, woven through a fabric of discolored air.

"Sure," I say.

It is dark out and I am paranoid because there are a dozen Fangs on the far side of the parking lot, directly in front of us in the shadows. I can see their teeth from the exit.

"Do they always stand in groups like that?" I ask.

"What do you mean?"

"They're like soldiers."

"I like their obedience," she says.

Selena's voice is so calm that I am ashamed to have noticed the Fangs at all. I deepen my voice and sheathe my nervous insecurity in a baritone of annoyance. "They don't even look real. They look dead."

Selena hums as she walks through the broken glass from the parking lot light near my car. All of the lights in the parking lot are out and Selena's hum seems anxious.

"The Corolla," I say and pop the trunk.

The Fangs are gone and they didn't make a sound when they left. Maybe they have made their move. If they did, they are in the air.

"Where did they go?" I ask.

She screams in a voice that is deep and rigid. A man with a night stick swings at her knees and misses. Selena backs away so fast that she trips and falls to the ground. Another man, twice as thick as the first, punches me in the ear. I fall more from fear than the punch. He wraps a noose around my neck once I fall to the ground. The lady with the chocolate lips, her husband and mother are attacked too. Brutally hungry, the fangs eat the husband before he is thrown into a black van. His body showers thick gobs of blood on the ground, the muscular parts are torn from his body and his tendons hang like loose strings.

The man's moans make my body ache with fear and a part of me is relieved when he is silenced by a fang that defiles his throat until his entire body deflates. The women's screams fade when the van drives away with them inside. I hold my key in my hand like a shank and I stab the thick fang in his eye. It sticks in the socket and I yank it out. The eye ball hangs by a loose ganglia of flesh and the fang falls to the ground. I assume I have defeated him for the moment and I move to Selena who is motionless on the ground. The other fang is gone and I grab her and place her in the front passenger seat of my car.

This was not part of the plan. I did not even know that I had a plan, but Selena has been my obsession since the last time we fired words at each other like daggers. We exit the parking lot and Selena moans.

"Did they hurt you," I ask. I am so eager to touch her that my knuckles sweat.

She reaches in her pocket and pulls out a small black container. She looks away as she sprays me in the face. The chemicals feel like a thousand tiny fires set ablaze on the surface of my eyes, but the real fire is the empty failure I feel inside. The thought of her smile when she first saw me in the store flashes in my mind for a second, as the right side of my heart shatters I stop the car and lock the doors.

"Why did you do that?" I ask.

She sprays mace into my mouth and the acrid liquid clogs my throat. I struggle to breath and place my hands over my eyes as they swell.

"I'm sorry," she says. "I thought it would be easier than this. Don't fight."

We are quiet for a moment, she reaches over and unlocks the doors, and I hear the car door open on her side. I am grabbed and dragged out onto the street. No one speaks except me, but the words I say are empty.

"What happened?"

My wrists are bound and I am forced inside the trunk of my own car.

"The police are coming," Selena says, but she is not talking to me.

When she sprays me a third time her hair brushes my face and her lips touch my cheek as she sniffs from my earlobe to my neck.

"I just want to make sure that we are safe," she says. "I know I did something wrong, but it was an accident. It's not my intention that you get hurt."

"What?"

She grabs my head with both of her hands and kisses me on the forehead. I am not sure, but I also think she licks me. The pain in my eyes is terrible, but noticeably mollified. The kiss feels nice and it seems genuine. She hugs me again and grabs my other hand for a moment.

"Men can be violent in unpredictable ways," she says, her voice low. "My father was the worst at that. You never knew when he would flip and punch holes in the wall until his wrists shattered. He would wear a cast for weeks, then he would get mad while drunk in the darkness and punch the walls again. He never forgave himself, but I want you to forgive me."

"I forgive you, I forgive you, now let's get out of here. Can we get out of here together?"

I cannot see, but it sounds like she is crying. "It will be safer for you in the trunk. I'll be able to lose them once I start driving."

"Who are those guys?"

Her gentle hands rub down my lower back. She remembers how that makes me feel. Everything is silent and I want to tell her to kiss me one more time, but she lets go of my hand. She sprays me in the eyes again. This time the spray does not burn at all, but it makes me drowsy. My entire spinal cord vibrates and I lay down in the trunk as my body fades away.

"I really want you to forgive me," Selena says and presses her mouth to my lips to suck the cellular layers like they are fat. She leaves a trace of her own saliva on my face like a dog marking its territory before she slams the trunk shut.

I wake up on a bed, my ankles and wrist are restrained with handcuffs to the bedframe. In front of the bed are fangs. There are two of them and their teeth are sharp and yellow. One of them is chubby with a gray beard and the second is the one I stabbed earlier absent a left eye. Selena walks in with a blade in one hand and a foot in the other. It does not hurt, but I look down to see the severed flesh where my foot used to be. We are silent in the room for a while as Selena eats. The other two study my face as I watch her and they could not be more amused. They start with my gut once they become hungry. I don't mind the sight of my own bones, but I am not prepared for the sound of them chewing my body parts. It would be better if they played music or closed the door, but the sound of swallowing is haunting. My inside parts coat the inside of their gums and I can hear them suck parts of me from their teeth. The worst part is Selena, who carves chunks from my legs and never once looks at me.

About the Author

My name is **Uko Tyrawn Okon**. I studied English Literature as an undergraduate student at Arizona State University. I self-published one fiction novel in 2008, Racist Infatuation, and one book of poems, The Love Mindset. I host a podcast every Monday called the writing junky podcast at www.anchor.fm/thewritingjunkypodcast. I also host a YouTube channel that reviews novels, poetry, and short fiction. It can be found by searching U2OKON on YouTube. My blog has the same theme as my podcast, but with a focus on Shakespeare and classic novels. It can be found at www.thewritingjunky.com. I describe my fiction as bordering between Urban Fantasy and Magical Realism. I enjoy using magic to make readers think while entertaining them.

ROBERT AND GOYLE GO TO THE MOVIES

by Ryan James Lamb

The dull green Daihatsu Sedan pulled into the car park with a grunkling sound and came to a crooked stop between two bays.

'Don't forget the bag.' Robert said stepping out of the driver's side.

'Yeah, yeah, yeah.' Goyle replied holding one of the backpack's straps in his mouth and hopping out of the car. Slinging the bag over his back he bounded on his knuckles and feet after Robert. 'Hey, wait for me!'

'Hurry up, please.' Robert said, walking with his cheeks squeezed together. 'I don't want to miss any of the previews.'

'Aww, I hate the previews.' Goyle said. 'What's this movie called again?'

'A Most Violent Year. It's supposed to be a cinematic triumph.'

'Aw, wow. Like The Nutty Professor.' 'Nothing like The Nutty Professor!' Robert said as the glass doors parted before them and they entered the lobby. 'Great. There's a line.'

'I hope they sell outta tickets.' Goyle said as they took their place in the queue. 'Then we can see Spongebob Square Pants.'

'We are not seeing the Spongebob movie.'

'Aw, why not?'

'It's a child's movie. And it's completely vulgar.'

'I hate you.'

The child ahead in line turned to face them. Her eyes widened as she saw Goyle, standing on his knuckles like some early and repulsive link in human evolution. His bulging eyes stared back at her without blinking and his top teeth were exposed as though his upper lip were scared of his lower.

'What're you lookin at, Rat Features?' he asked her.

She yanked her Father's hand. He turned and recoiled.

'Jesus.' he said. 'What the hell're you?'

Goyle shot the man a sideways glance and stood on his hind legs like a meerkat. 'I'm a Goyle. What the hell're you?'

'I don't like it, Dad.' the girl said, her head buried in her dad's side.

'I don't like it either, Kiddo.' The man said putting a hand on her shoulder and glaring at Goyle. 'Don't talk to my daughter again.'

The man turned back toward the counter, he and his daughter inching closer to the people in front of them.

'See what you did?' Robert said. 'Why can't you just keep your head down when we're in public?'

'My head's already down.' Goyle said. 'It's really close to the floor.'

'Not what I meant at all.' Robert said as the line moved on. 'People aren't used to seeing something that looks like you.'

'Hey,' Goyle said scratching at Robert's leg with a long and filthy nail. 'I told you not to call me a something.'

'Ow,' Robert said rubbing his leg. 'Yeah, you're right. I'm sorry I forgot. But please try and see it from my point of view.'

'Yeah all right. Can we get popcorn?'

'Aww.' Goyle moaned as they stepped up to the counter.

'Hello!' The girl at the ticket booth said with a grin. 'How are you tonight?'

'My goodness.' Robert said under his breath. 'Umm, quite well thank you. We'd like two for A Most Violent Year.'

'Oh,' the girl said craning her head to look down. 'Do you have a child with you-' She stopped as she saw the humanoid monster perched on the floor. Dressed in running shorts and a checkered shirt both caked in dirt and grime, it stared back at her.

'Hello.' Goyle said waving.

The girl raised her hand in a rigid wave and swallowed hard.

'That's two, adults then?'

'Yes.' Robert said glaring down at Goyle.

'Anything from the candy bar?'

'No, thank you.' Robert said. 'I don't tend to eat much sugar.'

'Aww, but what about the colas and chocolate in the bag?' Goyle asked.

'Quiet, Goyle!' Robert said. 'He's only joking. That bag just has our gym stuff in it.'

'It's really fine.' the girl said handing him the tickets. 'Cinema three.'

'I haven't paid for these yet.'

'Oh right. Threnty, uhhh, twenty-three.'

'My God.' Robert said as they walked down the hall toward the cinema, Goyle sniffing at the sticky carpet for stray pieces of popcorn.

'No one's dropped any.' Goyle said. 'It's normally everywhere.'

'I think she was the most beautiful girl I've ever seen.' Robert said.

'She was alright. Kinda funny lookin.'

'Am I crazy or was there something there?'

'Meh, heh, heh!' Goyle laughed. 'Yeah right.'

'She was stuttering toward the end there. Seemed a little flustered. And she tried to give me free tickets.'

'Maybe she's just a bit spazzy.'

'Aww, man, that popcorn smells good.' Goyle said snorting in nosefuls of crowded cinema air.

'I wish we hadn't had to sit so close to the front.' Robert said rifling through the bag and pulling out a wet can of cola. 'Dammit.' he said squeezing the can. 'One of the colas has leaked in the bag.'

'That's yours then.'

'I don't think so, Goyle. You probably weren't careful enough with the bag. Here.' He said handing Goyle the half-empty can. 'Enjoy.'

'Aww, crap.' Goyle said licking the side of the can. 'It's all flat.'

'Can youse two shut up?' Asked the thick-necked man in the seat in front who had turned to face them.

'Ah, yes. Sorry.' Robert said putting his can of cola in the cupholder. 'Please try and be quiet, Goyle.'

'Can I have some chips.' Goyle asked.

'Alright.' Robert whispered passing him the bag. 'But try to be-'

There was a loud crackle followed by a pop as Goyle pulled the bag into two pieces sending a flurry of chips into the air like a bunch of salt and vinegar butterflies. The thick-necked man turned and glared at them. It was when he turned back that Robert noticed the markings of a tattoo printed on the man's freshly shaved head, indecipherable in the dark of the cinema.

'Goyle,' Robert whispered. 'Please try to be quiet.'

'Aw, it's only the previews.' Goyle said gathering chips off of the floor and munching them.

The thick-necked man turned once more. 'This is the last time I'm gonna ask yas. Shut the hell up or I'll drag yas outside and kick the crap outta yas.'

'Alright.' Robert said, his voice frail. 'I'm really sorry, Sir.'

'Just shut the hell up.' the man said turning back and putting an arm around the girl beside him.

Robert closed his eyes and gripped the seat and took a deep breath. As he exhaled he heard an aggressive and exceptionally sloppy raspberry erupt from the seat beside him. He opened his eyes to see the man wipe a hand over the back of his head before inspecting it.

'Oh no.' Robert said. 'Goyle, what've you done?'

The man rose like some heavy beast awakened and turned.

'Which one of you did that?' he asked. His voice was low and calm which only fuelled Robert's terror.

'It-' Robert said. 'It w-was-'

'It was him.' Goyle said pointing at Robert. 'He said you should take your ugly missus home so we don't have to smell 'er.'

'What?!' Robert cried.

There was a sharp movement in the dark as the large man seized Robert's throat. There were mutters and gasps from movie goers witnessing the altercation as it was silhouetted against an advertisement for McCarthy's Jewellers.

'Drexel, what the hell?!' the man's companion said standing and slapping him on the back of the head. 'Cut it out!'

'Aw, no.' Goyle said as Robert squirmed. 'Hey, let him go!'

'Get out of it, or you'll get it too.'

'Aw, yeah?'

There was a booming cry as Goyle's teeth sunk into the man's arm.

Some people, obviously deciding that this was about to become a most violent evening at the movies, had begun to get up from their seats and head to the exit. One of these was the lady seated next to the thick-necked man who stood just as he pried his arm loose from Goyle's mouth. The bloody forearm collided with the old woman's head, sending her over the seat in front of her and into the laps of some teenagers.

'Oh crap!' The girl cried. 'Look what you did, Drexel!'

'Run!' Goyle shouted to Robert who was already retreating through the aisle of seats with no regard for the people in them. The result was a Mexican-Wave of knees and feet lifting off of the floor and a chorus of curse words and one person expressing his wishes that Robert die in a fire.

His shoulder hit the heavy cinema door with a thud and he stumbled into the brightness of the foyer, his arms and legs flailing as he struggled to stay upright. There was a crash then as he collided with a puny teen carrying a large popcorn and drink combo. Robert sat up and wiped his soggy face in time to see Goyle bounding out of the cinema followed by the thick-necked man who in the well-lit foyer turned out to be quite thick altogether. He seemed not to notice the door, running through it at full speed and sending it thwacking against the wall and rigorously testing the durability of its hinges. As Goyle disappeared into the crowd of confused, amused, and in the case of the puny teen, severely abused patrons, the thick man's gaze fixed on Robert, now scrambling to his feet.

'You're dead!' he cried as Robert bolted for the door, his scuddy Converse crunching the teen's glasses as he fled.

It was around this time that Robert's adrenaline finally kicked in. Time slowed down and he saw his path of escape clear. The excess fat around his middle jiggled with each lunge of his chunky thighs and his greasy, curly hair flowed behind him like nothing very majestic. It was quite surprising that in this heightened state of focus Robert failed to see the identical and equally puny twin of the crushed teen, whose mangled spectacles were still clinging to Robert's sole. The only real noticeable difference between the two boys in fact, was that the second had opted for the extra-large popcorn and drink combo and these exploded in a larger radius than his not-so-greedy brother's.

There was no time to wipe his face this time as Robert felt two gorilla-sized hands seize his ankles and begin to drag him across the carpet.

'Help!' he shrieked. 'Somebody help!' Quite unsurprising was the fact that none of the patrons wanted to intervene in the abduction of a pudgy, twenty-something man who had just wiped out two young boys in the space of about fifteen seconds.

'Jesus Christ! Someone help me!' These were the cries Goyle ignored as he battered the knees of patrons on his way toward the counter.

'Oh my God!' A woman shrieked.

'What the fuck is that thing?!' An old man implored someone, anyone, to tell him.

Goyle paid them no mind either. As the counter came into view he beheld a glass cube containing enough popcorn to fill he and Robert's bathtub.

'Can I help anybody?!' The manager called from behind the counter in an attempt to wrangle the scattered patrons. 'Anybody?! Who's nex- Oh my God!' he said as he saw Goyle crouched before him. His jaw hadn't quite descended entirely when Goyle leapt onto the counter and propelled himself into the popcorn machine with amazing fluidity.

The manager's head swivelled from one side of the counter to the other searching for someone to help him. There was not a staff member in sight and it appeared that things at the other end of the foyer were just as dire as patrons jumped and cheered and a large man dragged something into the men's room.

Turning to watch as the grotesque creature buried its head in the mound of popcorn he sprinted to one end of the counter where a fire extinguisher hung on the wall. Returning to the popcorn machine he pulled the pin, levelled the nozzle and discharged the extinguisher all over the monster's back. There was a cloud of white mist and some in the crowd turned to view this new spectacle. There were the sounds of choking and flailing within the mist and as it cleared the thing stood facing him, now powdered white.

'What'd ya do that for?' it said, its yellow teeth the only thing of colour on its person. 'Ya ruined it.'

'What the hell are you?!' the manager cried.

'Mehhhhhhhh!' it hissed before lunging at him. The extinguisher hit the floor with a hollow thud and the two tumbled over the counter onto the carpet. The manager squeezed his eyes shut, held his arms over his face, ready for the blow of the creature's fists, the tearing scratch of its claws. When nothing came he opened his eyes and saw it charging into the crowd leaving a faint cloud of mist behind it.

'Please!' Robert cried as he and his pursuer came to a stop in front of the urinal. 'It wasn't me! It was-'

He was silenced by a boot to his ribs.

'Shut up!'

Robert rolled onto his side and looked up at the thick man. 'What are you gonna do to me?'

The man only pointed to the urinal.

'What? What do y-'

'Lick it.'

'What?!' Robert cried rolling onto his back.

'Lick it!'

'I can't! That's disgusting!'

'You're disgusting!' The man said, pointing a finger down at him. 'You spat chips on the back'a my head! You insulted my missus! Ya smashed into those two kids! Now lick it!' Leaning down and taking a handful of Robert's oily hair he held his face up to the stainless-steel surface of the urinal.

'Please.' Robert begged.

'Do it!' the man said twisting Robert's hair.

'Alright!' he shrieked. 'Alright.' Closing his eyes, Robert's tongue inched from his mouth. His face wrinkled like the sultanas in his fridge (which he had bought when they were grapes) as he tasted the pissy steel and then snapped his jaw shut.

'I said lick it!' The man said. 'Don't just touch your tongue to it!'

'Oh God!' Robert said spitting and sputtering.

'Lick it like you like it!'

Robert poked his tongue out again when the bathroom door swung open. The thick man turned to face the intruder, pulling Robert with him.

'What the hell's goin on 'ere?!' the policeman asked.

'So you're tellin me your friend bit this man. Then you ran into two kids and knocked em both flat?'

'Yes!' Robert said sitting on one of the sofas in the cinema's lobby. 'But he strangled me! He made me lick the-'

'I wouldn't be pointin fingers, Mate!' the officer said. 'I'd be thankin ya lucky stars the parents and the cinema aren't pressin charges! You are gonna have'ta pay for all that popcorn ya friend ate and to get that fire extinguisher refilled.'

'But that wasn't me!'

'Well my partner hasn't been able to track down this friend or thing or whatever it is, so I'm afraid you're on the hook. Like I said, count yaself lucky.' The officer turned to where the thick man stood, smirking, his girlfriend by his side. 'You guys're all good to go.' he said extending his hand. 'Thank you for ya cooperation.'

'My pleasure.' the thick man said shaking hands.

The manager unlocked the door for Robert, offering him one last glare as he did. Robert put his wallet back in his pocket and walked out into the night, the taste of urine still lingering on his tongue. He reached his car, now the only one in the carpark save for the paddy wagon, and got in. He lurched against his door as the passenger's opened and a white figure scrambled into the car.

'Oh.' Robert said. 'It's you.'

'I had to hide in the bushes.' Goyle replied. 'That cop lady was lookin for me.'

'I hope you're happy, Goyle! That whole incident was entirely your fault!'

'Aww, what'd I do?'

'Don't start with me!' Robert said. 'You owe me a hundred dollars.'

'Aww, what for?'

'You just do.' Robert said as the car struggled to life. 'Hey, did you manage to get the colas?'

'Just this one.' Goyle replied pulling the can out of the bag, half-crushed and leaking.'

'Ah, good. Give it here. I need to get the taste of urine out of my mouth.'

'Aww, sorry, Robert.' Goyle said glugging from the can. 'This one's mine remember.'

Robert gritted his teeth and yanked the car into reverse.

'Meh heh heh heh!' Goyle laughed as the car pulled out of the car park and into the street.

About the Author

Ryan Lamb is a writer from Western Australia. His writing is inspired by authors such as Terry Pratchett, Haruki Murakami as well as all of the weird people he has met in his life.

BEER BEFORE LIQUOR

by Daniel Davis

Ronnie's brother, who'd been in our shoes himself after graduation, bought us a case of Natty Lite and left us alone in their basement. We had a bathroom, snacks, a TV, an Xbox, and a sofa. Everything, we understood, that we would require.

Ronnie immediately went to town on a bag of mixed nuts, spilling some as he popped them open. "I can't believe we did it," he said.

Cole took a deep swig of beer. He was the only one of us who'd drank regularly through high school.

"Well it's done," he said, and belched. "Gonna pussy out?"

Ronnie rolled his eyes. "I said surprised, fucker. That's all."

Ronnie's surprise seemed genuine, which struck me as odd. His was a military family, going back five or six generations, depending how long you listened to his father drawl on about it. Pictures of men—and, if one looked carefully, only men—in uniform lined the walls of their home. Medals, too, though not a great many. They were a family happy to serve, even without distinction. Ronnie had been brought up knowing he would enlist one day, just like his brother.

Cole was the one who was most bemused by the whole thing. He'd barely graduated, his diploma more the result of the football coach's influence than any academic success, most of which came from copying—poorly—off my homework. I would never have said it to his face, but he'd long ago struck me as something of a stereotype: not good at much except being a friend, following orders given by a larger and tougher superior, and acting older than his age. Higher education was not for this young man, and his parents had been laying recruitment brochures out since eighth grade, letting the idea sink in. He didn't let on, but I think he dug the idea, knew that he needed the discipline. He wasn't good enough to walk onto a college football team, not even Central Illinois Community College, where all you had to do was toss the ball moderately well and take a hit without crying.

I tried to match Cole's swig with my own, and managed not to choke too obviously.

I hadn't developed the taste yet, but the thought of getting plastered was appealing. I was terrified. Scared absolutely shitless, in a way the other two, though nervous, weren't. And it's not like I'd been pressured into enlisting. My parents had been against the idea, actually, and I could see their point: I wasn't a genius, but I wasn't an idiot. I could get an Associate's Degree—maybe even a Bachelor's at State, though let's not push it—and support my inevitable future Midwest family on a respectable blue-collar career. Future Moose Lodge Member Walker Wainwright, at your service. Shit, if I *really* did good, maybe Chelmsford Country Club Member Walker Wainwright. Wouldn't that make the folks proud?

But the thought made me nauseous. I wasn't bad at school, but I hadn't liked it. I had almost strutted across the stage the previous night. Thought of flipping the principal off as he handed me my diploma, though I never in a million years would've actually done it. But college made no damn sense to me. Why pay to go to college and learn when the Army would pay you to join them and do the same thing? Plus free room and board. Travel the world. All that brochure shit, which appealed even though I knew half of it was horseshit. The money, though, the training and the education—those were real. College would provide parties and girls and a nice piece of paper, but that was nothing compared to what the Army had to offer.

Plus, and this was the one thing all three of us would admit, we just wanted to kill terrorists. *Shove Old Glory up their ass until they choke on it*, as Cole sometimes put it.

So we'd enlisted, all at the same time, the way we'd gone to senior prom together—with dates, of course; dates who, it turned out, didn't much like each other—and the way we'd had birthday parties together and camped out together and done pretty much everything else together going back six, seven years. Cole had football; I had baseball and golf; Ronnie had coin collecting and that freshman experiment with basketball. The rest, we pretty much shared, which generally made things easier to predict. *What am I doing Saturday night? Well, what's Cole doing? Yeah, and Ronnie'll be there, too.*

The way we were rebelling tonight, if you wanted to call it that. Ronnie's brother knew, obviously, and his parents had conveniently decided to spend last night congratulating their son, and tonight visiting some family upstate. One had to wonder how far back this tradition went in the McConnell family. Had his granddad gotten sloshed on moonshine while his great grandad skipped stones or whatever the hell they did back before color television? It struck me as a nice tradition.

We put in Ronnie's brother's *Call of Duty* and played Zombie Mode for a while. Ronnie liked to make "pew-pew" noises, despite the realistic—or was it?—gunfire from the game. Cole, as usual, took it a bit too seriously, elbowing me when I failed to kill a flying zombie-thing—looked like a turd with eyes and fire—which directly led to his death. Ronnie and I lasted long enough to find a David Hasselhoff Easter egg, then promptly died, and we started it all over again.

Cole held his alcohol best. But after an hour we were all feeling it. Making stupid mistakes in the game. Finally, when we realized it was useless to continue—only Cole insisting on one last attempt, then throwing his controller down when he didn't make it five minutes—we turned off the game and found Adult Swim on the TV.

As we watched cartoon creatures do adult human things, Ronnie said, "My uncle died in Desert Storm."

We knew, of course. There was almost a shrine to him upstairs. But in our drunken stupor, Cole and I were awed by this sacrifice.

"He died saving his brothers," Ronnie said. "That's what they told us."

Cole sighed. "Man, if that's how I gotta go, then let me go like that." He meant it. Him, or the beer.

I nodded. I did not mean it. Not that I was against sacrifice. I just didn't want to fucking die, which struck me as a perfectly realistic view to take. Can't you save your fellow soldiers and live, too? Why isn't that ever an option?

Ronnie said no more on the subject. The three of us took turns using the restroom. We had already broken into the Cheetos. Ronnie's brother had supplied us well. Knew what it was like.

"I wish I had a basement like this," I said, and Cole said, "We're gonna see some shit, boys."

We thought about what said shit would entail. Ronnie probably pictured a legacy, glory enshrined behind framed glass. Something his own kids would discuss one day. Maybe a parade on his return home, where he would use his service to get a good job—his grandfather had been a cop; Ronnie had often spoken of becoming one himself. Cole probably pictured a career of it, a second family where everyone was your teammate and you had their backs and they had yours. Not something to pass down to those who come after, but a foundation upon which to build your own life. Ronnie wanted a past; Cole needed a future.

Which begged the question—I asked myself, almost aloud—what was it was I searching for? A future, sure, but not a career. Hope, maybe? Money? Could it be as simple as money? And, if so, was there anything wrong with that? Wasn't that what public school was supposed to prepare you for—go out into the world and contribute to society? And most people only contributed by making, and spending, money, right? Just all a part of the great big American machine, making me yet another product to get shat out into the world—

"Hey," Ronnie said.

I blinked. The world swam back into focus, which was how I noticed it had been out of focus in the first place. I was sitting on the floor somewhat slumped over; Cole was on his back beside me, staring at the stucco ceiling and tracing patterns with his fingers. Ronnie lay on the couch, turned onto his side as he fumbled between the cushions. His hand disappeared; I thought of a big fish swallowing up a smaller fish. I thought of a vagina, though I'd only seen one in person once, and not much had come of it. Then I thought of a fish with a vagina, and laughed.

Ronnie pulled his hand out, clutching a fifth of something dark and sexy.

"Hey," he said again.

Cole sat up. "Cool," he said.

I just stared. Was that what I thought it was?

"Yeah," Ronnie said. "Whiskey."

"Gimme," Cole said.

Ronnie gave. He said, "Patrick must've forgotten about it."

I didn't think that was likely.

"Me neither," Cole said, then took a quick pull. He winced, and part of me trembled. If even he, the seasoned drinker amongst us, didn't care for it—

He coughed. "Not bad." He said. He handed it to me. "Don't think, Walkie, just do it."

So I did it, threw up a little in my mouth, swallowed that down and did it again, then passed the buck to Ronnie.

"We're gonna hate ourselves in the morning," Cole said, but he was grinning.

Ronnie barely pushed the whiskey down. He belched, and it looked like it hurt. My head swam. Surely it was too soon for that?

"Chaser," Cole said, handing me a fresh beer.

"Thought you were supposed to use Coke."

"Read that in a book, nerd?" But he was just teasing, and we both grinned as we drank our beers.

The whiskey enlivened us. We gave *Call of a Duty* another fruitless go, but even Cole didn't get angry when we all died spasmic deaths in the first few minutes. So we switched back to the TV and it seemed funnier, even the commercials were a riot. My vision alternated from not seeing much to seeing two or three of everything, but I always found my way back to the beer can or the fifth of whiskey, which I took shorter and shorter pulls from. Ronnie was the first to pass out; one minute he was laughing, the next I glanced over my shoulder and he was gone, mound hanging open and drool trailing out.

Cole laughed. "Shit," he said. "I had money on you, Walkie."

"I don't think I feel too good," I said.

He frowned at me. "Gonna puke?"

I shook my head, which wasn't a good idea so I stopped. "No. Just...not good."

He looked at me for a moment. I couldn't see his face very well so I couldn't read him, but when he spoke, his voice seemed heavy, and I somehow knew it wasn't just the alcohol.

"Me neither," he said. Either he shook his head, or my vision swam. "And not because of this, man. I mean...because of all of this."

I wanted to say something profound, something intuitive and brotherly, to express my gratitude at his friendship, to show how the three of us were still in this shit together, even though we'd been pushed out into the real world, where we were about to be split up for the first time ever. I wanted to say what I felt, which I couldn't quite understand but knew he shared, that this was the end but also the beginning and middle, that life could end but go on just the same. I wanted to say all of this, and more, because there was so much more to share, there was an endless universe of possibilities at play here, and I opened my mouth to tell him as best as I could, and that's the last thing I remember.

The next morning, we were miserable, taking turns vomiting in the toilet and moaning on the floor, chugging the water that Ronnie's brother brought us, popping Excedrin like they were Pez, and mutually agreeing we'd made a terrible mistake but not really meaning it. A few months later, the three of us were in the desert. It went about as well as expected.

About the Author

D.W. Davis is a native of rural East-Central Illinois. His work has appeared in various online and print journals. You can find him at Facebook.com/DanielDavis05, or @dan_davis86 on Twitter.

TALK TO ME

by Bonita LeFlore

At three months of age, Maria Lopez Ruiz's eyes turned blue. Not just any ordinary blue, but turquoise, the color of the sea near Porto San Sebastian, where Sophia Lopez Vargas, Maria's maternal grandmother, lived. She, too, had turquoise eyes.

It was a sign; Maria's brown-eyed mother told the rest of the family that her child, the fifth daughter of a fifth daughter, would be a woman of great importance.

Maria's father worked at a grand resort in Las Almandas, which was over three hundred miles from Porto San Sebastian. Because of the distance, he only came home twice a year: the month of August and the week of his birthday.

It was in January of Maria's sixth year that her mother died with the fever, leaving the family adrift. Maria moved in with her grandmother, Sophia, in the small house that overlooked the sea.

***

"Being successful, Maria," her grandmother always began her stories, "requires being in the right place at the right time." As she continued to braid her granddaughter's hair, she repeated the adventures that led her to Porto San Sebastian.

"My first marriage was arranged, or that is what my husband believed. He was from Madrid and I was from Las Rozas. He had seen me..." Her grandmother went on to describe how, at the age of fifteen, she had used her turquoise eyes for the first time. "I have not always lived in this quiet village," she said, ending the story the way, she ended all of her stories. "And you will not, either," she added.

"When you are fourteen, you will leave here. You will go and live with your oldest sister in a faraway place. You will become independent and a woman of great importance."

***

Maria leaned against a pillar on the platform of the Christopher Street Subway station and rubbed her belly. She was in her fifth month with her first child and the heat was the one thing that felt familiar. Taking a deep breath, she considered how far in ten years she had come to be in this place so removed from San Sebastian.

That evening she told her husband: "If I close my eyes for a moment, I am transported home: the thick air covers me, and I can almost hear the sound of the waves."

He laughed.

"Why is that funny?" she said.

"That's not why I laughed it's just..."

Maria sighed as he kneaded his fingers deep into the arch of her right foot.

"I'm proud of you. Remember when I introduced you to my aunt? We agreed to make her think I was seeking her approval," he said.

Maria smiled and looked toward a window where the air conditioner hummed relentlessly. A sound so familiar and yet so far away, a steady summer wind rattling her grandmother's house in Porto San Sebastian before a storm.

"Your aunt took me into her lavender bedroom, she pulled the shades and read my cards by candlelight. I know she whispered the readings to you, mi amor. It was a good thing that you had already proposed marriage, or you might have changed your mind."

He furrowed his brow.

"You are a beautiful woman," he said. "When we walk down the street, people stare at you. I don't think you even notice."

***

It was at the age of twelve that her grandmother told Maria about men who were only interested in the superficial.

"We are like *this*," she gestured toward the sea with one hand, as they sat in old wicker chairs on the stone patio sipping cold tea. "Men see what they want to. It is useful."

***

Maria's boss, Xavier Batista, was one such man, expecting to get his way with anything and everyone he touched. Xavier moved in all the right circles at Telemundo.

"Brilliant!" He clapped his hands. "But, why just New York, Maria? Think bigger. This country is changing. You have a story to tell, use your biography. Remember my mantra: *demographics*. Women are our audience; this show will speak to them.

"You have been so generous to me, Xavier." She turned her eyes toward him and could see the heat rising into his face. "If the network buys my show, how will I repay you for your advice?"

He looked at her, smiled and reached out to touch her arm. "Tell your husband who the father is." When he began to repeat his dream of how they would move to the city of angels together, Maria moved away. "We are meant to be together—a team."

"It is too soon to talk of these things. My husband thinks..."

He pulled her toward him. "We will work this out." His face was now flush with color.

For several months Maria let Xavier think what she needed him to.

***

A scent of bitter fruit infused the air as Maria felt the rumble of the Number 1 train before its lights turned from the tunnel and flooded the tracks ahead. When she entered the crowded subway car, Maria stood in front of a young woman.

"Oh! Sorry," the woman said jumping up, offering her seat. Maria sat, closed her eyes, and started to review the presentation of her show *Háblame: Talk to Me*.

Thirty minutes later, when she walked off the elevator onto the twenty-first floor of an office building in mid-town Manhattan, she spotted her secretary, Julia, leave her cubicle and run toward her.

"The presentation has been postponed; something happened this morning."

Maria let Julia take her briefcase and watched as the woman put her finger to her lips.

"I'll explain in your office." Julia twitched like a small sand bird, weaving her way through the maze of gray cubicles.

As she followed Julia, the young employees, heads focused on screens, sat quietly typing. They didn't look up. It was not their usual morning buzz over prefabricated walls where they stopped to welcome her.

"Xavier has resigned," Julia said breathlessly as she closed the office door. "I mean he has been fired—resigned is what his memo to the company said."

Maria took out her phone and saw for the first time the messages, starting twenty minutes earlier from her staff, multiply with every second.

Julia went over to a table where a carafe of coffee waited to be poured. She turned and looked at her boss.

"Are you surprised?" Maria said looking up from her phone. They had never discussed the rumors about Xavier.

"Some of the interns had problems with him," Julia said. The cup rattled on the saucer as she walked across the office.

Maria flinched. A few years earlier one of the production assistants told her something suggestive Xavier said to her. She remembered laughing. Now the child inside of her rolled and pulled tight against her.

"Talk to me, while I get up to speed." Maria sat adjusting a pillow on her back and logged into her computer.

"There's an executive committee meeting in fifteen minutes." Julia handed Maria a printout of Xavier's letter to the company. "I told them you would be there," she said.

"How are you feeling?" her secretary asked.

"About this...or just in general?"

"You work...worked really closely with Xavier. Did he ever...?" Julia's voice was trembling.

"Of course not, a total professional since the first day I met him. I'm shocked." She rested her hand over the kicking inside of her. "Give me a few moments."

"Can we meet?" read the text from Xavier.

Maria waited and when a second text appeared on her phone she read: "Are you there?"

"Can't. It's crazy here," she responded. She was walking toward the Board Room.

"I need to talk to you," he wrote.

They all will have stories, Maria thought. Even now, on the other side of the building, the President of Telemundo was finishing telling his to the media.

"None of it is true," Xavier added.

Maria knew he couldn't possibly know everything everyone was going to say.

About the Author

Bonita LeFlore was born in New York City. After receiving a BFA in painting from Syracuse University, she began a career in advertising. Today Bonita lives and works on the North Shore of Massachusetts. Several of her short stories have appeared or are forthcoming in: Front Porch Review, Mulberry Fork Review, Work Literary Magazine, and others.

THE ALLEYWAY FIGHT

by Taylor G Mauck

The annoying ringing in my ears is the first thing I hear when I start to come to. Ugh, my head! How did I even black out? The only thing I can even register, is something firm but at the same time soft against me. The ringing in my ears died down a little, and I can start to hear some muffled voices.

"...vid...ear...e...?! ...ease...!"

I try to muster up enough strength to open my eyes. It takes a few seconds, but I eventually do open my eyes. Above me is a person; although, I can't make out who it is. I blink a few times before I'm able to see who it is. My eyes widen at who it is. It's my boyfriend Jacob! What's he doing here?!

"David!" Jacob exclaims.

"J-Jacob?" I asked, while trying to sit up from his lap; which is what I am laying on.

"Stay down! Makayla thinks you have a head injury! Possibly a concussion!"

"Wait, Makayla's here?!"

"Yea! She was the one who heard some crashes coming from here! She wanted to check it out, and we looked in time to see you getting your head slammed against the wall! You can imagine how pissed she was, and how worried I was!"

I'm about to say something, when I hear a thud. I look over to see Makayla slam her fist right in a guy's nose. The guy lets out a yell as he slams on the ground. A moment later, she turns around and blocks an incoming attack from behind. Oh right. I keep forgetting she was living on the streets for 5 years and taught herself how to fight. Back in early high school, I never knew she would one day become one of my best friends. As Makayla went to block another blow, everything started to come back to me.

A kick to the chest.

I get jumped and dragged into the alleyway.

A hit to the jaw.

"You think you're so cool!"

A sprain to the arm.

I get a punch in the gut. I get slammed into a wall.

Makayla yells as she charges again.

"You deserve this! After you expelled us senior year! You and your stuck up

boyfriend! What makes you so special for being gay anyway?!"

Makayla blocks another attack.

They slam my head against the wall behind me.

Makayla dodges.

Black.

Now I remember. I know they didn't like me in high school because they thought I was stuck up, especially when I started dating Jacob, but I didn't think they would go this far.

"David?"

I look over at Jacob to see that concerned look on his face.

"I'm ok," I try convincing him.

"Like hell you are!"

I glare at Jacob before looking back at Makayla's fight. In that moment, she looks over at us, and her eyes widen.

"David?!"

"Makalya!" Jacob suddenly shouts.

I suddenly see one of the guys running up to her. She doesn't have time to react as she's suddenly knocked off her feet and is pinned to the ground. Jacob suddenly stands to his feet.

"David, if anyone comes after you, yell!"

I don't get a chance to respond before he runs over and tackles the guy off of Makayla.

"Don't touch her!" I hear him yell.

Makayla stands up and takes a moment to run over to me, while Jacob tries to fight.

"Thank god you're awake," she says as she kneels down next to me. "We were worried there for a bit. Thankfully you aren't bleeding, but we still need to get you to the hospital, Do you think you can walk?"

I nod. "Yea."

She sighs. "Alright. Just hang tight."

Makayla stands up and turns around, only to be met by the guy with the possibly broken nose. When did he...?!

He's suddenly grabbed by the ponyhair and yanked on the ground hard. He groans as he makes an impact, and we look to see Jacob glaring daggers at him. After a few moments, he looks at us.

"Are you guys ok?"

"Yea," Makayla says while I nod.

"Good. We need to get moving! Now!"

I stand to my feet, only to wobble and fall against Makayla. Judging by the way she flinches, I'm guessing she's off guard.

"David!" Jacob suddenly shouts.

I shake my head and push off Makayla.

"I'm fine! Just got a little dizzy is all."

"Don't say you can walk, if you actually can't," Makayla rolls her eyes.

"But I-!"

"David, I love you. I really do. But you're seriously an idiot sometimes!" Jacob glares at me.

I roll my eyes. "Gee thanks. Love you too."

"Let's just go! We're wasting time! Jacob, help with him!"

Jacob nods, and left me no room to protest. As Jacob prepares to grab my arm, I suddenly hear a smack. We look over to see Makayla smacking one of the guys in the face. Wait, weren't they just knocked out a moment ago?! Damn it! Makayla was right! We wasted too much time with arguments! Makayla's back is turned to us as she charges at the guy. Within a few moments, she suddenly stops, and starts backing up a little.

"U-um...w-was David by any chance stabbed, Jacob?"

Jacob and I look at each other confused before Jacob quickly inspects my condition.

"No. Why?"

"Because this guy has a knife!"

Jacob and I look at each other in shock. What did she just say?! How does he have a knife?! Oh god! What would've happened if these two didn't see me getting ambushed?!

"M-Makayla?" Jacob suddenly stutters, but then Makayla charges at this guy again. "Makayla! Ugh! Damn it! What an idiot!" He then looks at me before making me sit on the ground. "David, I need you to hang back. Make sure those two other guys don't move!"

I look to my left to see the three other guys Makayla and Jacob knocked out. When I turn my head back, Jacob was already fighting alongside Makayla. It's obvious they're both heavily on the defensive side. Wait a second...weren't there five of these guys? I looked back to the three guys unconscious, and back to the guy with the knife. That's four. I look around the alleyway, but I didn't see him anywhere. Did he simply just run away? No, he wouldn't when it's 3...I mean 2 against 5.

Suddenly, small pieces of gravel fell on my back. I flinch at the sudden impact of it. It feels like it came from above. I look up, only to find out where the fifth guy is at. He's on top of one of the buildings closest to the alleyway. He has something in his hand, but I can't make out what it is. It kind of looks like a...wait, is that a gun?! Shit! He points his gun forward. He points it towards Makayla and Jacob. Shit! Shit! Shit! "Hey, get down!" I shout, causing my head to suddenly throb.

Makayla and Jacon look confused, as the guy with the knife nearly stabs Makayla.

"There's a guy on the roof who has a gun! Get down!"

Everyone looks up towards the roof before they hit the deck. A shot rings through my ears, but I could tell it was a blank.

"What the hell?!" Jacob exclaims.

"Ugh! That bastard!" Makayla shouts as she makes a run for the fire escape.

"Makayla, wait!" Jacob yells after her, but she doesn't pay attention.

He looks back at the guy with the knife. I get to my feet and walked over towards the two. Something tells me Jacob's going to need help.

"Jacob!"

He looks at me. "David, what are you-?!"

"Shut up with your talking already!" the guy with the knife charges at us, barely missing Jacob in the process.

Jacob gives me a glare as if saying he will lecture me later before he went in for another attack. My head pounds and throbs, but I can't just sit by and watch any longer. With Makayla after the guy on the roof, it's Jacob vs a knife wielding maniac. As I begin to try and run into the fight, Jacob is clutching the guy's wrists as if he was trying to get khim to release the knife. I can see this either going very well or very wrong. I run towards the fight, and the guy sees me. He kicks Jacob in the gut as Jacob lets go of his wrists and falls over to the ground.

He then swings his knife at me and I barely dodge. Damn it!

He smirks at me as he swings the knife near my head. Holy shit! Is this guy *actually* going to kill me?! What exactly happened to him after his expulsion from school?! I try my best to dodge his attacks, but my head wouldn't stop spinning the more I dodge. Eventually, my legs give out and I collapse to my knees.

"Well look who finally stopped being a pest!"

He raises the knife, and that's when Jacob comes out of nowhere and basically tackles to guy to the ground. That guy has a knife Jacob! What the hell are you thinking?!

"If you even *think* about hurting him, I'll kill you!"

All I can focus on beyond that point, is my pounding head and everything around me spinning. Damn it! Why does this have to happen?! Why?! My hearing begins to go as well as all I can hear is that annoying ringing again. I clench my eyes shut as I silently pray for the dizziness to stop. Damn it all! Why did those guys bring me into this after all these years?! Why did *they* get dragged into this?! They had absolutely nothing to do with this!

The dizziness stops and my hearing comes back. I open my eyes to see Jacob once again getting kicked towards the ground. The guy approaches him, knife in hand. Jacob looks like he's still recovering from that blow. I bit my lip as I look to the roof above. Makayla and that other guy aren't there. I really hope Makayla's alright.

I look back to see the guy was a foot away from Jacob. Shit! I had no idea my body even moved until I'm suddenly standing in between Jacob and the other guy. And then...pain! The best way I can describe how this pain feels is just...white, hot and agonizing. I hesitantly look down to see the knife lounged right into my side. I don't even have to turn around to see the horrified look on Jacob's face.

"You little pest!" the guy pulls the knife out of my body and kicks me towards the ground.

I can't stop myself from screaming out in pain as I fall. My body falls on something, and I look up to see Jacob, looking at me with terror.

"David, I...you idiot! Why did you do that?!"

"I...I..." I don't even have the strength to talk.

Jacob lays me down gently, and he glares at the guy.

"YOU'LL PAY FOR THAT YOU MONSTER!"

Jacob charges full speed, knocking the guy over. I'm able to make out Jacob beating this guy senseless and ruthless. Everytime the guy tries to get up, he's immediately back on the ground. My vision swims heavily and it's making me feel nauseous. My shirt clings onto my skin as I felt the blood flow beneath me.

"Jacob, stop!"

I look up to see Makayla pushing Jacob roughly off the guy, who is now unconscious. When did she get back?

"He's done, alright?!"

Jacob glares at her. "He *stabbed* David!"

"Wait, what?!"

She looks over at me before rushing over. Jacob isn't far behind her. I look up at her, and her eyes widen as she looked at my wound.

"Holy shit...!"

Jacob looks like he's about to be sick.

"Oh my god! Oh my god, Makayla! He's bleeding badly! David, you need to stay with us! Makayla, do something please! He's gonna die! He's gonna-!"

SLAP!

Jacob immediately got silent as soon as Makayla left a huge red mark on his cheek.

"Shut up! Calm down! How about instead of freaking out like an idiot, go call an ambulance?!"

Jacob blinks before gulping.

"Ah, right!"

He frantically grabs his phone before shakingly pressing the numbers. Makayla sighs as she looks back down at me.

"David, can you hear me?"

I look up at her.

"Ma-Makayla? I-I...don't...f-feel...good..."

"I know, but you're going to be fine. Just stay with us, alright?" her voice shakes slightly.

I stare at her as I find myself getting more and more sleepy. I know she wants me to stay awake but I'm...so tired. So very tired. Sleep sounds so good right now.

"David!" Jacob comes into my view, tears forming in his eyes. "Just stay with me ok!" He holds my hand. "You'll make it! You just have to just listen to my voice, ok?!"

Every second, my vision gets more and more blurry. Every second, I can barely register Jacob's plead for me to stay awake. Each one sounds more desperate than the last. Jacob please just...shut up. I'm tired.

I very vaguely am able to hear the sound of sirens in the distance. Hearing that made me realize I can finally get some sleep. My vision goes black shortly afterwards.

...

I opened my eyes slightly, and the first thing that floods my vision, is a ceiling. My vision is hazy for a few moments before it clears. When I look around at my surroundings, I notice I'm in a hospital. Everything that happened starts coming back to me. I quickly realize the pounding in my head has lessened, but it was still there. It was uncomfortable, but at least it isn't unbearable. I go to sit up, when a sudden pain went through my side. Oh right. I was stabbed protecting...

I quickly look around again, before I see Jacob resting his head in his arms on top of my bed. How long has he been here? How long have *I* been here? Should I wake him up? My silent question has been answered when Jacob stirs slightly and opens his eyes. He then looks over at me, and he immediately froze.

"D-David?"

I give him a weak smile. "Hey."

He immediately leans back roughly in the chair, nearly falling over in the process.

"Oh my god! David! You're finally awake! How do you feel?!"

"Well, my head hurts from all your screaming."

"Oh," Jacob blushes. "Sorry. But seriously, how do you feel?"

"Well, my head hurts a little. My side hurts too."

"The doctor said that was to be expected. That is, if you ever woken up."

"What?"

Jacob bites his lip. "Well...you had a concussion, plus you also got...you know, stabbed. You've been unconscious for a week, and the doctors weren't completely sure if you were going to wake up due to falling asleep with a concussion plus bleeding out. But look at you now!"

I felt numb in that moment. There was a chance I could've died in a coma?! That's...

"Y-yea..."

I look up to see Jacob having tears in his eyes, which caught me completely off guard.

"Wha...Jacob?!"

"I'm sorry. I'm just so relieved that you're ok! You had us all worried sick!"

I chuckled weakly. "Well, I'm sorry to worry all of you. Wait, where's Makayla?"

"Oh, she had something to do. She said she'll be back later," Jacob tells me as he wipes the tears from his eyes.

"Oh, alright. So what happened after I blacked out?"

"The ambulance and the police came to the scene, and the paramedics loaded you quickly onto the ambulance. The police arrested the five guys who attacked us, and took Makayla's statement, and my statement. They want us to expect a call from them on the matter. We're going to have this case taken to court eventually. We didn't get arrested because they classified our actions as self defense. Especially since one person had a knife and another person had a gun. Makayla basically beat the crap out of the guy with the gun after she got the gun away from him."

I look down towards my lap. "Oh."

"Yea..."

Jacob suddenly leans over and kisses my forehead, before he stands up quickly from the chair.

"Shoot! I have to go tell the doctor you're awake! I'll be back!"

Jacob runs out the door immediately afterwards. I sigh as I stare at the ceiling again. How long did this fight even happen? A few minutes? An hour? Honestly, it felt like it lasted forever I knew they hated me for expelling them in high school, but I never thought they would try to kill me. Would I be dead right now if it wasn't for Jacob and Makayla? That's what scares me the most. I know this won't be the last time I'll see them. But is their motive to fight me actually because of them being expelled, or is it something far more deeper than that? I feel that will be a story for another time.

About the Author

Taylor Mauck: I am 20 years old and I was born, raised, and currently live in western Maryland. I'm currently going to a community college to get my associate's degree in general studies and planning to graduate in August 2020. After graduation, I hope to work in a library as a librarian technician while also trying to work on my creative writing and getting my work published. I've grown up loving to write creatively and reading. I hope one day I can make people happy with my stories as much as many well known authors have made me happy with their work.

THE SULLEN ROAD

by Susie Gharib

I fell in love with his shadow which wavered every time he passed by my window, a profile with no features, but whose footsteps echoed in a rhythmic fashion that made me wish it would continue for evermore. No one knew his name, whence he came and whereto he went. He kept his face submerged by a hat and was nocturnal in his habits. He left his apartment as soon as all traces of the sun were obliterated from the horizon of a very quiet neighborhood. There was not a single pub in our area, and children went about their business with hushed voices and any boisterous child got his proper chastisement. No wonder ours was called the Sullen Road. The only sound that reverberated for nearly five minutes was the rhythmic treads of Mr. Unknown. Respect for privacy had over the years become the norm in that suburb which boasted amity amongst its neighbors but with measured aloofness, so no one tried to befriend or approach the new neighbor who apparently preferred solitude.

His comings and goings became the hands of my clock. My life began ticking as soon as his footsteps penetrated my wall. I stood mesmerized before my curtained window and patiently waited for his shadow to fill my eyes with warmth. His strides became an alphabet that constituted a language of its own. I learnt it letter by letter and by the time I got addicted to Mr. Unknown, my ears could comprehend each footstep that was audible in my camouflaged room. My curtains allowed me to see through without jeopardizing my reputation as the most serene and self-sufficient woman in the neighborhood.

Louisa, the only friend I had, asked me out on several occasions to dinner but I had to decline each invitation because it would deprive me of my daily dosage of romance. I ran out of excuses, so I had to confide in her for she elaborately expressed her mortification at my shunning her out of my world. Were we still friends? She kept pestering me with unremitting remonstrance that enjoined a response.

"I'm in love," I said, taking Louisa by surprise, as we were having a breakfast of buttered scones in our favorite cafe in a shopping mall.

"What!" Louisa responded, her face looking like a rainbow in the wake of a storm.

"I am enamored with ...," I stopped, not knowing what to say next.

"With!" repeated Louisa in the manner of an angry parrot, bent on teasing the surrounding spectators.

"A neighbor's...," I stopped again, feeling an utter sense of helplessness.

"A neighbor's good looks!" said Louisa, hoping her intervention would unleash my tongue, but utterances refused to leave my throat.

"Joyce, take a breath and spit it out. There must be something wrong upon which you are choking," said Louisa with contrived calm.

"He's a shadow," I said, with tears fast filling my shadow-tinted eyes.

"What do you mean by shadow?" Louisa responded, placing her hand on her forehead, her way of showing alarm.

"I have not seen him face to face," I tried to explain.

"But you have spoken to him," said my worried friend, hoping the answer would be in the affirmative.

"No," I answered, unable to maintain eye contact.

"You have dumped my many invitations to dinner for the sake of a mute shadow," said Louisa, with a tone of bitter disappointment.

"I cannot explain Lou. He is a presence. When he passes by my window, he charges me with energy. I vibrate the whole evening and would not be able to sleep before his return, which is as punctual as Big Ben," said I.

"What if he disappears one day, or should I say one evening. You do not know his name or even his face. This is self-torture, Joyce," she pleaded with sudden softness.

"I dreamt of him the other day. He took off his hat and revealed his face to me, which became lit with the silver of the moon and he had inky eyes, dark blue and magnetic," I said, hoping that the texture of a dream would endow my affair with actuality.

"Inky!" exclaimed Louisa in a semi-scream.

"The color of the sea when seen from a ship, far away from land," I continued, with no intention to upset my friend.

"This sounds like a fictive character that has come to life from some book you've been reading," said my pal, with disbelief contorting her features.

"Lou, it's real. Do you want to see him tonight?" asked I.

"Yes. Let's sort this affliction out, you and I. When do you expect your bundle of shades this evening?" asked Louisa, with apparent relief.

"At nine-thirty," I answered with a resigned voice.

"Nine-thirty then," said Louisa and abruptly veered the subject to her ailing cat.

We stood opposite the window the next evening, I trembling with anticipation, Louisa with apprehension, until his footsteps resounded in the room. I beckoned to Louisa to keep calm, so she stood transfixed like a pillar of salt. As he passed by the window, the shadow looked agitated and for the first time paused for a few seconds then resumed his usual pace, but with discordant steps. Distress took hold of me. Had he seen Louisa standing next to me?

"Joyce, I have to leave. This has unsettled me. We discuss this tomorrow morning," she said, rushing out of the house as soon as the shadow's footsteps faded.

I waited the whole night for him but he never graced my window with his silhouette. Louisa called the next day and told me that she was feeling indisposed, so we postponed our meeting to an indefinite date. Nine-thirty came with no footsteps to enhance my heartbeats. The shadow vanished from the neighborhood and Louisa never called again. For years I frequented our café hoping to accidentally meet Louisa and restore our friendship, but she disappeared from our favorite spots and never returned my calls. When I gave up, I learned through an acquaintance that she recently passed away and was given an address where I could offer my condolences.

I arrived at a beautiful house the next day and hesitated before ringing the bell, not knowing what sort of reception to expect. A tall man opened the door and ushered me in, then with an agitated face asked me to wait for Louisa's mother to get dressed because they were not expecting any guests. Before I could utter a single word of apology, he picked up a hat, whose contours I knew by heart, and abruptly left the house. I learned from Louisa's mother that the man with the inky eyes was Louisa's widowed husband, so with a single sigh, I left the house without paying my condolences.

About the Author

Susie Gharib is a graduate of the University of Strathclyde with a Ph.D. on the work of D.H. Lawrence. Her poetry and fiction have appeared in multiple venues including Down in the Dirt, Three Drops from a Cauldron, Inspired Magazine, The Opiate, Mad Swirl, The Blue Nib, The Poetry Village, Blue Unicorn, A New Ulster, Adelaide Literary Magazine, The Ink Pantry, the Pennsylvania Literary Journal, and Miller's Pond Poetry Magazine.

FOR YOU, BLUE

by Anna Schaeffer

"Eighty-two."

Lina Vaduva woke up with the number thrumming in her head like a dial tone. The clock on Lina's phone read 3:45, but silence was rare in Lewiston, even in the mornings. Somewhere, a dog was barking and the wet hiss of wheels on damp pavement announced the first of the morning commuters making their way across Androscoggin river to the city center. A toilet flushed in the apartment downstairs. Beyond these sounds, or behind them, maybe, Lina heard the number repeating. *Eighty-two, eighty-two, eighty-two.* Lina could hear it like the sound of her own voice in her head, incessant and perfectly clear. The dog had woken her up and continued to bark, but the phantom number pushed her fully from sleep. She rolled over in bed and muffled her ears with her pillow but neither the dog nor the number fell silent.

While God was walking down the street,

A dog was barking

When god came back, the dog was dead.

When Lina's mother had first told her the prayer to silence barking dogs, Lina had snorted, "all that's going to do is make someone call the ASPCA on you."

The sound of the voice still echoing in her head, however, concerned Lina more than the dog. *Eighty-two*, it insisted, *eighty-two*. Fully awake, Lina knew that the voice wasn't some fragment of a dream as she had first thought.

"Shut up," she whispered to the voice," please."

The voice only continued. Lina reached for her phone, it's solid weight in her hands and blue-tinted glow calm her. The screen was like a window, Lina could peer through it and stare at the crowd of tiny strangers who stood on the other side, arguing and laughing with one another or looking right back at her. *Eighty-two* the voice muttered, sullen at being ignored. Lina struggled to divert her focus but typed into the search bar.

Hearing voices is an auditory hallucination that may or may not be associated with a mental health problem. It is the most common type of hallucination in people with psychotic disorders such as schizophrenia. 2. However, a large number of otherwise healthy individuals have also reported hearing voices.

Lina breathed out in relief and repeated the last sentence out loud to herself several times. *Otherwise healthy*. Otherwise healthy individuals might experience and recover from a short break from reality, they might be able to ignore the anomaly until it passed. *Eighty-two,* the voice said. Lina pretended not to hear.

When Lina padded down the stairs at ten after ten, the number had quieted to a soft mumble. Lina's mother was seated at the wide kitchen table.

"Morning," Lina yawned. Maria had her steepled hands pressed against her chin in morning prayer and said nothing in reply. Ignoring the number her head, Lina poured a cup of coffee and sat down across from her mother.

"You're up late."

"My alarm never went off," Lina said.

"Then it's a good thing that the bennet's dog was barking it's head off." Maria took a sip from the cup of coffee that Lina handed to her. "Mike won't be up for a while either."

"Mm."

"Bizon," Maria spat the insult in Romanian before pressing her lips into a bitter line, a feather of her dyed cherry colored hair bobbed in the draft.

Maria's exasperation with Lina's stepfather wasn't new. Mike was a drinker, in the same way that other men his age were lawyers or mechanics or teachers. Lina looked over at the small statue of the Virgin Mary that sat on a plastic alcove over the sink, her neutral smile and raised, open hands shrugged in amiable resignation, *What can you do?* She seemed to say.

"I noticed that he hasn't fixed that window in the stairway yet either. Like he said he *would,*" Lina said

Maria's mouth, already painted her favorite raisin-maroon, twitched at the corners and she sighed,"It's ok, Lina, you know I'm perfectly happy to shame him by myself."

Lina only shrugged, feeling the burn of her clumsy attempt to relieve her mother's lonely indignation. The number eighty-two bounced in her mind and filled up the familiar silence that had fallen over the conversation until Lina left for work.

At seventeen, Lina had secured a job at the Shop n' Save deli counter at the Lewiston Mall just three bus stops away from their triple-decker apartment on Holland Street. Lina liked the work, she liked pushing the fat mounds of meat into the slicer and watching them come out on the other side in silky, sandwich-ready heaps. She liked decorating the glass case where the pastrami, turkey and ham rested in herds under the fluorescent light. The bright-colored labels and orderly aisles made up a world that was separate from the one outside the Shop N' Save's sliding doors and Lina had become a part of it. Lina often thought it was something in the native familiarity she had of the deli counter that had kept her there so long.

A small punch clock sat beside the employee table in the break room. Lina had memorized her PIN number within her first week of working at the deli counter some six years ago now. Numbers weren't her strength, but Lina could memorize anything. Lina could recall sitting after class with Mr. Baker, trying to understand what it meant to add four and four together, desperate to leave for lunch or recess. Eventually, Lina taught herself that the two fours, who were all lines and angles came together to make the rounded and elegant shape of the number eight. *Six eight five two nine. Employee Lina Vaduva clocking in for another day at the Cold-cut Colosseum, the Meat Mansion, the Pastrami Palace, that's right folks, number six eight five two nine, coming in hot.* Lina raised her thumb, the paint on the numbers had faded from the pressure of countless fingers-

Lina snatched her hand back as if she'd touched something hot. Repeated over the LED screen moronically, and at least a dozen times was the number eighty-two.

"Little early this morning, Lina Helina Bo-Bina," Lina's supervisor brushed by her, taking no notice of the haunting strand of numbers on the punch clock. Lina prodded the backspace button until they disappeared. "What's five minutes between friends, Tristan?" She said, "Makes up for all the times I've been late doesn't it?" Lina's voice shook, but Tristan took no notice.

"That is *not* how it works. But you beat Amber at least."

"She's late every day and I never hear you say anything about it," Lina grumbled.

"She's too sensitive," Tristan said

Lina snorted loud enough for Tristan to hear it from the break room, but he only smirked and lumbered out, tying the white apron around his broad stomach. Sometimes, with his pinkish complexion and shock of dyed blond hair, Lina thought that he had come to look a little like the ham hocks and turkey rolls he had spent so long slicing. His personality too, was rich and indulgent like honey ham and sometimes as hot-tempered and raspy as the cracked pepper that coated the pastrami. Maybe, Lina thought, in ten or twenty years time she too would be just like a roll of smoked turkey breast in a white apron and Dr. Scholls No-Slip work shoes.

Eighty-two, the voice interrupted Lina's unpleasant thoughts, this time with more authority, somehow louder Lina's head as she took her first order of the day. *Eighty two, eighty two Br-*

"-Sorry I'm late Tristan, Cassie was puking all this morning. Hey Lina."

Amber blustered in at quarter-past twelve and brought with her the smell of cigarettes and cotton candy hand lotion.

"Is she sick? I'm not getting sick again, Amber." Tristan began pumping disinfectant gel into his cupped hands.

"No, she's a kid, Tristan. Jesus. Kids always puke..."

"Six eighty-five for the roast beef," Lina said

"Well if I get sick I know where it came from."

"You're paranoid."

"Amber, can I get a quarter pound of the turkey ham, extra thin?" Lina said.

Amber pulled her rubber gloves over her large hands and walked to the slicer. Often, Lina had to remind herself that she and Amber were the same age, they'd gone to high school together. Amber stood several inches shorter than Lina, but her stocky body echoed strength and perfect competence. Lina felt that her own long, bony limbs moved through space precariously, unsynchronized with Lina's mind. How did Amber find the time, Lina wondered, to have a child? For Lina, time passed in a straight and unbroken line, but somehow Amber had managed to create an entire human life in the time since leaving school. Not to mention the time it took to persuade the male half of the equation, Amber's boyfriend Sunny, had been around on and off since the sophomore year. Lina couldn't imagine sustaining a lover for that long. Lina thought of sex as something of a brief refreshment, like taking a drink of water, washing the glass and returning it to the cabinet.

"A pound of low sodium oven roasted chicken,"

"That's eighty-two eighty-two please," Lina said

"It's how much?!"

Lina paused and returned her attention to the computer screen.

"No. No. No. My mistake, it's four dollars, thirty-nine cents, sorry."

"That's what I *thought*," The man tilted his head back.

Customers waited in line, and made their purchases. Lina sliced meat and passed package after package of cold cuts over the counter. At eight minutes to six p.m. the phone rang.

"Hello, Shop and Save Deli counter, Lina speaking, how may I help you?"

"Oh hey, Leen, it's David, is Tristan around?"

"He's restocking right now," She said.

"Oh damn. Can you tell him that the plumber is coming on Tuesday at three-thirty instead of Wednesday like he said he would?"

"Yeah, lemme just write that down," Lina said, grabbing a spare piece of wrapping parchment from beside the slicer.

"Ok, bye now."

Lina pressed her thumbnail into the end-call button and rested the phone back on its cradle. She looked down at the paper, where she had written the message while David spoke.

Lina's stomach dropped several feet below it's normal resting place just above her diaphragm. She had written nothing about the plumber coming at four-thirty on Wednesday instead of Tuesday, or whatever David's message was. Instead, in her own familiar, neat and rounded print, Lina read;

82 Broadhurst Avenue, Monmouth, Maine.

Lina never heard of or visited the address that she'd written in such firm print on the paper. For a full thirty seconds, Lina couldn't move her eyes from it.

"Lina, who called?" Tristan lumbered out of the tiny bathroom. Lina snatched the paper and stuffed it into her pocket, and shrugged.

"Just David," she said. "Wanted to tell you that the plumber's coming on Tuesday instead of Wednesday."

"Oh God damn him,' Tristan spat. Whether he referred to David or the plumber, Lina didn't bother to ask. *Eighty two Broadhurst Avenue*, the voice said, now confident, somehow excited. Tristan spent the rest of the night in a foul mood, snapping at Amber when she sent a wet handful of knives clattering to the ground. Amber had the news playing on her phone in the break-room, Lina caught snippets of stories, *something something gun violence, something something, Iran, something something viral video of a boy singing in a Walmart*. How had all of the feverish confusion of the outside world found its way into her own, Lina thought, as the phantom address repeated itself faster and faster in her head.

When her shift came to an end, Lina forced her face into a neutral expression, wiped the sweat away from her hairline.

"See you, Tris," She said into the dish-room.

Tristan lumbered out, "Have a lovely night, Lina, I'm sorry for being an ass today,"

"Don't be," Lina said, "You were a ray of sunshine."

"Oh, shush."

"See you Amber, tell Cassie to get better for me."

Lina waited for the bus outside in the dark-blue gloom. A man slept on the bench in the bus stop shelter and Lina took care to stand sideways, keeping her eyes on both the oncoming traffic as well as the latent heap three feet away from her. His sleeves were rolled up past his wrists, which were dotted here and there by a track of flea bite sized scabs. He murmured something under his breath. From the edge of her vision, Lina saw someone making their way towards the bus shelter. Another man had joined Lina and the homeless man at the bus stop and rested like Lina against the other side of the shelter.

"Is that Lina Vaduva?"

Lina looked up from her phone. The man's face had the deflated look of someone who had once been very fat and lost a great deal of weight too quickly. Purple smudges hung under his eyes and his skin had a dry, flaky texture not unlike that of the man at the bus stop. Nonetheless, something familiar lingered around that face.

"Lina!" The man said again. "It's Mr. Baker, remember me!" he said. The words of long and lost acquaintance came out of his mouth sounding somehow wrong. Demanding, rather than asking Lina's remembrance that she couldn't quite recover. While she knew that the man in front of her had indeed taught her third grade mathematics, his pale and somehow foul face remained abstract in its familiarity, like a shape or a street sign. More than his face, what struck Lina as familiar was his habit of licking his lower lip and sucking it under his significant overbite. What had the class called him? *Rabbit boy.* Lina toyed with the word in her mind, *rabbit, rabbit, rabid*. Rabid seemed more fitting to Mr. Baker now, Lina thought, with his skinny limbs and the way his eyes darted from her to the sleeping man and back.

"Yee-es," Lina said at last. She drew the word out slowly, hoping to make up for the sparseness of conversation that she could offer him.

"Well, it's been a long time since Longley Elementary hasn't it?" Mr. Baker said, "A very long time." He paused, giving Lina an opportunity to respond which she didn't take.

"I don't blame you if you don't remember me." Mr. Baker said. "You look all grown up now though, don't you?" He said, somehow accusing her of it.

"Well," Lina said,"What can you do?"

Mr. Baker skated over her reply. "Such a smart kid too, those big bug eyes..."

Lina swallowed, "Are you still working at the school," she said, her mouth had gone dry.

While God was walking down the street.

Lina flinched. The voice that had haunted her all day had begun to speak.

"No, I'm not working there anymore" Mr. Baker looked away from Lina for a moment. "Those days are over. For the best, I think" he said, "school board never had a clue what it was doing anyway..." He spoke more to himself than Lina, talking a cocoon around himself and trying to draw her into it with him. Lina kept perfectly still, struggling to ignore the voice and unable to discern if her stillness was her own response, or a paralysis induced by Mr. Baker's encircling words.

He returned his gaze to Lina, "You have kids of your own now, I assume," He said, the softening interest on his face turned her stomach like lemon juice in a glass of milk.

While God was walking down the street. A dog was barking

"Don't know what would make you say that," Lina said.

"Well, you know, parenthood is such a gift, such a miracle," he said, "It's so much like teaching- I wish I could've had the opportunity myself. I understand children, maybe it's because I am childlike myself, I've always been that way, immature, maybe some would say...It's true, I'm not perfect. No. I'm not."

"Mm-hm,"

"Everyone makes mistakes in their lives," Mr Baker said, the sudden urgency in his voice startled Lina, "is it too much to ask to simply set mistakes aside? To ask complete forgiveness?"

When God came back

"Sometimes, yes," Lina said, staring at a heap of roadkill on the other side of the street.

"You're christian, aren't you? If you believe in God, you *have* to believe in forgiveness," Mr. Baker said.

"Well, I'm not sure," Lina said, "I think it was said that you only have to forgive seventy-seven sins in your life."

"That is *not* how that parable goes!"

"Really? Maybe not." Lina looked into Mr. Baker's wet and pleading eyes and shrugged, "Oh well."

The dog was dead.

The bright lights of the nine-oh-five bus blinded Lina and the shriek of old breaks drowned whatever Mr. Baker had said in reply. Heart pounding, Lina climbed onto the bus without another word, the bus driver took notice of him either and closed the door after Lina boarded. As his figure shrunk in the distance, Lina realized how poorly dressed the old teacher had been for the weather, in a pair of khakis and an off-white collared shirt. The bus turned a corner and Lina saw nothing else behind her but the bruise-colored hills and the telephone wires that swooped from pole to pole.

On the weather station, the meteorologist had said that any day now it would snow. Lina looked around at the passengers. The driver sipped from a half-empty bottle of Mountain Dew. A young man listened to music loud enough to hear it through his white earbuds. A woman in a yellow scarf slept with her face pressed into the window that she fogged with her steady breath. Lina had seen many of them before. The bus lurched to a stop and Lina got off the bus alone.

Only the kitchen light was on when Lina came in. A droplet of water dripped steadily from the faucet and although Lina could still smell food, the room was empty. Lina turned her eyes to the blue draped statue of the Virgin over the sink. Mary's face had changed since the morning. The hands that had shrugged with apathy so many hours before, were outstretched in celebration, triumph stretched the small smile on her porcelain lips as she extended a tiny glass foot to deliver the fatal stomp to the green-painted serpent underneath it. What was the word for the feeling on the face of the Virgin perched above the kitchen sink, what was the word for the dislodging, excision, and slow ascent that Lina felt just below her ribs?

Days passed in layers, unhaunted by numbers and street addresses, covering up the peculiar one until it was almost forgotten. A week later, Lina came to work to see that Amber had arrived before her and was looking down at her phone.

"Hey, Amber," Lina said, tying her white apron around her waist, the strings were becoming threadbare and she wouldn't wear it much longer. Lina was sick of the apron anyway, sick of the deli. Amber said nothing, but continued to stare at her phone.

"Ugh." Amber said, tucking her phone into her pocket at last. "Just disgusting." she said.

"What is?" Lina said, refilling the soap dispenser with a new bag of blue liquid.

"This article I just saw. You remember Mr. Baker? From third grade?"

Lina felt her stomach flinch.

"Yes?" Lina said.

"Yeah ok, well, get this, apparently he *died*. Yeah, so sad, right? But that's not even the worst part, because when they found him the EMT's said he'd been dead for like- a pretty long time, like he was *slightly decomposed*, it says. It's like that story about the lady in New York who'd been dead in her apartment for so long that her cats started to-"

"-How long had he been dead?"

"-Eat her. I don't know," Amber shrugged, "A while, I guess. No one came to check on him. Not surprising, the guy was *such* a creep. You know what he got fired for from the school right?"

"Does it say anywhere, how long he'd been dead?" Lina asked.

"No, Lina. Jesus. Stop being so morbid," Amber said.

Lina stared at her open-mouthed.

"Fine, here, just look at the article yourself it's nasty, I'm glad they didn't put any pictures in." Amber handed Lina her phone. Lina looked down at the wall of text in her hand, she struggled to read the tiny print on the screen but a single passage leapt to Lina's eyes from it.

"Alexander Baker was found dead at his home at 82 Broadhurst Avenue, in Monmouth. Apparent heart-failure, first responders said it was likely that Baker had been dead for two to three weeks before his body was discovered. Baker had taught third grade at James B. Longley Elementary school before being discharged six years ago."

"Wow," Lina said.

"Yeah, wow," Amber said, "fucking gross, right?"

"Mm."

"I would never want that to happen to me," Amber said, "Being so alone like that? No one noticed he was gone for weeks? God, it's so sad," she said. "I always thought there was something kind of weird about him though," Amber squinted out over the counter as if she were looking for Mr. Baker himself amongst the shoppers wandering from aisle to aisle. "Even as a little kid, I always felt bad for you because you had to spend so much time in after school tutoring with him."

"I couldn't do fucking math."

"I remember this one time, I came back from lunch a little early, and Mr. Baker was in his homeroom alone, and at first I thought he was on the phone, because he was just laughing. Just laughing at nothing, and when I realized he wasn't talking to anyone, I just tried to back out of the room, but he saw me and got really, really quiet and we just stared at each other till I ran back down the hallway. I think that was the moment I knew something wasn't quite right with that guy." Amber tucked her phone into her back pocket like a judge striking a gavel and turned to Lina.

"What," Amber said, "Are you sad or something?"

Lina smiled, raised her palms and shrugged, "Why would I be?"

She shared none of Amber's pity, disgust or even entertainment in hearing the story. There were other things to think about. New things. Lina looked out the window. The world outside didn't seem to feel much like mourning either, because, like confetti, fat snowflakes had begun to fall, covering the dead earth and silencing the world around it.

About the Author

Anna Schaeffer: I work as a Park Ranger in Maine. In my writing I like to explore how larger social issues manifest themselves into the humdrum of daily life when we are least likely to notice or address them. My goal in my writing is to shed light on the ways that the same issues which our nation and world face currently are often ignored when they show up in our daily lives, particularly when they relate to families, work and the household.

ALTER IAGO

by Marcia Eppich-Harris

"The soul is as important as the sinews," the orientation speaker had said on my first day of medical school. "Here at St. Hearthguard University, we believe that the best doctors are those who learn empathy and compassion. We will teach you hard science, yes. However, we will also strive to feed your souls." I kept my face neutral, but internally I grimaced. *Feed my soul? What if it's not hungry?*

The only class that fit my schedule was Shakespeare. In addition to Brain Development and Cell Biology, I would also be studying the human condition via the 16th and 17th centuries – back when they treated practically every disease with bloodletting. *What cutting-edge curriculum!* Our professor gave us seven plays to read, three of which were being performed by the local Repertory theatre: *Othello, Richard II,* and *Two Gentlemen of Verona*. We were required to attend the theatre. I asked a couple of girls in the Shakespeare class if they'd like to go to the shows with me. Make it a girls' night.

"Fun!" Chloe said. "I'll make us a reservation at Le Poisson Rouge, so we can have dinner before the play."

"How expensive is it?" I asked, thinking about my meager savings.

"It's moderate," Chloe said.

Chloe drove a BMW, so I wondered what she considered to be *moderate*.

Le Poisson Rouge was the first restaurant I'd ever been to where you couldn't substitute onion rings for fries. The wine glasses were huge, but the sommelier – a job I never knew existed – only filled them about an inch. I watched my companions' behavior for cues. My etiquette training was about as sophisticated as eating baked beans from a can, but I managed not to spill anything on my black sweater and jeans skirt. I called it a win.

Once we arrived at the theatre, I felt the next hurdle was going to be harder to jump. I opened the program to find a synopsis but landed on the cast photos. A picture of a man with curly dark hair grabbed my attention: James Giles as Iago. He wasn't classically handsome, but his eyes were stunning – a dark circle outlined each of his pale irises. I stared at his eyes for too long; the lights dimmed.

The man whose picture I'd studied entered the scene. James Giles had a voice like silvery music. When he spoke about his general, Othello, passing him over for a promotion, I empathized. Iago was an outsider, trying to be an insider – just like me. I spent most of my time trying not to be an impostor. My soul and I had been waitlisted for medical school. It wasn't until other accepted candidates had abandoned S.H.U. for the sanctity of the East Coast that I was admitted into the program. Like Iago, I was no one's first choice.

As the play went on and Iago showed his villainy, I felt I couldn't help admiring his ingenious persuasion, despite his villainy. He spoke and moved with seductive charisma, enchanting Othello, and frankly, me, with his linguistic acumen. *I've never been in love with a villain,* I thought. *But I want to wrap myself around this man.*

At intermission, the stage went black, and the crowd relished the electric darkness for a moment before thundering into applause. The house lights came up, and my companions looked at me expectantly. I smiled like an idiot.

"What do you think?" Daphne asked, giggling at my expression.

I said. "I think I might be in love."

"With Shakespeare?" Chloe asked.

"With Iago."

"I'm partial to Cassio myself, but Iago is okay," Daphne conceded.

"His voice," I said, "I've never heard anything like it. He could read Shakespeare to me anytime."

And I'd actually understand it, I thought. He made it seem easy.

"Why not try to meet him at the stage door afterward?" Chloe said.

I felt a kindling of hope. "Is it possible to meet the actors?"

"Yeah," Daphne said. "I've done it loads of times. Why not?"

When the show resumed, I felt sorry for Othello and Desdemona, the victims of my glorious villain, but Iago's manipulation, while pathological, wasn't nonsensical. After all, if you work hard, do all the right things, and then you still get shoved aside, it drives you insane. My professor had given us a different interpretation of the character entirely. But knowing how I felt about my past rejections, and seeing the way James Giles played Iago, I understood the character in a totally different light.

At the curtain call, I leaped to my feet when James reentered for his applause. My sudden flight caught his eye, and he smiled in my direction just before bowing. I clapped so hard that my hands burned. Is this what it meant to have your soul fed? I had never reacted so strongly to any other encounter with the arts, but then again, I had never experienced an actor as smooth and thrilling as James.

I pulled Daphne close to be heard over the cacophony.

"Where do I go to meet him?" I asked her.

We threaded our way through the buzzing patrons. Outside the stage door, around fifteen people stood patiently in line, waiting for their favorite actors to re-enter society as mere mortals. I planted myself at the end of the line, my heart throbbing with anticipation. I did what I always do in nerve-wracking situations – I listed the elements on the Periodic Table in my head. *Hydrogen, Helium, Lithium, Beryllium, Boron, Carbon...*

Chloe and Daphne talked about the play and the garish lighting of Desdemona's murder scene. *Garish lighting*? I hadn't even noticed. While they analyzed, my mind slipped from elements to think about all the things I could do with the actor playing Iago on that gauze-curtained bed. *This is so unlike me*. I started over, *Hydrogen, Helium, Lithium, Beryllium...*

Eventually, the man playing Othello exited the stage door and started signing programs, and then, out walked James Giles. My stomach twisted with excitement, and he followed Othello's suit, signing programs down the line of admirers. When he finally came to me, Iago – James Giles – held my stare without saying a word, and I smiled with rapture. His eyes turned out to be pale blue inside those dark outlines, and up close, I could smell a faint whiff of cologne mixed with sweat.

"Hi," he said.

I handed him my program, saying, "I couldn't take my eyes off of you when you were on stage. You were perfect."

He laughed and wrote a sweeping signature on the cast page.

"Thank you," he said. "Most people don't like the villain."

"I loved Iago," I said. "He was the smartest person in the whole play."

"She means, 'the sexiest,'" Chloe said over my shoulder. I reddened with embarrassment.

James/Iago looked at me, assessing my reaction.

"Any interest in a drink?" he asked. "Some of us are heading to the bar around the corner. It's called Red's."

I looked at the girls, and they nodded encouragement.

"We'll meet you there," I said.

When we were settled in with drinks, James leaned in to be heard over our friends and the jazz band in the back of the bar.

"What's your name?" he asked.

"Annie," I said. "Annie Stephens. I'm a med student at St. Hearthguard."

"Medicine?" he said. "That's a great career for donating to the arts."

I laughed. "I think that's what S.H.U. is doing with their new program. They're making med students take classes in the arts, so our 'souls will be fed,'" I made quote marks with my fingers. "And then maybe we'll feed artists, too."

"We do make hungry where most we satisfy."

"Is that so?" I asked.

"Well, that's Shakespeare, anyway. He gives me my best lines."

"I'd never seen a Shakespeare play on stage before," I said. "Now, I think I'm in love."

"It makes a difference seeing it. I didn't have a wealthy family growing up. We didn't even have cable. I watched PBS all the time. I saw a performance of Shakespeare's *King Lear* on there once with Ian McKellen –"

"Gandalf?" I asked, surprised.

"Yeah, he's a great Shakespearean," he said.

"I had no idea."

"A lot of great Shakespearean actors that are famous for other things – Patrick Stewart –"

"Professor X?"

"Ian McDiarmid–"

"The Emperor in *Star Wars*?"

"Yeah," he laughed. "Anyway, when I saw Gandalf as *Lear*, I thought, 'I know what I want to do with my life.' So I started acting in high school and continued in college."

"That's so great."

"It is now," he said. "My first paying gig as an actor wasn't so great."

He told me about seeing an ad for open auditions in college. It said, "Actors will be paid," but when he received his contract, the stipend was only $25.

"So I was 'paid,'" he said. "But not a living wage or anything."

"Talk about false advertising," I said.

"Yeah, it wasn't even a clever, like 'Red Bull gives you wings.'"

"Right," I said. "Who would ever be stupid enough to believe they'd sprout literal wings by drinking Red Bull?"

My idiot boyfriend in college did, actually, I remembered, but I kept it to myself.

"I had to be a lot more critical about auditions after that. I had to pay rent, you know? It took a few years before I stopped worrying about that constantly."

"Med students still have to worry about that," I said.

"Well, sacrifices pay off sometimes. It doesn't make it any less hard, though."

I immediately felt more comfortable with him than I did Daphne and Chloe. I was surprised how relaxed his off-stage persona was compared to his bad-boy Iago. As Iago faded and James came into focus, the manipulating villain vanished, leaving behind a genuine, interesting, sweet alter ego – *alter Iago* – James.

"I have to see *Richard II* and *Two Gentlemen of Verona,* too," I said. "Are you going to be in those plays?"

"Yeah. Iago is my big role this season, though. In *Richard II,* I play Henry Percy. He's more commonly known as 'Hotspur.'"

Appropriate, I thought.

"Then, in *Two Gentlemen of Verona*, I'm playing a servant character named Launce."

"Which role do you like best?"

"Oddly enough, I think I like Launce the best, even though it's a smaller role."

"Why is that?"

"Well, he's funny, for one. But he's also the only character in all of Shakespeare's plays that has a dog – like, actually on stage, there's a dog."

"Are you a dog person?"

"I like dogs," he said. "But the thing I like about Launce is how much he's willing to sacrifice for this animal. He takes a beating, so the dog won't be punished. He sits in the stocks for him. It's incredible. Launce isn't smart like Iago, or valiant like Hotspur, but Launce has integrity, you know? He'd do anything to protect the one he loves."

"I thought you'd be more like Iago," I said with mock disappointment.

"You like the bad-boy type?" he asked, arching an eyebrow.

"Not *usually*," I said.

"Sorry for the false advertising," he said, putting his hand on mine. "I know how disappointing it can be."

"I might be able to get over it," I said, inching closer to him.

The next day, Daphne ran up to me before class.

"So?" she asked. "I noticed you ducked out last night without saying goodbye."

"Yeah, sorry," I replied. "I had to work on a class – Soul Cultivation 101."

"That doesn't sound like you," she grinned. "Aren't you more into the hard sciences?"

"Yes, today I'm running an experiment on how long a medical student can stay awake after being up all night with a gorgeous actor."

"Let me know how that goes."

Four years later, James and I got married on that stage where he'd played Iago. Shakespeare provided the readings for our wedding, but it was the actor behind the words that truly fed my soul.

About the Author

Marcia Eppich-Harris writes fiction, plays, and poetry. Her fiction most recently appeared in Furtive Dalliance, The Breakroom Stories, The Bookends Reviews, and Mused. A full list of her publications can be found at

www.meppichharris.com.

DID I STUTTER?

By Alan Berger

No one ever in any of Joe's classrooms starting from kindergarten ever thought that he would ever be P.H.D. material.

More like P.H.Duh material.

So thought the students, the teachers. And Joe occasionally, here and there, himself.

His folks believed in him only because they were supposed to.

Just don't ask them to take a lie detector test.

Joe had a terrifically, terribly bad stutter problem.

But only when he spoke.

Which was not too much.

On the outside he was a stupid comedy.

In the inside he was an intelligent drama.

After high school he didn't want to disappoint his highly educated parents by not making the debating team of any college that would not accept him, so, he joined the Army.

After three years of saluting this and shooting that, he moved to The East Village in New York City and became a restless peace officer.

He didn't have to wear a body cam during training at the academy, but he did have to wear one on the job.

No big deal.

He didn't plan on doing anything wrong and maybe he would save a life and be on T.V. one day or night or both.

He liked that his beat was Washington Square Park.

The structure made him think of Paris although he had never been there.

He still didn't talk much.

He didn't have to because his partner, an old timer, talked enough for the both of them, thank you Christ very much.

One day when they were patrolling the park, the senior of the un-dynamic duo was again spending more time on the park toilet than on the beat.

He didn't handle diary that well after a half dozen free cream filled donuts.

Joe had a cigarette and waited nearby as was the familiar custom.

Joe heard groans coming out from the toilet facilities which was nothing new either.

Soon he realized they were coming from the ladies' room and not the men's room.

Then he heard that magic word coming from a woman.

The word was help.

He rushed in without even taking out his gun and saw a guy choking out a woman on the floor.

He kicked the guy in the head and grabbed him by the neck and squeezed as hard as he could while the woman rolled away.

He yelled for his partner who had heard the whole thing but was still mortally attached to his toilet seat.

His partner yelled out, "Read him his rights and I'll be right there, good work".

Joe started to read the guy his rights but could not do it without the stuttering.

They threw the case out of court on account the defendant did not get his precious rights read properly for all to see and hear courtesy of the body cam and Joe was kicked out of what by now he called, " The New York City Police Farce".

He a job with Uber and thought about finding a maybe opportunity of being a vigilante like Charles Bronson in those ," Death Wish", movies.

One day he picked up a familiar face.

It was the face of the impetus of his former cop days.

He pulled into an alley and the face asked what was going on.

Joe got out of the car and opened the back door had once again, by the neck squeezed as hard as he could.

A choking blurb of a sound asked him what he was doing? and Joe flatly and very clearly said, "I'm going to beat the Hell out of you".

The guy said ,"What"?

And Joe said," Did I Stutter", Like Charles Bronson would have delivered and went about his un-official business.

He gave himself a five-star rating for that particular ride.

About the Author

Alan Berger has written and directed two films on Netflix. Has had over forty short stories and poems published since 2018. He shares an apartment in West Hollywood with a cat named 'Iron".

THE OLD FRONT PORCH

by Ruth Deming

He was a man who never cussed in front of women. Just inside his own head. The black head of retired Major Robert O. Brown. Thanksgiving was on its way. In the cupholder of his battered 1973 LTD he had a silver Thermos of hot black coffee with two teaspoons of sugar – real sugar – not that fake stuff – and real cream.

A huge map of southern New Jersey was spread out on the passenger seat. For a dozen years he'd been promising himself to visit Great-grandmother Alicia on the family farm. He'd call her every year and her voice kept getting weaker and weaker, like a player piano missing half its keys.

She had been a former slave, not like Obama, a decent enough president, slow to the draw, but now he would sit down with her and they would shoot the breeze.

He drove nice and slow. Cops were hiding behind bushes in the middle of the median, the black and white cars were as camouflaged as Humvees in the Afghan. He wasn't gonna get shot dead by the bastards before he sat on the front porch with Granny.

He pressed the buttons on the radio and summoned far-off stations like New Zealand – yes! The Kiwi State – where he heard commercials to save the koala bears. Not surprisingly, tourists would kill them for their warm fur and the country was in crisis.

Static crinkled on the station. *Remain calm*, he thought. *All things pass*. He made sure his seatbelt was on. He imagined a cop stopping him. What! He should show him his medals from the War in Vietnam? They were in his study, in a glass case, his granddaughter Arielle polished with Windex and ammonia.

He'd warned Arielle that ammonia could knock you out. Once, he was pushing a shopping cart at the Shop-Right, and a large man was down on the floor, seemingly dead. The Major, who was called Robby, lifted him up by the collar, stared hard at him, then blew his own breath over his face, and the man bolted upright.

Robby wore a warm leather jacket he and his wife, Sarah May, had bought over at Target. It was not cheap. She was a coupon saver and it only cost them two hundred dollars. He wondered, as he drove, what he had in the pockets. Many surprises. Possibly a pair of tiny red gloves that expanded when you put them on.

He found them in the middle of the street. Their street. Edge Hill Road. A cul-de-sac. The GI Bill enabled Robby to buy a three-bedroom rancher with a stone front and a fireplace that burned real logs. The heat lit up the whole house.

"Get out of there," he'd yell at the cat. "Ya wanna end up like Fra Savonerola burnt at the stake for heresies?"

Sarah May was out shopping at Whole Foods today. She had her canvas bags ready as they aimed to save the world from climate change.

He kissed her goodbye, feeling her soft skin, but saying nothing about where he was going. That's all she needed. To have her "worry meter" set on "high."

He adjusted his sunglasses and looked out the rear-view every few seconds. If anyone got too close, he'd let them pass. He watched as they looked at what they believed was his old jalopy.

Wrong! In his garage, he and some neighbors installed modern engines that could out-gun your average car. Then off they'd go to "the track" - Millville, New Jersey - to test their engines along with other so-called "amateurs."

Accidents are frequent.

If you looked carefully at Robby's index finger, the tip had been sewn back on. His buddies raced him over to the nearest hospital – the tip was kept warm in his mouth – and the only way you could tell was if you had a one of them magnifying glasses used to read small print on medicine bottles.

Up the hill he drove. Gulp! Robby swallowed hard. These upward slopes caused congestion in his ears. He pushed back his red Phillies' baseball cap and thought, *Doin' good, man, doin' good.*

He swung over to the shoulder and got out of the car.

A series of still-green bushes hid his black ass as he took a whiz.

I am ready now, he thought. *Granny here I come*.

What a perfect time for a cop car to approach. Robby wasn't a praying man. What good did it do in 'Nam?

Sure enough, he watched the red light atop the car pulsating and pulled over immediately.

A slender police officer, dressed in civilian clothes, walked over to his cocoa-brown LTD.

"Nice car you got," said the cop. "Sure don't make 'em like this any more."

"Thank you, officer. She's in better shape than she looks."

The officer said he figured that out, since one of the bumper stickers read, "Association of Antique Cars of New Jersey."

"Where you off to, today?"

Robby explained he was going to meet his Granny off some lonesome road near Crampton, New Jersey.

"Well, you drive carefully, son," said the officer. "I know where she lives. She's not long for this world."

Robby nodded and set off again. He paid attention to the landscape, miles of bleached grasses, where a film director like Tarantino or Scorcese could make a film.

He pulled up to the house.

His was not the only vehicle there. A rusting green John Deere Tractor rested itself as if awaiting a decent burial.

He went over and patted its yellow seat.

Then took off his cap as a mark of respect.

A side window of the house had yellowing lace curtains.

Granny stuck her head out.

"Can't hear you, Robby, just know you're here by the rumbling of your car," she said in a voice that sounded like it had been sleeping for one hundred years.

"Gonna make you the best breakfast of your life. Wait outside" – she had a fit of coughing – "on the front porch until I gives you the okey-dokey to come in." She muttered something about being tired of cooking just for herself.

He walked up the steps to the front door.

The loose boards tried to make him fall, but he walked carefully. It reminded him of those IEDs in Vietnam. He blinked hard so's not to remember his fallen comrades.

He sat on the front porch in a rusty glider that faced the dry hills.

Thank you, Lord, for keeping Granny alive till I got here.

Gray clouds above threatened a downpour. He could, of course, spend the night if need be. Why had he never noticed how beautiful they were. Gray. A simple gray like news anchors with gray hair. Walter Cronkite, for instance, who unashamedly cried when JFK was murdered.

He stood up and walked from one end of the front porch – which was as big as the house was wide – picked up a broom – and swept off the dead leaves.

A tiny mouse lay in the corner with his feet up. Robby swept it away. Newly dead, he thought, or else it would have been eaten. And, there was the cry of a hawk and then a bluejay squawking and he was certain he heard a barn owl.

The barn was behind them.

Who lived in *there*? *Runaway slaves?*

Robby knocked once on the front door and entered.

The overpowering smell of buttermilk biscuits and mold and rot entered him.

Granny wore a long black overcoat to keep herself warm.

She stood at the black stove – glanced over at her grandson – waved hello and said,

"Gimme another minute or two. I ain't gonna die yet."

"Promise?" he asked.

She laughed. It sounded like a wheeze. Like she had pneumonia.

"Take these flapjacks and sit yourself on the porch. I poured real maple syrup on top."

The dish she found for him had flowers all acrost it. Could it have been from the days of slavery?

He sat outside on the top step of the front porch. The stack was high, golden brown, the syrup falling off the plate.

He licked his fingers.

Was it an exaggeration to say he'd never tasted anything as good in his life?

He took his time eating. What, after all, was the rush?

He chewed slowly, gratefully. His tongue washed over every tiny bit. Soft as silk, toasted in all the right places. Better than Sarah May's sweet potato pie.

He patted his belly, then stood up to see what was in his pockets.

A beige napkin from Starbucks and a coupon for Libby's pumpkin filling.

"Gran?" he shouted. "Darn good, darn good!"

He refused to enter the house just then.

He knew what he would find.

And he did.

About the Author

Ruth Z. Deming has had her work published in numerous lit mags including Mad Swirl, Scarlet Leaf Review, and Pure Slush. She lives in Willow Grove, PA, a suburb of Philadelphia. She belongs to the Beehive Writing Group where a dozen writers share and give gentle feedback to one another.

DELUSION

by Ibrahim N. Al-Huraiyes, translated from the Arabic by Essam M. Al-Jassim

He threw the pen aside and collapsed on the lumpy chair, resting his aching body. Dazed, he silently stared into the distance. Last Monday, a strange ethereal shadow had appeared out of nowhere, settled over his head, and loomed over him ever since. He was able to bat it away, sometimes, but it still peeked out at him from time to time, and felt as though it could engulf him, all of him, at any moment. Strangely enough, he could neither discern what it was nor fathom its nature; he didn't know why this specter had invaded his body and soul. He winced at its presence, his face contorting with both misery and dread. Every time the shadow overtook him, he felt overwhelmed by deep confusion and dejection.

Was this the harbinger of age, systematically invading his body, declaring the imminent end of his mission? Was it related to the recent decrease in his literary output? Had his creative genius run dry at last, with nothing left to offer? Over the last two weeks, he'd hardly been able to write even a page of his new novel.

Perhaps it was connected to the immense grief he still felt over his wife's death, though she'd left him five years ago. Was it his recurring sense of deathly loneliness? Verses from a poem he'd read many years ago had been weighing his heart down.

Who will finally get my arm?

To whom will my ribs and heart go?

To whom will my steps go ...rambling?

To whom will my blood turn ...my shores?

To whom will my long talk go?

To whom shall joy prevail?

Who will laugh more—

Is it the one who strops the butcher's knife?

Or the one who was butchered?[1]

Whenever these verses crossed his mind, he shuddered. The words moved him into another dimension, almost transformed him into a different entity. They had a great impact on his spirit, sailing as it was through uncharted waters.

He thought a stroll might help him forget. He swayed to his feet, dragging his coat behind him, and wandered out onto the narrow gloomy street, suddenly realizing he wasn't sure where to go.

As he ambled restlessly, alleys absorbed him, passageways drove him, and junctions spat him out until he found himself sitting in a crowded café. He wanted to talk with the other patrons about their feelings, to meditate on their problems, penetrate their souls. This was what he'd always loved about writing—creating characters from all walks of life, etched from those he observed coming and going before him. He had perfected the art of creating personas, brilliantly interweaving events. But now he was unable to delineate even his own personality, incapable of understanding his intrinsic nature or comprehending what he sought.

He took a pack of cigarettes out of his pocket, fumbled in the other for a lighter, and blew out pale, white clouds that framed his craggy face.

He sipped his coffee as he idly watched employees hurry to work and tourists drag their whining children through the city. Staring reservedly into the distance toward nothing in particular, he became absorbed in thought as if nothing else was around him.

Tales have always walked before me. Dozens of them, with or without purpose. Do these people perceive that we're sucked into a giant swirl willy-nilly? Or are they just deaf and dumb puppets, being moved and ordered to talk because there is a power manipulating them? Our actions are not our own but are carried out through us on behalf of another's will. We are completely helpless, powerless, and weak-willed, simple playthings. All that's important is what needs to be said and done through us as human tools. Maybe we utter the opposite of what we think, and do what we don't want to achieve. Even our facial expressions and physical movements are but masks we hide behind so we don't expose what is inside of us.

We are afraid of being shamed over simple private behavior. These traits must be entombed deep in the soul, so it may hurt here or feel good there, just to satisfy those who are like us. However, what if we don't recognize our inner selves? What if we can discern no difference between the mask and the real face? As if we pass our days wandering in a labyrinth—we may not know where we started, where to go, or what truth we seek. We are never really lost, but we can never quite see where we're going. Liable to fail and go astray, life is simply a delusion in nothing other than a state of limbo.

He gathered up his shattered soul and left the café as anxiety ripped through him. He walked for a long time, no doubt giving those who encountered him the impression he was weighed down. His steps led him to a public park where he peered through the metal fence at the human masses that scattered in every direction. The rattling of playground equipment nearly drowned out the children's hustle and bustle as they rushed to and from the different rides. Women calling to their kids to remain in sight distracted him. The rustling of the trees, the soothing babble of trickling water, the abundant verdant vegetation—it all captured his senses. A momentary sense of peace encouraged him as he sat on one of the adjacent wooden benches. He sat still like a stone statue, barely moving his eyes and silently contemplating the buzzing world around him.

Because life has disciplined me through its days and years, as it has against the will of everyone, I chose to discipline it through the pages of my books; people called me a man of letters. But am I actually still? Am I still able to fill up—with fountain pen ink—time, people, and things and confine them between two covers? Or has life triumphed in the end, as is its perpetual habit?

Life kills those who grasp its tactics and tire it out by fleeing. Life is aware of its abilities to do this, from the first thread of light that disturbs every newborn's face. It deceives and continues this game till some people think they are outside of its reach. In their moments of carelessness, life seeks retribution from them. Does life possess us, or are we the ones who control it? Do we breathe it, or is it life that breathes us? It confounds me.

While his mind wandered, he turned his head, suddenly realizing someone was close. A child sat beside him. He studied her face thoughtfully, reminiscing faintly upon the giddy days of a childhood fallen into oblivion.

Pointing toward the carousel ride, where the child's attention was fixed, he asked, "Why don't you play with the other kids?"

"The ticket man at the entrance refused to let me in."

"Why?"

"He asked for a ticket, and I told him I don't have one. He wouldn't let me in." The child's voice broke as the words stumbled out of her mouth.

The bitter words, wet with tears, came from her heart and fell into his.

"Why didn't you buy a ticket?"

She sighed and shrugged. "I don't have any money."

The child's poverty manifested itself through her tattered dress and worn-out shoes. Spontaneously, he grabbed the girl's hand and led her to the carousel. He bought the ticket and helped her onto the ride. The ride spun and turned, carrying her into another world. Her smile, laughter, and lively, bright eyes snuck into his aching heart.

Her joyfulness delighted him. He viewed her as a magical seed that had just been planted, sprouting at a supernatural speed, becoming a fruitful tree, basking in the glow of the sun. They rushed from one ride to another with an eagerness he hadn't known before. At that moment, he forgot everything—even himself. No longer did he feel the pain and grief, not even the bitterness of disorientation and alienation. Light suddenly filled his world. The sea of sadness and delusion that had clouded his eyes dwindled to a tiny puddle, which he trampled underfoot as he made his way to another ride with the girl.

Was it only a coincidence that this happened? Or was it his courageous maneuver against life as he instinctively took advantage of the moment without hesitation? He didn't give those absurd and fatalistic thoughts the chance to permeate and tamper with the remaining fragments of his exhausted body and soul. All that mattered was that the girl was a saving grace, the buoy that helped salvage what was left of him.

At sunset, he left her with a firm promise to come to the park tomorrow at eight o'clock in the morning. On the main street outside the park, he hailed a cab to go home. On the way, he stopped at a restaurant to buy dinner. He entered his apartment and asked the doorman to wake him at seven in the morning.

Lately, the rhythm of his life had become hectic and fast-paced. He no longer had enough time to achieve what he wanted. The most important thing now was to wake up early so he could go to the park to see the light flowing from the eyes of that little girl, filling the whole world with new hope.

After he had finished his dinner, an overwhelming desire to write overtook him. He headed for his office and wrote nonstop until he finished a whole chapter of his new novel. Then he went to bed, happy with what he had achieved. Peacefully, he set the alarm for seven o'clock and laid his head on the pillow.

At half past ten in the morning, the doorman knocked on the apartment door for the fourth time.

No answer.

The doorman had been away from the main entrance of the building all morning, watching and waiting for the tenant. But the writer hadn't appeared, hadn't left his place. More worryingly, that morning's daily paper still lay by his door. The alarm clock in his apartment also screamed for several minutes until it stopped automatically. The doorman knew it wasn't the writer's habit to stay in his apartment so late.

Neighbors came outside as the doorman's knocking became louder and more urgent. They gathered at the apartment door, and when the doorman told them what was happening, they insisted on breaking it down.

On the other side of the bustling city, a little girl sat on a wooden bench ... waiting.

[1]Nasrallah, Ibrahim. "The Heirs." *Autumn Balconies* (Beirut: Arab Institute for Research & Publishing, 1997), p. 7.

About the Author

Ibrahim N. Al-Huraiyes is a Saudi short story writer. He graduated from King Faisal University with a degree in Foreign Language Education.

About the Translator

Essam M. Al-Jassim is a Saudi translator. He taught English for many years at Royal Commission schools in Jubail, Saudi Arabia. He received his bachelor's degree in Foreign Languages and Education from King Faisal University, Hofuf. His translations appear in a variety of online and print Arabic and English literary journals.

NONFICTION

WHITEBOARDS AND COURAGE

by Beth Burgmeyer

The house that love built. I remember the slogan, but never really knew what a Ronald McDonald House was. Until now. Until tragedy brings me to the house in Iowa City. From the moment I walk through the doors after four days of hell—and however many more are to come—I feel that love, that grace.

The house manager takes me on a tour, although I don't hear much of what she says. My head and heart are still at the hospital, my body ready to collapse from exhaustion. After she shows me to my room, I sit on the bed and look through the welcome bag. There are toiletries, a coloring book, a notepad and pen, a voucher for a toy when my child leaves the hospital. It's the blanket that makes me break, that makes me feel the love. I pull the thick soft fleece around me, curl up on the bed, and cry.

***

I don't know why food is love, but it is, especially in a crisis. The kitchen at the Ronald McDonald House overflows with food. Every night a group or a family comes in and makes supper for all of us who stay at the house. I'm still raw, still tear up at the slightest kindness, like someone making supper for me.

Almost everyone in the house gathers for supper. The groups become obvious from their conversations. The parents with babies in the NICU huddle around the kitchen. They speak in a language of ounces—sometimes grams—lost or gained, feeding tubes, and ventilators. They dream about discharge dates.

The parents with kids in the PICU bond over the illnesses their children fight. They sit together at tables, looking exhausted, like they're fighting the illnesses too. In a way they are.

The kids who are there for cancer treatment sit in the dining room with their families. Masks cover their faces except when they take bites of food. If they feel well enough to eat. The little girl at the next table, puts her head down, telling her mom her head hurts, that it hurts too much to eat.

I sit alone in a quiet corner of the dining room, avert eye contact, hoping it will make me invisible. I dread the thought of someone asking about my child. What would I say, especially to the mom whose toddler is getting her fifth round of chemo?

***

The whiteboards bring my guilt to a new level. Every door of every room has a whiteboard. *Welcome! Feel free to share your story*. That's the message on everyone's whiteboard when they first arrive. I read the stories as I walk down the hall.

Michael and Anthony came into the world at 25 weeks. They're 15 and 18 ounces, but they're fighters.

Ten-year-old Bella is getting a stem cell transplant for Leukemia. We're hoping she'll go into remission. She's a fighter.

At five years old, Aidan is having his third heart surgery. He has an amazing spirit and will to live.

The stories go on for the length of the hallway. My heart shatters for these families and for their amazing children who are fighting to survive.

I reach my room and look at my whiteboard. I spent my own terrifying days in the PICU, wondering if my daughter would survive, but even those days were spent in isolated guilt. Now she's stable enough to move to a different unit.

None of that's on my whiteboard. It's blank, but I write it every day in my head: *My fifteen-year-old daughter Madilyn: fighting to die.*

I want to tell her story, how she also has an illness that tries to claim her life every day. But so many people don't see it as an illness. Instead it's a choice, a frame of mind, a flip of the switch that can be cured by an inspirational quote.

Just get over it. Pull yourself up by your bootstraps. It's mind over matter. Words Madilyn and I have heard too many times. It's that easy in the eyes of so many who haven't lived it.

How do I write that on my whiteboard in a house where other children are just inches or ounces or one cancer treatment away from death? Maybe I should write it, because my silence only feeds the stigma.

My hand hovers by the marker attached to my whiteboard when the mom next door to me carries her bald eight-year-old girl down the hall toward their room, both exhausted from today's treatment. I give her a nod, a quiet *hi* before I open my door.

Maybe I'll write Madilyn's story tomorrow.

About the Author

Beth Burgmeyer writes fiction and creative nonfiction. Her work is scheduled to be appear in Bending Genres in February 2020. Beth won first place in the CIBA Somerset Awards for Contemporary and Literary Fiction. She was also a finalist in the 2019 William Faulkner-William Wisdom contest and the 2018 Sequestrum New Writer Award. Beth lives near Des Moines, Iowa with her family and a menagerie of rescue animals.

POSTMODERN MUD

by Iggy J. Louis

In Lieu Introductions and Frontiers

A perfect ideology is as rare as common sense. There are near a billion perspectives when looking at what's wrong with the current station of society. And that's without upending widely scattered foot-holds comprising the frame—the language and the logarithms (as when scrutinising and reforming our interpretive fiscal-skeleton and its meat)—and what post-modernism comes to try to portray is a penultimate subjectivity and the plastic nature toward reality. Kinda like the obsidian of the Western World as nothing but false impressions, by dialogue and established conventions and misguided inferences, all stemming from modernism.

The movement has gained a fair wack of traction recently for anyone paying attention. Where this writer can't help thinking about it in curiosity and faint interest. But yet now, leads me to be conveying a few points' query in so far as its efficacy. First lets touch on its own definition and late antiquity.

Postmodernism originated sometime in the late 20th century in response to literary studies (things like philosophy, the arts, architecture and even criticism itself) however, due to its widespread shell-fire, the sanctity of *universalist* notions of reality's objectivity, morality, truth, human nature, reason, language and advance, all became prey to (what is in this writer's opinion) the chemical-weaponry of its own caustic countenance. To go deeper: isn't the existence of postmodernism that's corrosive and poison, it is individuals blinded by hazy emotions and ignorance and, in many cases, flatly fanatical corruption. That that leads you to question your own sanctity, along with those you're subjected to interact with in such ways, by and by.

See, these new-age, bite-size stanza's you will have caught popping up as memes in the newsfeed—you know the type: purple-haired girl shares, acquires nominal and ubiquitous heart-reacts, her content just as radical as reciting the anarchist cookbook on a phone-line in the 1990s—albeit emotionally stirring, altogether seems to forget the very *mettle* in each transient layers' singing history, to idly disregard the proto-conglomerate arrow-body. I can't help think it's an awful namesake for ourselves in this Age of Information.

(What? In where education is deemed redundant to now technologically-swayed low-frame-rate attention spans, the vast downsizing of interpretive tolerance and cerebral capacity; the heavy flowing torrents of disenchantment and disillusion cast with each news scandal, centred over them that were propagated [*vis.* puppeteer-ed] by overseeing corporate conglomerates, or the elite's ambiguity. . . furthering decay and mistrust; then the so-called "silent majority" populating with such variety against main-stream media and reflective population idiosyncrasies; you may just get the USA electing Donald Trump, conspiracy media, and a census's bleeding-heart renaissance for devious political gain [the reaction-ary-arsonists' flames popping up countless Earth's corners]).

People are looking for emotional nur-turing in a cold dystopia, down in their own subjectivity. Insecure and hate-filled. They claw at blank canvases, creating—and its no wonder people lap it up like last night's dinner—maybe they can pin the precise culinary definition that was lulling their tongues the first time around.

Quid Pro Status-Quo

Back in Terra Firma, it is a slightly differing narrative. A majority-milieu of conservative effulgence and other shit-eating physiog-nomy, where characters' attitudes are even less likely to be expressed in the online vacuum; I won't bother naming the peak newsfeed oligarchs' present on Facebook or Instagram, with their tendency to snuff out *peculiar* (cough) self-expression and realising and liberty . . . proto-subjectivity shunned, through hashtags and reams of comments' sniggers (including mine, but sure, I'll say it clear, *including mine,*) so.

So several mates and I delude each other to the point of a naive kind-a fanati-cism: a crescendo of glamour and creativity staining the retinae, like a wide-eyed artsy child stepping off colouring books into the blank canvas world, a fresh palette on the lee side of their naive mind.

I tell Brek things I tell anybody (I mean my associate Brek, an upcoming Sydney rap artist). And one of my comments I made is how when somebody feels the rub against community dialogue's most heart-felt cur-rency as being mostly shit, it is easy for said-somebody to radicalise and become a writer. *Or*, at least, it is what was the ef-forts of past generations' creatives did. So maybe the more experimental and busi-ness-minded become typed artists.

These days the comedians are artists of the online era; memers and admins the unsung heroes of apathy, community, even progress. This evolution is perhaps harm-less in its pissy synergy . . . So (me and Brek—*for the sake of continuity and brevity*) have however unknown to us, a kind-a malnutri-tion around pragmatic action. We identify as professionals and artists for all the cu-rious reasons cognitive dissonance evokes, lapelled onto our filmy identities' rebellion to the status quo.

Brek has always been the kind of indi-vidual that completely understands com-monality and normalcy but has always preferred pioneering his own flavour—in response to the internet's easy access and popularity for journalists' publishing, swaying outrage, he has enough sense (like most Australians) to fall in-line. His (now, more) private-circle humour, is random-spat nouns, made articulate with weird vocal intonations to provoke erratic loss of com-posure between audience and him. It's similar to predictive text from a future AI algorithm's proclivity to just take you for a spin. He calls the language 'vision,' which I think is candid (and maybe even a bit genius regarding its grande overstatement).

He meets the pressures of industry standards at eye level, saves the blind jest for his weekend's off. His beats and music videos are inspired by legendary greats, Travis Scott and Kanye West and Drake, yet this Americanisation of the sound is mixed with the local bottle-o vodka-soaked talking and rhymes, the half-drunk accent of Australians. *What it seems like*, is Brek is reconfiguring the proponents flecked in the skin patterns of culture's design, on the frontier of the Australian music direction for those unsullied by conventionality (lack of industry framework, neuroticism in critics to boot), he writes his lyrics spontaneously and with near professional ease, only his stories are rooted in a very subjective and personal scope. He diarises with intimacy, drawing some of the hardest pressures of his developing manhood public.

This bold experimentation is only "truly" found in established artists hoping to air their dirty laundry—now you're with them you may as well hate them—but this presupposition may not necessarily be naive; the rap consulate feeds just as much grandstanding and egoism as you'll find Western media gutting and bleeding with new-faces in front of crowds, contestants and unknown artists, for money and ratings, and more money. Each with their own simple and common vagaries. The main aim is pulling anyone led sympathetic's heartstrings for ratings. And everybody and their mother know the game these days.

Contemporary Society, with all outlined decay and postmodern media, has this ability to alienate the weak believers of postmodern cause until they radicalise; yet a sort of entrepreneurial schtick by Brek is just the kinda provocation to the more creative audience (with their subsequent open minds) to gel--how tragic does one's cliche have to be to stick? It's just that. His musical success echoes tell-tale attributes of something that'd never of existed some years prior. The by-gone modernity, lost holiday luggage's depression; start new and start fast; but fuck the effects, gung-ho son.

Perhaps the personal style of Brek's more heartfelt tracks is his nod to the reminiscent faculty of postmodernism's grande, mud-stained and driving epiphany force: we as humans are pulchritudinous, hard-wired to search for meaning in a sea of information's murk. We hope somehow the pressing boot will lift off our proverbial necks—but maybe with the milieu surrounding oppressive notions, we can recycle data and dialogue, escape.

Maybe, in a postmodern community's widespread reworking, it is your timeline articles protagonist that you can grow to recognise *yourself* in. You would today, need to forget the established judgement which comes with adulthood's suppression of widely accepted tropes, everything you now identify with as *instead* and *established*, collating the open-minded congress and kin where the irony and sympathy and networking are all advocated existentially—a universality fed by audiences *engaging*.

What a fucking lucky guy you are, your circle sharing theories, as such—it might just make publish; sway *harrumph* sized census.

P. S Fiscal Finishes

They say the best creative inspiration strikes in the midnight hours. The half-borne dream-time reveries, which is why I always take time to re-read my writing the following day with a freshly washed palette's clarity. On an essay topic of postmodern thought, maybe the *social influence* (as outlined in the early-presented definition) suggests it is this very "solitude" I should be salving. Growing this essay's merit in itself: a subject reading this very essay may enjoy its analysis of entrepreneurial idealism towering over the boredom of conservative notions, the now-vacuous fluidity in common-sense. And an ulterior subject may despise its fanaticism and inability to transfigure much other than the explicitly stated faculty, the far-flung impalpability. So.

I sit writing at the industrial-style IKEA table overlooking an under-watered and meekly flowering frangipani lit by pale moonlight, in the late Wednesday midnight-hours. I feel the grit and ugly hope running out my fingers for the original draft, and think a truer thing could not be said for postmodernism's cynicism and novice mode . . . the wind of these memories' comforting me, laid in print. With nothing to do for Brek and me but release our art, hoping it strikes true, and inventive and plentiful, prior to the establishment of an audience's mud-spattered subjectivity. Which, all in all, is a root cause of the irony. An ensuing smirk.

As I reflect back over this, the ultimate dishwater in this essay's crux is its *personal interpretation*, with little to no direction for the two figurehead characters other than straying from the convoy-wagons' back-seat Navman, to figure out how to make Boulevard's West by their own accord . . .

To dare to be different is a lost art in most popular circles in post-modern Australia, nobody wants to be the guy with a few crazy beliefs. To flunk creative, miss the fiscal finishing in lieu. Maybe adopting a more rational attitude from this conversation's roots allows the slipstream for creatives, perhaps a flung Molotov to the frontier of new-age fascism--a system's defunct depot--a renaissance of serious synergy, of being. Note: good art is the very individual's totality remodelling as either new or affirming objective truth, so perhaps the taboo is the salvation in itself for us as Contemporary Australians.

My good friend, who we'll refer to as Garry, believes in all sorts of greater-picture criticisms of our established society's framework. He and I are very opinionated, where they, extraverted and drunk, espouse anti-system cynicism and extremism to my wavering understanding, or my dismissal. So. Sometimes biting back with my own loose-tongued intoxication, one point of bitter difference is 'the free-spirited and ill-defined individuality with *harrumph* queer attributes,' is in itself is maybe too rickety and mapped with a shaky, unfeasible charter for the career prosperity, the community values of said person too alien to congeal. How straying far from normality is a filmy poise; the atypical beings' chaos, in the face of . . . *Yes*?

'Who is left to trust then,' I ask. The air of the lounge-room snaps still and in the bleak and tightness, as their face falls bleak. A second passes while unidentified bird coo with a late-afternoon soliloquy.

'Yourself,' they say, mocking pep and zeal. 'Just yourself.'

About the Author

Iggy J. Louis is a short story and narrative essay writer and a poet, hailing from Sydney, Australia. His work has so far appeared in Southerly and Independent Australia.

THE PEOPLE I USED TO KNOW

by Nate Tulay

Yesterday my best friend who I haven't spoken with in two years called. And as his name and number appeared on the caller id, my body began to shiver because we hadn't spoken since the infamous accident. Chills slowly crept down my spine and my fancy plaid shirt and designer jeans could no longer protect me as the fierce cold air engulfed the heat within the dimmed and narrowed hallway. And when the telephone rang, my body became stiff, motionless and consumed by the burning sensations of a paraplegic. After a few minutes, the sound of the loud bells jingling stopped. His number and name slowly vanished as his voice started to disturb my silence through the machine.

"Hi bro, I am just calling to check up on you because it has been a while since we last talked, and I am hoping you've gotten over what took place that morning. I miss you and the guys; and we should catch up like old times. Call me back when you get this message. By the way, I am going to be a father soon. Effy is pregnant and we want you to be the godfather," he said in a deep piercing tone.

This cannot be real I told myself as his nagging voice disappeared into the steep and silent air. This nigger didn't just call me; he didn't just ask me to be the godfather to his unborn child. I have to be dreaming, I slowly repeated to myself as I forced myself to wake up. But I couldn't escape this nightmare; it was far too real to be a dream. Suddenly, I noticed my right hand reaching into my left shirt pocket for the joint I had rolled up earlier. And as I pulled it out, I noticed the dimmed and dusty photo hanging above the phone. It was a photo of us before the accident. Effy was smiling, her slender body was leaning on Flo's jacked tannish shoulder as his middle finger drifted towards the camera pretending to be a thug.

Flo was a basketball player, and like most ball players, he was tall and slim. His powder-blue eyes were envied by the guys and admired by the girls; and because he wanted to be identified as black, his silky black hair was always cut low to his wavy scalp. He spoke in a uniquely soft tone and was one of those guys who wore their emotions on their sleeves. His nickname was Sweetie, and he always complained about it when we were in public, especially when we were around girls. But that never stopped us from messing with him, especially LeoNell.

Leo was the middle linebacker on the varsity football team and a year older than as well as my best friend though he was indeed a jerk and bully. He was also very shy and insecure about his speech growing up given that he was a heavy stutterer when we were young. And though others teased him about his speech, especially Flo, it didn't bother me because I had gotten used to it over the years, plus the teasing just seemed wrong. Yet, that didn't stop the teasing from getting to Leo after a while. And as a result his brown skin slowly mutated into a shell. A shell he only left around me like a fearful turtle. And as a result we became very close during those dark years. I got to know the aspiring writer hidden within the shell. The kid who wanted to change people's perspective of the world and free their minds of all the illusions created by their societies, nations, church and ideologies. And he made me believed there was more to life than hanging on the corner and partying every weekend. Most importantly, I got to know the kid who turned his suffering into a pure source of knowledge and wisdom. And that kid became my best friend and someone who I also encouraged and helped with his speech. But as the years went by my best friend transformed into a tall muscular guy blooming in the self-confidence of being the first freshman to ever start for the varsity football team after his stuttering gradually disappeared. And the success on the football field also changed his personality too. He became very loud and developed his infamous "I don't give a fuck attitude", which led to our infamous accident and his unapologetic voice mail earlier.

And as I turned to walk away, I suddenly remember why I shunned the photo and why I couldn't get rid of it even though I hated the emotional pain it triggers. And so I slowly walked over to the front door. Through it, I went gently making my way down the stairs and towards the backyard to sit on the old rusty swing. The swing was a few feet left of the evergreens and their branches hovered above like a sun umbrella protecting my brown skin from the blazing rays of a midsummer sun as I lit the perfectly rolled joint and gradually began to ingest the cannabis. Which effects I also began to feel on my body near the half waypoint of the joint. And by that I mean my body had caught a buzz and my mouth had developed the metallic, bitter, salty and sour taste, and my mind had stopped wondering. And as a result all the toxic memories that burned in my head like blistering flames began to fade as the weed began to stimulate my mind. My high wore on, and my body began to feel wearied, and I dozed off as Effy floated into my mind. Elizabeth (Effy) Pratt was very tall. Her black dreadlocks sagged below her shoulders like a bronzed garden of vines, for they had been dyed bronze like her cosmic skin. And her hazel brown eyes brought out her natural beauty and were also gleaming like the sun from her smoothly carved face. A preppy red plaid shirt loosely camouflaged her baby bump and lithesome shoulders as her arms loosely swayed below her waist.

"I thought you stopped smoking? Didn't the doctor tell you it's bad for patients with heart failure," she said in a melodious tone.

"He did and I quit afterward but started again after Flo left. Do you want a hit?"

"Come onnnn, you know I can't anymore because it's bad for the baby, and you also need to quit... because you promised him that you will look after me."

"My bad, I forgot, plus it's not showing... and WoW... you haven't forgotten that?"

"YES, I remember everything about him... he was my first everything," she said with a grin.

"I know... that's why I still can't believe you broke the CODE..."

"I had too..."

"Why?"

"You know why. It's the same reason you started smoking again."

"HUH?"

She grinned again but didn't reply and vanished into the mild breeze a few seconds later.

I waited but she didn't return. And so I turned from the swing and walked calmly toward the house, carefully dragging my feet against newly trimmed lawn as the dank, musty air tiptoed into my nostrils and down my lungs. And as I treaded across the lawn, an irritating, stuffy feeling settled beneath the bridge of my nose and erupted as I hiked up the condensed and narrowed steps. Leaving the steps, I strolled into the old Levitt house and marched down the moist hallway. And as a walked the hallway my heart began to thump rapidly, and I became scared as sweat started to slip down my steaming face. And again my fear of death, the invisible god became real to the point that I started to pray and weep for my soul in spite of not being a believer in Allah. But as I prayed to Allah to spare my life, my mind started to reminisce about Leo and his free verse poems. And I grinned as Leo's "Misunderstood Man" came into my head. And suddenly I began to repeat the following words:

if life is the never ending cycle of
suffering, shouldn't death be
the never ending cycle of peace,
love, freedom and happiness?
And so isn't it true that we hate
things we don't understand, and
are fearful of people who are different,
and cling onto the ideas we love,
even though they might be wrong?
Don't we cry when death takes away
our loved ones but cheer when it
takes our enemy? Don't we complain
about death and claim we are looking
for ways to eradicate it in-spite of us
being its biggest supporters and fans
given that we kill for pleasure, revenge
and retribution? And so isn't it true that
through our actions and deeds death
has become infamous for being unknown,
hated and fear for being different in spite
of those things being ideas that might be wrong?

Afterwards, my heart began to thump at its normal pace, and so I grinned as fear left my body. Then I slowly stood up and walked towards and through the bathroom door and began to wash my hands and face. And after I got done I lifted my head up and saw my own reflection through the mirror. It was an image of a young loser given that I had evolved into the young man I once vowed never to become. And as I stood staring at myself through the mirror, the honest evidence of shame overpowered me and so I left the bathroom and went into the living room and sat on the warmed red leather recliner and calmly dialed Leo's telephone number.

He answered on the fifth ring and said,

"Hey bro, it's been a while, and thanks for calling back because you didn't have to. And I'm sorry for the unapologetic voice mail earlier. It was out of place but I really needed to talk to you, and that was the only way I could've gotten your attention," in a giggling tone.

"It's cool bro, plus your plan worked... I'm on the phone with you... something I thought would never happen again; but what do you want to talk about because I wanted to talk about Flo and what really happened that morning. I think it's about time... that we put our huge egos aside..."

"Yea, you are right and I wanted to talk about Sweetie too."

"Okay... so what happened?"

"We got struck by lightning twice."

"Huh, what do you mean by that?"

"Come on bro, open your mind... it was a freak accident... even though I was under the influence."

"Under the influence? Under the influence of what?"

"Calm down bro... it was alcohol and weed, the usual house party shit."

"So you guys were coming from a party?"

"Yea, it was Sweetie's bawd sweet sixteen. He didn't tell you... he didn't want Effy to know he was cheating on her."

"Hold on... Flo had a side girl when he was going out with Effy?"

"Yeah bro, he was actually messing with two other chicks. You know Sweetie always had something to prove."

"WoW... but yea... what was he trying to prove that night?"

"Nothing really, it was all about getting laid that night. The girl's parents left for the weekend, and so we were going to sleep over after the party but the plan fell apart."

"What happened?"

"The first freak accident."

"Huh, there were two accidents?" I asked.

"Yes, around 2AM, shrieking cries interrupted the bonding process within my room. And the loud echoing led the bawd's friend and me to the master bedroom. And when we got through the door, Sweetie was on the bed gasping for air. His body was twitching as his eyes rolled toward the rear. The chocolate nightstand right of the bed was covered with white powder," Leo said.

"White powder? What the fuck bro, I thought you said it was just drinks and weed."

"I didn't know... about that shit bro... then Sweetie's bawd came up to me, and her eyes were engulfed with water."

"I told him to stop... he didn't listen, he wouldn't slow down... He said he was a pro, he had done it before... and nothing happened... now he won't stop twitching... do something please..." she said.

"What do you want me to do? I'm not a doctor... call the ambulance... tell them to hurry... he overdosed on cocaine," Leo said in a loud tone.

"No."

"What the fuck?"

"I can't, my parents will find out... they don't know about my night life."

"WHAT THE FUCK... do you think his grand-mom knows he smokes or drinks???

Plus he never sipped a lean before...we don't fuck with that shit... what the fuck... how am I supposed to explain this shit..."

"I don't know..." the bawd said.

"Drive him to the hospital" the bawd's friend said. She had Sweetie's head cradled in her arms. His body had stopped twitching.

"Hurry, he's breathing but slowly," the friend said again.

"Fuck, I can't drive... I'm faded," Leo said.

"You have to, he's dying... his body is cold... if you don't hurry Flo will die," she said.

"Fuck, where is the keys?"

"It's in his pocket," the bawd said.

"Where's his jeans?" Leo asked. The bawd quickly ran around the queen size bed. The denim was lying on the flood, left of the bed and by the huge chocolate dresser. She reached into the right front pocket and pulled out the blue Conwell-Egan key holder. Coming back, she ran passed me and through the door. I walked towards the bed, reached over and grabbed Sweetie. His body was unpleasantly cold. I cradled him and went through the broad door, quickly making our way through the massive hallway and down the lanky stairs and towards my silver Crown Vic. When we got there, the right rear door was opened and I gently laid Sweetie into the rear seats and ran towards the driver seat and started to drive.

It was foggy. I tilted my head around and looked at Sweetie. He was still breathing but his body began to shiver from the cold and mine did too. We had forgotten to put proper clothes on when we left. And so I turned the heater on and gently stepped on the gas without removing my right foot. And after all hope seemed lost, we passed the (D9-2) sign, which had two miles beneath it. I tilted to the rear to check on Sweetie. He was still breathing and so I grinned, but as I turned my head back I saw a beaming light from the right and it floated rapidly towards us turning my memories with Sweetie into memories that still burn in my head like a creek of flowing lava.

About the Author

A wise man once said, "That which does not kill us, makes us stronger." – Nietzsche. My name is **Nate Tulay** and I am an aspiring Liberian-American poet. I was born in Liberia during a civil war with a tied tongue and some deafness in my right ear and also experienced another Civil War when I was four and lost my childhood innocence to it. Furthermore, I also did some things in life when I was 12 and 13 that I too am not proud of and cannot truly forgive myself for which along with my other experiences and struggles made me a philosopher sooner rather than later in life and are still my motivations to strive for greatness and be a fair and kind and friendly and loving and understanding and compassionate and honest person one day at a time.

WE THE LOSERS

by Matthew Conte

I was standing by the oven when I saw them, clamped together tight as lovers on a station platform, beating each other. It was a midsummer Saturday at the boardwalk restaurant I've worked at off and on for the past decade, meaning there were a lot of people in the building. It's a counter service joint filled with bennies and families during the day and drunks and weekenders at night—my shift. A graveyard shift if every night were All Saints Day thanks to the summer rental houses and the two bars across the street. A shift for those with a little tougher skin, as steady streams of jukebox hijackings, over-orders, and fist fights could get taxing.

I quit my job as a reporter with a newspaper so that I could time things right to come back to Gee-Gee's, where I could work as many hours as possible. Back living in Katie's grandma's second floor thanks to the fire that took our first apartment, I decided to buckle down for the summer and spend the four months or so trying to make enough money to move to Philadelphia. I would put in around 50 hours a week plus another 20 or so at Brielle Recreation's summer camp program in the mornings. Both the job I left and the one I left it for were hectic at times, with deadlines at the paper and long lines at Gee-Gee's. Both could feel trivial, had a way of making the worker feel like they were meaningless and shouting into something that could just swallow them up if it wanted to. Whether I was writing a thousand words on an uncontested school board election or making a pizza that someone was going to pay for, throw up on, and then leave for me to clean up, I was typically asking myself why any of this was happening in the first place. But one was a lot of sitting, a lot of manners, a lot of middle-aged suburbanites yelling at me for this or commending me for that. Meanwhile, at Gee-Gee's I lifted things, I fought with teenagers over the auxiliary cord, and I ended most days with a beer. At the end of holiday weekends I slept on the beach, woke up with a swim, and brought the beach home in my shorts. I ran into the paper's manager at the annual week-long fireman's fair, one of the biggest weeks of the year in Manasquan. She told me at least I had the summer to prepare and relax before I moved. I didn't bother to tell her how unrelaxing it was.

* * *

One night, a Fourth of July weekend night during my last summer there, Hazy Davy and his girlfriend Crazy Janie came in, yelling back out the doors. I had played Little League baseball with Davy and he was a year below me at Manasquan High School. His dad was one of two people in my life who called me "Matty." I didn't know him too well but when we drunkenly bumped into each other at the senior formal at Roger Williams University, me as a guest of a student and he as the guest of a senior, we were so shocked at the sudden familiar face that we, the polite party fringes, the beach bums who still recognized each other in ties and clothes with buttons at this fancy-ass, seafood-serving ball hugged and danced together and got each other drinks at the open bar.

This particular holiday weekend had so far seen its fair share of wild conversations with customers. One told us she had been running a one-woman drink chip-for-pizza slice deal with various employees for years and needed a new trading partner. A pair of 25-year-olds made their way up onto the grill stage to try to coerce the college-aged boys on the fryers into some free food, slipping on a pair of greasy aprons. A former employee stepped behind the counter to pound out some dough. After closing, we watched from our encampment on Riddle Beach as a man stumbled from a house with the sunrise, fully clothed with beer in hand, and walked straight into the ocean without stopping. When he came out sopping wet and continuing to drink from a 50-50 split of Bud Light and saltwater, we asked how long he had been drunk. He asked us what day it was, which is sort of all the answer you need to that question.

* * *

Modern day jukeboxes are controlled mostly via iPhone apps and touch screens. At Gee-Gee's, I witnessed joyous Elton John sing-alongs, intoxicated faux-karaoke battles, and birthday wishes granted. But there's always someone with the mindset of teenage John Mulaney, a comedian with a story about playing the same song over and over again to see what would happen. I once heard "Higher" by Creed playing, and thought that was kind of a funny song to put on. People like to shit on bands like Creed and Nickelback because they're not good and they're very successful, but I learned to let go of any music snobbery I might've had back in college. It's stupid and useless; Creed is harmless and even though it's probably playing through a jukebox ironically, I don't really care. In the hectic workplace of the pizza ovens, it wasn't until a few minutes later that I realized that "Higher" by Creed was still on. When I came up to the counter, I didn't even have to say anything before the cashier girls said, "You have to do something." Apparently it had played at least four times already, so I found the remote and turned the jukebox off. A few minutes later, a guy came over to me and yelled over the counter that the jukebox was broken.

"Oh, yeah," I told him. "I don't think it was broken, somebody just put on the same Creed song over and over again, so I turned it off."

"Yeah! I put in $5 and I didn't hear all my songs."

I then realized he was the Creed guy, so I tried to change my tune hoping that someone who was drunk enough to spend $5 to hear "Higher" that many times was also drunk enough to lose himself in this conversation. "Oh, yeah, it's broken, sorry," I said.

"This is horseshit!" he said before turning on his heels and stomping out the double doors.

He and his friends came in again on different nights, mostly playing the same song. One time, I turned it off and they just gathered around and sang the song acapella. It became a tolerable and sometimes welcome distraction. The story got around, with the Creed guys gaining a little mythic notoriety amongst those clocking in and out. At the end of the summer, the last late shift of the Labor Day weekend, in the flimsy barrier of moments between the end of summer and the beginning of Local Summer, we closed the place down—swept and mopped the floors, plunged the toilets, shooed the nappers from the porch, tossed or boxed up or ate cold any remaining pizza. We left the jukebox on, paused, with the volume all the way up. We parked ourselves on the sand near the water and sat there with the case of drinks the bartenders had traded us for boxes of pizza, going for a swim when we had to piss, passing around joints and stories and insults, dodging the tractor sweeping the beach, waiting for the lights to come on. We gave the openers a little time to settle in and turn some appliances on before we, a ragged group of beards, teenage-boy dishwashers, college-girl cashiers, single moms, calloused burnt hands, ex-Navymen, sand-covered calves, teachers, struggling artists, bloodshot eyes, Soundcloud rappers, rent-a-cops, bartenders and backs, moonlighters, addicts, dropouts; we of the night who make your food and take your shit and thank you for it; we who fall asleep to the robins' dawn chorus, who huddle in the fringes of big nights out for sleeveless New Yorkers and rich young professionals, for tight dresses and popped collars; we who've been told by our wages are minimum; we the fiery, the sleepless, undereducated, greasy, we the losers slow-motion rolled in before service to the sound of a maxed out jukebox playing "Higher" by Creed and the exasperated sighs of the still sleepy eyed breakfast crew.

* * *

Davy and Janie were basically regulars. On a normal night we might have exchanged casualties or a story or two about his brother, Killer Joe, who was my wife's sister's husband's best friend. I didn't know Janie well but had seen her name occasionally in the sports section of the hyper-local newspaper I worked at her success with lacrosse in college beyond the borders of Manasquan. On this night, I came over to see what the commotion was, as the job of makeshift bouncer often fell to me. Once he calmed a bit, he told me of an encounter just outside the doors with a few guys who had just walked out, which began when they called him a "faggot."

"Which like, I don't really care, whatever," he said. "But then they kept calling her a slut." Apparently these guys could only insult someone in some relation to the variety and frequency of their sex lives.

He steamed there in front of the pizza display, his hands in fists and his face deep red. Janie wiped tears from her eyes. I asked them what they wanted to eat. This was a couple that came in often, almost never too drunk, and never caused a problem. They were locals who were usually alone, occasionally with a few friends. He got a grilled cheese. She got a 'tie-dye' slice, which is a disgusting concoction of fried chicken, buffalo sauce, barbecue sauce, and ranch dressing that inexplicably flies off the pan once the calendar turns with the stroke of midnight. I told them it was on me. A pizza pie only needs to sell about two slices before it becomes profitable, and bread and melted cheese isn't exactly breaking the bank either. We give out free slices all the time late at night. To former employees, to people we're flirting with, to friends or family or other service workers or cops or people we're just trying to impress. Sometimes even strangers with drink chips. Davy and Janie were both so happy, they thanked me over and over again and left a nice tip for the girls at the counter.

* * *

It was post-2 a.m. when I stood up on the pizza station and hollered down at the two combatants in my substitute teacher voice. Only these weren't grade schoolers, they were a 32-year-old man and the 17-year-old he was apparently too drunk to know better than to fight, who had most likely been smoking weed on the beach under cover of the darkness. I went up and over the pizza display window, down the steps, and through the circle of seconds and sidekicks to try to grip onto him. He was using his fist and the shaggy-haired kid, a local for sure, was using his elbow. They were both bleeding from their faces, dripping onto the pavement. With his belt buckle in my left hand and his arm in my right, I was pulling and prying when an officer came running down the macadam and took him straight from my arms. When the officer who took my statement—a former cook at the same joint and my wife's co-sibling-in-law—I told him the big guy was on top and the kid was defending himself. I don't know how it started but for some reason, maybe because he was punching below his weight class, or maybe because of a misguided need to protect my home and people from the rowdy three-to-four-month invaders, I found myself slanting the details to put the big guy in the wrong.

He wrote it all down in a little notepad while I got down on my hands and knees with a bucket of soapy water and a hot rag and washed the blood from the pavement.

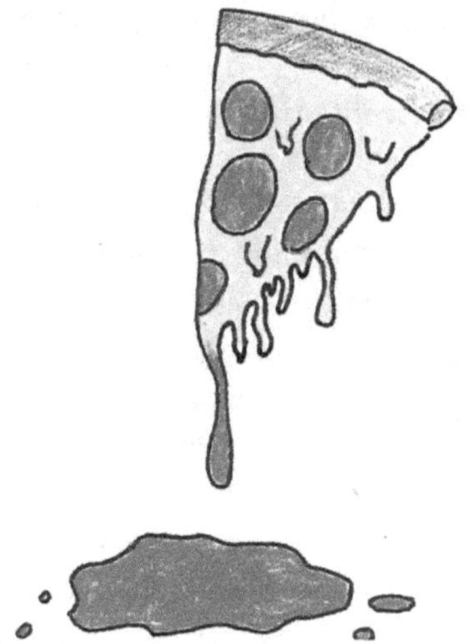

About the Author

Matt Conte is a New Jersey-born writer with an MFA from Rosemont College. He lives in Philadelphia and makes pizza dough.

BAD FORTUNE AROUND MEETING THE PRESIDENT

by Kurt G. Schmidt

Since my father had threatened Mom with a .22 rifle, life had been reasonably calm for over three years. However, the cat population at our house during this period had risen to twenty-one. Mom and my sisters had become addicted to the cuddly things and allowed feline sex lives to run rampant without any thought to giving them away or getting them spayed. Some of the adult cats became fed up with overcrowding and headed for the woods. And though some died, there always seemed to be pregnant female ready to replenish the supply. One round-bellied cat rejected the towel-lined carton Mom had placed near the warmth of the wood stove and insisted on sleeping at the foot of my bed until, in the dark of the night, she gave birth there to the first of four, carried it to my pillow, and caused me to wake up screaming for Mom because I thought there was a mouse in my ear.

In the summer the cats stayed outside mostly and hung around the barn at feeding time or whenever I returned from fishing with a pile of small sunfish and tossed them to the hoard of growling, hissing competitors. In the winter pregnant females and kittens were allowed inside, although once after a heavy snowfall, a black-and-white, long-haired male named Piachi returned from a two-year absence with a wild demeanor that prevented Mom from coaxing him into the house but allowed her to feed him in the shed for a few days before he disappeared again forever, knowing perhaps that becoming a stud in this house meant a shaky life in which two rabbits had joined the fray and become targets for kittens that jumped off chairs onto their backs.

But the cats were minor problems compared with those that arose during the summer when I was sixteen, when harebrained behavior had nothing to do with rabbits. First, there was my introduction to President Eisenhower. Then, my family's introduction to Bud Blake, a local stud with a huge belly that jiggled on top of a low-slung belt. Other than both men being bald, and both being infatuated with power, the President and Bud Blake had nothing in common.

That spring began with my selection from the high school's a cappella choir to be in the All-State Music Festival. I could be excited if it were all-state baseball, but the J.V. baseball coach thinks I'm too small to hit the ball any distance, even after I blasted some scorching line drives. Big disappointment. Being a reserve on the team is killing my dream, and the uniform is too big.

The all-state chorus creates an exciting sound, but my mind is on the whack of the bat hitting a baseball. I hardly have a chance to play though, and then only at second base, not shortstop. I think life is unfair.

In May the town's American Legion Auxiliary announces they will sponsor me to attend an event called New Hampshire Boys State — one week in June at the University of New Hampshire. The Women's Club will sponsor my friend Stuart. Organizations like the Lions Club and Rotary Club will sponsor nine other boys from our high school. Theoretically, Boys State is intended to teach New Hampshire boys about state government. But the guys gathered at UNH seem more interested in having fun than learning about government. So I find plenty of tennis action. And John Ineson from Rochester plays his guitar and sings Elvis Presley songs like "Hound Dog" and "Heartbreak Hotel." On talent night, Pete Wright and I sing "Tell me Why the Stars Do Shine," but the guy who sings Elvis songs is the star of the show. I think participation in the mock elections is worthwhile as long as I don't compete with the state's big wheels for offices like Governor, and so I'm elected Clerk of the Senate and supervisor of the voter checklist. Near the end of the week, administrators pass out a small booklet on state government, saying we'll be given a little test on the material. I don't know why such a fun week should be marred by a test, but I stretch out on the campus lawn with Stuart, studying the booklet.

Stuart says, "I heard a big 4-H group just arrived on campus. They're having a dance tonight. You want to go?"

I know I'd feel awkward being the smallest boy at a dance, so I say, "Nah, I think I'll stick around and study for the test tomorrow."

Stuart says, "That government stuff is boring. You'd have more fun at the dance. Just about all the guys I know are going."

Stuart is right. The dormitory is empty at night. One hundred and seventy-eight guys from Boys State must have gone to the 4-H dance. So I study civic government alone. The material is dry, but I think if I'm using it as an excuse to avoid the dance, I might as well try to do a good job on the test.

The next day the late-night guys and I take the test in a big hall. Most questions are true and false and seem fairly easy. I leave the hall with the satisfaction of having done my best.

The following day at the final ceremonies I sit with Stuart and the contingent from our school. Boys State administrators announce awards and certificates, while everyone whispers that John-the-Elvis-man is a sure thing to be one of the two chosen to go to Washington, D.C., for Boys Nation. You have to send a guy who can play guitar and sing "Hound Dog." So when they announce John Ineson's name, no one is surprised as John-the-Elvis-man walks up front.

They announce the second name, and I think it must be someone whose name sounds like mine. I don't move. My friends poke me and say congratulations. As I walk to the front, I hear someone say, "He got the highest mark on the test."

By some strange miracle, I'm going to Washington. It is the first time I feel special, as if the asterisk next to my name says something good instead of *too small*.

Newspaper articles over the next few days make it sound as if I am special, as if going to this Boys Nation thing, as if being the first boy ever chosen from my school, is a big deal. When my parents drive me to the nearby YMCA camp where I've been spending part of my summer each year, the camp director speaks to them for the first time. He has smiles and congratulations that he usually reserves for the affluent families. Somehow my good luck has elevated my family. I still doubt this change of fortune until I leave camp and my parents drive me to Boston and I'm on the train with John Ineson to Washington. Mom says if I meet President Eisenhower, I can tell him that he and Grandpa played cards in the same poker group when Ike was president of Columbia University.

John and I and some huge guys from states like Texas and Nevada are housed in the dormitories of the University of Maryland. The huge guys are kind to me and do not razz me when I challenge one of them to some Indian wrestling. I place my right foot against the right foot of a muscular guy from Nevada and grasp his right hand. I ram our clasped hands down and drive his arm behind his leg. He loses his balance, moves his back foot. He wants to try again. Same result. Others want to try. Same result. I am recognized as the Indian-wrestling champ. Low center of gravity has some advantages.

I am glad for this small recognition because the other boys are so mature and dynamic when it comes to campaigning for Boys Nation president and other governing positions. Particularly impressive are the southern boys, who talk like preachers about God and country and their view on whether to pass our mock Senate bill to abolish the electoral college system. John Lee Frye from Huntington, West Virginia, is the best, winning our election with ease. When we proceed through a reception line at the Capitol to shake hands with Vice President Nixon, John Lee Frye is out front with the American Legion chaperones, making that important first contact.

John Ineson and I meet New Hampshire senators Styles Bridges and Norris Cotton at the Capitol. They treat us to lunch and ask what we intend to do after high school. I can't tell them I need a college that provides a free education because my family can't afford a flush toilet. But Mom has suggested one of the service academies because they don't cost anything if you get in, so I say I'd like to go to Annapolis. I could say West Point, Air Force Academy, or the Coast Guard Academy too but want to appear decisive. Senator Bridges says to contact him if I remain interested in an appointment to Annapolis.

* * *

I am sixteen and only five foot two when I meet President Eisenhower. On the day of our White House tour, the American Legion chaperones for our Boys Nation group say we will not meet him. Big disappointment. The President is still recuperating from abdominal surgery. The tour ends, and someone tells us to wait on the White House lawn. Someone says Ike is coming out. The group forms a semicircle. I can't see over everyone. A chaperone notices my problem and leads me to the front on the far left-hand edge. Ike comes out smiling and says how we represent the best in the country. He moves forward to the center of the semicircle and shakes hands with John Lee Frye. Then Ike steps back and scans the front row until his eyes lock on mine. He walks directly to me, sticks out his hand, and says, "You're a small fellow. Where are you from?"

I shake his hand and say, "New Hampshire, sir."

Ike says, "I've been to New Hampshire a few times."

I know Ike likes to fish, so I say, "You should bring your fishing rod next time you come. I caught a five-pound smallmouth bass once."

Ike says, "Sounds like you're a good fisherman."

I smile. Ike says good luck and begins shaking hands with guys next to me. I level my camera for two close-ups of him. It's hard to believe the President picked me out because I was the smallest kid. I think maybe he did it because he is only a few inches taller than me. When I saw him on TV, he seemed tall. But Ike has empathy for small boys, and now something good has come from this handicap. Only a few more guys in the front row get to shake his hand before Ike waves and retreats into the White House.

I have the feeling my luck in life is getting better. If I achieve good grades my senior year, if I score high on the College Boards, Senator Bridges might appoint me to Annapolis. If I grow two more inches, I can meet the minimum height requirement for Annapolis. This trip to Washington, which never would have happened if I'd gone to the 4-H dance, has opened up exciting possibilities for my future.

A professional photographer captures the Boys Nation events, and I come home with an 8 x 10 glossy of Ike and our group, showing me clearly in the front row. I have another 8 x 10 of John Ineson and me with our New Hampshire senators. Mom tells me to bring my photos to Bud and Joan Blake's house, where we've been invited to socialize. She says Bud and Joan would be interested in my trip. I think my meeting the President might impress the Blake's attractive older daughters.

* * *

I can tell that Joan and Bud Blake are not interested in my trip to Washington. This situation is different from other homes we've visited, where the adults and the kids gather around the TV. The Blake's teenage daughters are missing, and it is only my sisters and me in front of the TV. From my vantage point, I can see Bud is flirting with Mom, and Joan is flirting with Dad. They are drinking beer together, but each couple's conversation is separate from the other. I feel as though something strange is going on.

When we arrive home, Dad wastes no time snapping at Mom. He says he knows what Joan was suggesting. "If you think I'm going to sleep with Joan just so you can fuck Bud, you'd better have your head examined."

Mom says, "You know how to ruin every social situation with your perverted imagination."

"If I catch you with Bud, I'll kill you both. I'll kill the kids too."

I hear a scuffle in the kitchen, and my fear returns to the shooting incident three years ago. Threatening to kill us kids is a way to control Mom, but I'm afraid he'll actually do it next time.

* * *

A couple weeks later Mom comes home from work with two brand new fishing rods. She says a friend at work gave them to her, and I should use them. It's mid-August, a good time to cast lures off Teddy Olsen's dock and try for a big bass. I'm walking down the road to the lake with the new fishing rods when Bud Blake stops his truck. His windows are open, and for a moment he just chews on his cigar butt and stares at me.

Finally, he says, "Where'd you get those fishing rods?"

I say, "From my mother."

People like Bud Blake squint sometimes when they're pissed off. Bud is squinting and talking slow and soft. He says, "I gave those rods to your mother."

"She said I could use them."

"Maybe. But I gave them to her."

"You gonna take her fishing?"

Bud keeps squinting and chewing the cigar. He thinks I'm too young and stupid to know what he's up to. I just want to kick that fat bastard in the balls and tell him to leave my mother alone. He doesn't give a damn about our family. The fat bald bastard with the soggy cigar thinks he's a handsome stud, entitled to whatever action he can find.

Finally Bud Blake drives away. I spit in the direction of his truck. I continue to Olsen's dock and try fishing, but I can't enjoy it. There are too many bad thoughts pounding in my head. I think Mom is poking the dragon again.

I walk home and remove the .22 rifle and the 12-gauge shotgun from the depths of the large storage closet in my bedroom. I dismantle each gun and wrap the pieces in newspaper. I hide each piece deep again in my closet in various locations. I feel safer now, but at night I have the same dream I have so often. A man with a gun is shooting at me, and I'm running to escape. I wake up sweating and gulping for air.

About the Author

Kurt Schmidt's essays and memoirs have appeared in Bacopa Literary Review, The Ravens Perch, Grown and Flown, The Good Men Project, Eclectica, Snapdragon, and as a "best essay" in the 2017 Adelaide Literary Awards Anthology. He also authored the novel Annapolis Misfit (Crown), won awards in technical writing, and had a coming-of-age memoir as a finalist in a Bread Loaf creative nonfiction competition. You can view Kurt's work at www.kurtgschmidt.com.

REFUGE WITH LAST BLACK MAN IN SAN FRANCISCO

by Mellody Hayes

"The only thing effective immigrant parents are doing is raising kids who will someday disrespect them," I said to my date, Vincent.

He is French. And African. His mother had eyes the color cyrene, and his father hailed from an African country whose name I didn't know. He said the name of the country three times, his French accent caressing and distorting the sounds to my ears.

Finally, I gave up and he frowned, stating that he was no longer surprised by how little geography Americans knew. I toss my synthetic braids behind my shoulder, amazed that after all these years in this country, he still doesn't understand what it is to be an American. Our ignorance is combined with arrogance --that therein is our American privilege. I willfully never bother to look up the name of his father's homeland and we are still scheduled for date number three.

On date one, he dizzied me. No, I was not in awe. I mean I was literally dizzy from how he guided us from store to store, in and out, without any overarching sense of direction. My internal compass points straight to the spirit world and I haven't yet found my true North in this one, so I am left to allow him to lead us through San Francisco's Mission District. He takes me to a jewelry store--*Love and Luxe*--and I imagine he thinks that the positive association of the beauty of these objects will be conveyed onto him. But my mind is meta, watching him watching me as I watch us in streams of sociology, psychology, and evolutionary biology. French and African, the colonizer and the colonized. Black and American, claiming freedoms spiritual and material. Man and Woman, biology with a question of chemistry.

On date number two, we watch *Last Black Man in San Francisco*, a movie poorly billed as being about gentrification. The film is about "story"--creating yourself through a narrative that inspires and empowers. A story that organizes your pain into meaning, your time into purpose. Dismantling the flat-bootied stories we have been handed. Usurpers, upstarts, lyrical geniuses, creators of new language, we write ourselves into being, using symbols of power and privilege that dominants stories say we could have never own.

Over dinner, he tells me that his father has this cultural rule that one must never touch the father's head.

"Yes", I acknowledge, "the symbolic meaning is that one must never threaten to take the throne."

But proper parenting, I tell him, has in it the seeds of insurrection. To be a good parent is to empower your child to think for himself and someday overthrow you, to disrespect you. This is especially true for some immigrant parents, I say, thinking of my own migrate childhood. My father is from the rural south, where he grew up picking cotton, putting it into guney sacks, sacks the women folk cut up to sew into sheets. These ambitious parents, if they did their job right, they push you far away from themselves through education and opportunities. Later, your best love becomes how to hide your dissimilitude, your consternation at their "backwardness."

They love you, push you, support you into not understanding them. Love becomes tinged with *tolerance*. Or, as a Sri Lankan friend described of her mother's weeklong stay with her, daughter now demonstrates her maturity by her *forbearance*, avoiding arguing, and not mentally overpowering her with the scientific knowledge she now wields professionally--that her parents lack. Fucking western education, steals the smartest, most eager and needy Black and Brown kids from their homes by estranging them from their families. The colonizer and the colonized...

His eyes and lips smile as reply to my comment and I see the gap in his teeth, the African sign of beauty--royalty. (We were all royal, ain't that right?) I had used that gap to flirt with him on the dating app.

"Yes, I can see you in two weeks when your family leaves town, but don't get braces in the meantime."

His reply two weeks later, "I checked and the gap is still here--can we meet?"

"Sure, just be sure you bring the gap."

I am mindful of the gap. Not just in his smile, but that narrows between us. I am from the land of children-are-made-to-be-seen-and-not-heard Mississippi, but he says he sees the African in me. We talk about our recent mutual overthrows of our fathers, both occurring weeks ago. He raised his voice, corrected his father aggressively, putting him in his place, clarifying that his father did not have expert knowledge on all topics. His elbow was on the table and I witnessed his bicep visibly flex as the energy from the recollected conversation flowed into him. And I—Southern, Holy Ghost-filled—swore at my father for the first time. My nephew had run away from my father's home and called me in desperation. He was barely able to speak through his tears and terror, his fear at going back to the apartment where his older brother had beat him for his poor report card. When I called my father, he took no responsibility for the fact that his 14 year-old ward was wandering the rough streets of Long Beach in the dark of night. Still unaware that parenting means accountability, my father erupted defensively, "I wasn't my fault when you ran away either!" Me, now the calm anesthesiologist, recently freed from residency, throwing off mental subjugation and gaslighting wherever I met its remnants, I cursed at him. F... ree.

The lights are low in the upscale Indian bistro but I am sure that our eyes shine with bloodlust as we recall these first swings at independence from patriarchy. These bold, late-in-life moves to be the person who sits upon the throne of our own minds. Laughing, I tease him, "You raised your voice, that's like coming after him with a knife." He smiles again and I see the slit of darkness between his teeth, a vacancy, an invitation--the space where whispered secrets first escape, slipping from behind white bars to be heard...

***

"You may be the last Black man that I date," I confess on date three. We sit over Japanese food and he introduces me to the Japanese set menu *omakase*, which he explains means, "I let you decide." He pours soy sauce into the small, blue, ceramic dish, mine first and then his own, as he explains how in his ten years working in China he vacationed in Japan frequently and became more than fluent in the cuisine. I confess that I am nervous because our initial match seems so good. He feels like the "everything" for which the old me didn't even hope to consider as a possible option. And then there are the unexpected paroxysm of goofy, belly laughter that erupt from "serious me" on each date. I explain to him that stakes feel higher when on a date with a Black man. In my heart, I wonder if will we overcome Chris Rock's dire prognostication. "Even if you meet the perfect person, it ain't gonna be at the perfect time," Rock jokes, "You're married, they're single. That's right. You're Jewish, they're Palestinian.... You're a Black woman, he's a Black man."

He is playful, charming, successful, and like me, he speaks Mandarin so—unlike the functionally monolingual American-Born Chinese I have dated, we can actually speak to each other in Mandarin. He is intense. His mind as analytical as mine, and when I listen and feel the powerful force behind his words and watch the way he moves in the world, I know that he is a natural leader. But around me he becomes the confessor and I his priestess as he tells me every truth. He hides nothing, wanting to be known and accepted at this price--a bargain, really. I mean, what is the going the cost of a heart that is recently broken, only months separated from his ex-wife?

In the car, his nerves bolstered by the *sake* we shared, he looks towards me with a downward tilted head, unable to look me directly in the eye, he breathes, "You are beautiful." He is shy with me, and I hear it again as a confession from the heart. My peak compliment of the last man I dated was, "You are discerning," because he saw my soul, my invisible parts, and superpowers. Part of me feels sad for this gentleman sitting across from me if beautiful is all he can see...

***

After the date, he emails me—"In November, if we are still dating, I want to go see this movie". There is a link that I click on and I view the trailer for "Queen and Slim". Suddenly I am catapulted into scenes of violence, tinged with the American's contemporary story of race and police violence. Because movies about White police officers and Black citizens having a nonviolent civic interactions are not yet being made, the plot of Queen and Slim is that the Black man kills the police officer in self-defense and a romantic first date between a Black man and woman turn into "Bonnie and Clyde on the lam."

After watching the trailer, I am filled with horror. My fingers move quickly over the keyboard, alarmed, and I write. "Look, there are are two purposes to storytelling. Storytelling reports and prescribes a reality. These have been the stories that they label as 'Black people stories.' Stories of violence, pain, and abuse. To imbibe them automatically is to continue to endorse them as a possible future reality. Unless you are an intentional visionary, like, say a Martin Luther King, Jr. or a Gandhi, one is merely reiterating the stories of pain that will be lived out for the next 200 years. Unless you raise the psychology, emotional expectation of a positive outcome, the same outcome is destined, because it is the outcome that has been pre-rehearsed on our visual cortex, in our imagination when are dreaming."

Spiritual writer David Dieda says that the superior man meets his woman's challenge with unmoving love. Yes, I challenge and he is unmoved. He doesn't respond to this monologue. And I see that in the reflex of fear, it had taken me taken me two days to appreciate the sweetness of his email. He had asked for a date in November, so many months away. Oh...in his visual cortex, his imagination, and in his dreams of a possible future...he sees me.

He is a tourist to this race story in America and wants to jump into the deep end first. Having grown up in the French countryside, the view outside his window sheep "baaing" (or what do sheep say in French?), he has the lookie-loo curiosity of an uninvolved foreigner. He rubbernecks on this race story and I wonder if he will slow my transport to more internal spaciousness with these topics ("I've never made love to a Black woman," he said and Spirit asks, "Is that really what I am?")

The movie I would create for our collective imagination? Thousands of boring, civic and professional police stops happening everyday because both parties have babies and dreams to which to go home. We don't have time to act out being each other's worst nightmare; Let's free each other from those projections. I want happy beginnings and endings for Black love stories. (Yet, my favorite love story—Love and Basketball, Sinea Lathan's character was perfect and loved Omar Epps, but he left her nevertheless. And she had to fight for his love. Black woman warrior, always at work. But I have learned to allow and receive...)

***

On Bastille Day, he makes brunch for us. He knows how to make perfectly soft boiled eggs and he shows me the way to decapitate the head of the egg. He says that he wants to read Black Rage and I ask him why.

"You have to know about the past, to know the struggle," he answers.

"Yes, I agree, but how are you going to make your vision for the future stronger than your knowledge of the past?"

How to walk into a new future, hopeful, confident, without being constricted by fear from the past?, I ask him. He's not Black American, why put those psychologies and programs in his head when he can live free? Why curse himself with this particular ghost —to be haunted by doubt in his next pitch meeting. Are they judging me? Are they holding within them the psychology that oppressed others? Why imprisoned himself in stories and expectations of the past instead of furtively creating a new future. Perhaps his mind, free of circuitously winding self-doubt and suspicion, can find more a direct path out of the maze in which I once found myself lost.

Does he think he can sample this indignation—oh, so righteous—and not have his brain changed? To take a hit and not be affected by newfound paranoia? This newbie wants to take on the high of the freedom fighter, of the cause so morally superior. Does he actually think he can stay whole without being connected to community and in spiritual traditions of love? I feel him wanting to storm the gates, to take in all that ammunition. Grabbing his shaved head, feeling the bristles his salt and pepper hair poke my hands, I squeeze his face tightly I say, "Stay French." Be free of this particular American drama, stay confused by it. It should never make sense to any of us.

***

I am confused by why I fought relaxing into the soft rhythms of being with him. With friends, French and American, we do a twelve-mile hike in Point Reyes and my new hiking shoes allow no flexibility in my foot's stride, causing a muscle spasm in my hip. I hide the pain, keeping it to myself as we lunch at the beach, but during the final miles, the pain deteriorates my walk into a limp. Meanwhile, he is still full of force and energy and seeing my injury, he asks to carry me the last bit of the way. My heart fluttered at the offer, but I declined. The idea wafted in my mind as a vision, so delicious, of being carried like a playful teenager, being uplifted, and my spirit experienced it as joy. But it felt so silly to grown-up me, this notion of being on his back, and I even worried that he might reference this moment of my frailty and weakness in our future. I was embarrassed to receive such an intimate gesture in the presence of the group. Later, however, after soaking in the Epsom salt bath he drew for me and letting him knead the spasm out of the muscle, he held me, not on his back, but in his arms as I slept the sleep of the exhausted.

Once so independent, having sampled this thing called togetherness with him, I feel changed. I am shocked by the joy in his face as he looks at me. Witnessing his smile is a complete experience--I feel moved and sated both. I love the sight of the muscles in his back as he raises out of bed, tired yet determined, to meditate with me at 5am. I am amused by our linguistic play as we say goodbye to each other in the morning in Mandarin—I tell him to work hard and he wishes me a good day in the operating room.

***

I remember a slow moment on an overnight UCSF call shift, between kidney transplants and emergency spine surgeries, lounging at the front desk with our multicultural crew. We were "shooting the shit" until our 7am release to go home. The topic of interracial dating came up and, remembering the smile of one of my dates, I remixed the classic "Once you go Black, you don't go back." With a faux moan, I offered, "Mmmm, once you had the curry, there is *no* hurry". And the OR nurses and staff each chimed in with their own, each from their own cultural background.

"Once you had the lumpia, you want some up in ya."

"Once you had Chinese, you'll be hungry in five minutes."

And the show stealer, "Once you go White, your credit is right!" And we roared with laughter until the next kidney transplant had to be started.

But what of this French (mixed with Burkinabe) kiss… "Once I've tried the brie, will my heart be free"? I always wanted to live in France, to experience the freedom that Baldwin and Baker said they discovered there. But he found me here…

Can love ever be free of sociology? Of power and of its shadow game —an attempt to escape feelings of shame and social vulnerability?

Love is free, but public commitment can be a power game. My thinking about why some people choose their partner changed completely when a White girlfriend told me the following story. She and her Black boyfriend were in Martha's Vineyard, walking down the street together. She turned to him, with what I imagine was Olive Oyl hero worship and said, "I feel so safe walking down the street with you." His response? "Really, I feel so safe walking down the street with *you.*" And then it hit me—the utter physical vulnerability some Black men may feel and the experience of safety and *possibility* that even the most "woke" brother may feel with a White partner to sponsor them into safety. Asylum seekers, like Salvadorans in San Francisco churches, finding refuge from the ravages of social violence. Like political satirist Baratunde Thurston's TED talk about race implied—that police stop may go more smoothly with a social safety sponsor in the passenger seat.

Asylum seekers all. Maybe that's what we are. I see the utter vulnerability of some Black American men, hidden in masculinity, and I wish them that shelter. For my White girlfriends over the years, they experienced refuge the first time they dated a Black man and realize that they could be "thick" instead of overweight, learning that they could love their ample asses. They got to be refugees from the crazy idea that all women are meant to be waif thin. Their walks even changed. Mentally I noted, "Are you poking your butt out instead of trying to tuck it in?" Free…

For me, it's can you shelter my dreams in your hope, faith, and confidence, even your male privilege, while I work to bridge the gap between my previous beliefs and my growing knowledge of the possibility we can create? Can I date to walk around in your freedom? I won't wear the pants, but can I share your worldview, that says ease, abundance and that life is a yes to me? Share a window into your reality so I can expand my sense of privilege, question the solidity of my old stories, check the reactions of a previously doubtful and vigilant nervous system?

***

A year ago, I went on an amazing first date with a Mexican-American lawyer, smart, sexy, athletic, who after explaining minutiae of the tiny laws that govern our society said that these laws were why Black and brown people "will always be on the bottom." His societal prediction made it our last date. I studied sociology of equality as a college student at Harvard, with book shelves full of documentation of the inequality in education and healthcare. I know the past and the present, but I disagreed with him about the direction of the future. Nah, Boo, your dreams of the future don't belong on a pillow beside my own.

***

"You're complicated," my French-African had said on our second date. And I laughed my laugh, the joy reaching high to the ceiling. See, I am giggly and bubbly between metaphysical discourse. "No, it's good," he reassures me. His utterance of "good" is guttural and expanded, "goooood" with umlauts and thick like camembert. He shook his head, relieved by the rarified paths my mind takes. His countenance looks befuddled, almost scared, as he mentally recalled conversations with others. His eyes widen, eyebrows raise, and he is nonplussed as he declares, "Simple people confuse me." He is spiritual, brilliant, a physical savant, energetic, and driven. And in his matching complexity, I experience refuge.

***

On date number one he had read me cold. "You are a strong woman who only recently learned to be vulnerable." The accuracy of that statement melted and scared me. And after each one of our dates, I told myself I wouldn't see him again. I dissuaded myself by saying that something was missing. But I was unable to resist each subsequent invitation. I would arrive, adorned with makeup, sporting high heels, glad each time his wide smile and open heart greeted me. My own heart has been in a multi-staged surrender. I remember my old mental image of my singleness—I was a gazelle that I would continue to run; the lion would have to take me down because I refused to be caught. I was alone, evading the predator, alert, regal, free, and definitely not weak enough to fall on the savanna.

But recently, talking to me while he roasted salmon for our dinner, he stopped mid-sentence and said, "Between seeing you, I forget how beautiful you are," and I think, "I could get used to this." The softness of being connected. The feeling of needing and wanting. Letting go of arid self-sufficiency and defensiveness, my mind shifts out of sociology, psychology, and history, and I am merely aware that I want to be his. It's on a sun-filled Sunday afternoon, that I fall from my mind and into my heart as I feel him sleeping against me. Watching his muscular chest rising and falling, wisps of *qi* sawing in and out, my mind and heart feel calm. I told him to nap and he was asleep in seconds, and I laugh inwardly at the amount of peace he says that I give him.

On our most recent date, we sit in the dark, watching The Farewell, a funny Chinese movie about the cultural differences in how to show love for someone. Knowing that I am likely to arrive having forgotten about dinner, a pattern leftover from my habit of busyness, he has snuck cherries into the theater for me. Letting language, shifting light, and laughter wash over me in the darkness, I pop rubies of juicy summer into my mouth. When I finish that Tupperware bowl, he finds my hands in the darkness to place another container of rubies in my hands for my joy. I find myself full. Instead of eating more, I reach out my hand for his and interlace my fingers with his own, feeling my heart held, carried, and uplifted.

About the Author

Dr. Mellody Hayes is a Harvard College graduate and UCSF trained physician-writer who lives in San Francisco. She works as anesthesiologist with a focus on palliative care. Founder and CEO of Ceremony Health, a psychedelic medicine clinic, she is passionate about creating peace and health for all people.

A MURKY FUTURE

by Jennifer Nelson

I thought I knew exactly what I wanted, until the morning I started bawling in the newsroom.

Tears gushed down my face, blurring my vision as I struggled to read my interview notes for an article about a local accounting firm. The clock was ticking. In an hour, my editor would scold me for tying up the editorial process and accuse me of slacking off.

Come on, just start typing.

Certainly, I could do that. After all, I had penned stories for the business journal for almost two years—and I had never missed a deadline. The adrenaline always kicked in when I had to produce copy.

I closed my eyes, searching for a Zen-like state that would allow sentences and paragraphs to flow effortlessly as they usually did. At one time, the newsroom had been my salvation, a place where I'd bonded with an all-male editorial staff while my marriage dissolved. But now, new owners were bombarding reporters with requirements for more stories. I couldn't hack it. I was a failure.

Hunkered down at my desk, I squelched my sobs so as not to be overheard whimpering like a trapped animal. Mark, behind the cubicle wall to my right, was conducting a phone interview. No sound came from Scott on the other side. He was probably out on assignment. I was safe. I could escape without anyone noticing. The article about Melissa Rosenberg's successful accounting firm would just have to wait.

The fresh air would clear my mind—and blanch my rose-colored cheeks and bloodshot eyes. Gingerly, I peered over my cubicle as I wiped tears from my eyes and stood.

"Where are you going?" Scott poked his head above the cubicle wall.

"On a walk." *What the hell! Why wasn't he out?* I lowered my head so he couldn't see my face.

"Is everything okay?" he said.

The usual "fine" that spilled from my lips regardless of my troubles at home refused to come. "Not really. I should go."

The ever-affable Scott approached me, a look of concern on his face. "Maybe you want to talk about it. I can join you on a walk."

"Don't you have a story to write?" I asked. I wasn't sure I should confide in him. For a long time—ever since my husband and I had separated—I'd taken care of problems on my own, not relying on others to ease the burden.

"That can wait. I've never seen you this upset."

"I need to get out of this place," I said, sniffling. "I can't go for long. John wants the story on Rosenberg."

Honestly, I no longer cared about Melissa Rosenberg growing her accounting firm into a multi-million dollar operation over four years. I was pissed at how I had called her three times before she'd released the company's revenues and profits—without those figures, John would not run the story. Didn't she understand we were a newspaper not a public relations firm? Scott grabbed his windbreaker from the coat rack; we descended the narrow staircase in the three-story, downtown building.

Outside, the warm, spring air refreshed me. I glanced at the cloudless blue sky. It wouldn't be long before we were blasted with heat and humidity, just around the time of my divorce in late June.

"At least, it's not raining," I said, in a feeble attempt to start a conversation.

"I can see why you're anxious with all the changes at the magazine," said Scott, a thirty-something want-to-be hipster. "I'm feeling it too."

Trust Scott to cut to the chase, though the break-up of my marriage also weighed on me. "It's insane what they want us to do now. I can't write three stories a week and two or three briefs every morning."

Scott nodded. "You can do it. Just interview fewer sources—and pick stories that are easy hits."

"I'm already doing that," I said. "And I'm completely stressed. I don't want to cover events superficially, but that's exactly what we're now doing."

"We had it good with George."

George, a former *Time* writer and founder of the business journal, had trusted his staff to cover industries in depth—and had given us time to craft insightful, analytical stories. The new owners believed readers wanted shorter stories—and more of them.

"Why couldn't George have waited another couple of years to sell the paper?" I lamented.

But, George's wife had complained about being the paper's office manager, and had convinced her husband that it was time to retire to their Block Island home. It had taken George two years to find a buyer who'd agree to his terms and conditions—except those maintaining a reasonable workload for reporters.

"The new owners don't seem that bad," said Scott, his curly blond hair glued to his head. "You'll get used to them. You're a hard worker."

"But, I can't work until 8 at night. I need to pick up my kids at 6."

"Could you come in early in the morning?"

"Not really. I get them off for school at 8:15."

"That's tough."

As we walked rapidly, I looked at the beautiful tree-lined street. The ash trees stretched upward, their branches strong and sturdy as if they could handle any disturbance.

"I just don't know if it's worth it," I said. "Maybe I should start looking for another job."

Scott sighed. "I'd hate to see you go. You're a good reporter. And you like journalism."

The snuffling resumed. "You're right about that."

Scott recommended that I not rush a decision. With time, he felt I could adjust to the workload, though initially I'd need to work longer days. Was there a babysitter who could help out for a month or two?

His suggestions made sense to me. But would I ever get used to cranking out three stories a week while raising three young children?

Scott gallantly opened the building door, gesturing me to enter. "If something's bothering you, I'm always up for another walk."

What a sweetie! I nodded, almost bursting in tears again. We climbed the staircase to the second floor. "Is my face red? It always gets red when I've been crying."

"A little. But it's fine." He patted me gently on the back before returning to his cubicle.

In the upstairs' bathroom, I splashed water on my face and caked powder on my checks to hide all signs of distress. Scott would keep quiet about my issues. No one else needed to know how I was drowning at my job.

Over the next few weeks, I churned out a slew of stories, viewing myself as a machine on an assembly line without any respite from production.

I no longer chatted with reporters, took hour-long lunches with colleagues at Attilios, or pondered over company reports. I interviewed sources in less than thirty minutes—on the phone, never in person. I allotted an hour to write a story—at most eighty minutes—as I raced to complete an article every day. Bathroom breaks were limited to five minutes, twice a day—and I never peered over my cubicle to gauge how others were coping. I evolved into an overworked and under maintained robot, my worth measured in terms of efficiency and productivity, not quality.

But I managed to leave the office at precisely 5:00 p.m. I couldn't keep my kids waiting at their after-school care program. The few times I'd been late, I'd gotten dirty looks, and a warning that if this continued I'd be charged extra. Besides, my children deserved a mom taking care of them for at least a few waking hours. Their father, too occupied by a business career, couldn't be counted on to pick them up by 6:00 p.m.

Back at home, I quickly prepared dinner: macaroni and cheese, ready-made ShopRite meatballs with pasta, and take-out pork fried rice. As the kids got ready for bed, I snapped at them for dawdling. Couldn't they hurry up so I'd have a few minutes to read some newspapers to get ideas for future business stories? I'd lose my patience when Patrick, 8, couldn't find his pajamas, or Emily, 10, refused to go to bed, or Nicholas, 9, teased his brother. Couldn't they just behave like little angels? I was too exhausted to handle even the slightest misbehavior.

Regularly, I fantasized about quitting my job. Why not move to my mother's mountain retreat in Lake Tahoe where the children and I could live rent-free? There, I'd write for the newspaper *The Bonanza* and only have a couple of stories to pen weekly. But my children's father wanted to see his kids regularly; he'd be devastated if we moved away, a lost Nordic soul with no joie de vivre. Besides, after the divorce, I couldn't legally relocate unless I got a job with a comparable salary that would allow a certain standard of living. A weekly newspaper wouldn't cut it—nor could I uproot my kids from all they'd known and loved.

So, I had two choices: adjust to the demands at *The Business Chronicle* or find another job. No matter what, I would bust my butt to hand in stories on time, and hope that the stress didn't lead to a nervous breakdown. Long term, I worried I would become a basket case. But I wasn't thinking that far into the future. Take it day-by-day. Keep in check my exhaustion by not over-scheduling myself on weekends. Most importantly, maintain a positive attitude that I could do it all.

At work one day, after a restless night of pondering my future, I approached Bill, a senior writer and editor. The door was open to his private office, meaning he'd welcome visitors.

"How can I help you?" asked Bill, a scholarly gentleman with a law degree, looking up from his computer. "Sit down. I hardly see you these days."

"There's too much work," I said, sitting in a chair next to his desk. "I barely have time to breath."

Bill leaned back in his chair, and chuckled. "It's the new regime. They're cracking down on us. You're keeping up with the work. John hasn't complained about you."

I breathed in deeply. "I don't know how much longer I can keep it up. I'm completely stressed out. I lash out at my kids. I'm always rushing. I don't have a second of down time."

Bill stared at me, his kind blue eyes sympathizing with my plight. "You're not thinking about quitting, are you?"

I sniffled. "No, I need a job. You remember that I'm getting a divorce next month."

"You could change your mind," he said, pushing back from his forehead his thinning blond hair.

"I'm not sure I will. We haven't lived together for years."

"You never know."

"I feel so drained. I used to have fun in this place. Now it's a grind. It's just story after story with no time for reflection."

"I agree. Our new leader doesn't want analysis. It's tough for me too. But I'm getting used to it. Just report less and write more. That's the winning formula."

I smiled—and I appreciated the simplicity of his solution. "It sounds like you're talking about winning a car race."

It was his time to laugh. "Jen, it's hard for you because you have to leave early to take care of your kids. You're under time constraints. I don't have that responsibility. This might not be the right job for you. Maybe you should consider teaching."

"Teaching?" I asked incredulously. *Didn't he know how I'd disliked teaching in Niger as a Peace Corps volunteer after college graduation? That had been twenty years ago—perhaps I'd never mentioned that to him.*

"Why? What's wrong with teaching? Remember how your predecessor Sarah left here to teach Spanish at a public school?"

I nodded. "She likes her new job?"

"From what I understand, she's very happy. She earns more money, works fewer hours, comes home when her kids do, and gets better retirement and health care benefits. I don't think she misses this place one bit."

"Her kids are young, right?"

"I think so. She was always pressed for time—just like you. Now, she's found a way to balance raising a family and earning a living."

I rubbed my forehead, thinking about the benefits of teaching, but my heart rejected such a move. "I like reporting and writing."

"For the past month, you haven't been happy. You don't smile anymore and I can't remember the last time I heard you laugh."

He was right about that. I wasn't enjoying life. I felt like a slave to the newspaper. It wasn't fair to my children to devote so much energy to my profession. These years would zap by, and I didn't want to regret being an absent mom. Did it really matter that my sense of identity came from being a journalist, and that I'd committed to the profession when I'd gotten a masters degree in journalism form Columbia? How many sacrifices was a job worth? Weren't my kids as important as my job?

"You know Bill, I used to wake up in the morning super excited to be going to work. I loved this place. I wanted to see you guys and go out and report on companies. It was the best."

Bill frowned. "It's changed—and I'm not sure it's for the better. It is what it is. I'll stay around for a while. But I'm also thinking about exploring other opportunities."

My eyes brightened—it wasn't just me who was considering a change. "Where would you go?"

"Perhaps Washington. I've been contacting government agencies. Maybe I could be a spokesperson or work in communications."

"That'd be quite a move."

"It's tough breaking into government work. But for you, teaching might not be that bad. You could teach English—and French. I seem to remember you speak French. There will be job openings this fall."

As Bill talked about the benefits of being an educator, I saw how it could work. I had a degree in English and I'd learned French as a child, though I hadn't used it in years.

"So, your French is little rusty," said Bill. "You'll remember it. You're going to know so much more than anyone in high school."

I glanced at my watch—ten minutes had vanished and what had I accomplished? No words had been written, no source interviewed, but Bill's insight had given me hope. Perhaps I should consider teaching. It would be a way to see my kids more often. Teaching couldn't be nearly as stressful as the newsroom. Was it so important to be passionate about a job once I had kids?

Nevertheless, I couldn't discount how my dad had encouraged me to find a profession I loved with interesting colleagues and tasks. After all, I'd be spending one-third of my waking hours there. I'd be miserable if I didn't like the work.

"Thanks Bill for your suggestions," I said, getting up from the chair. "I should get back to work."

"I'm glad you stopped by. By the way, I think you'd be a great teacher."

"Really? Why?"

"You're personable—and fun—when you're not stressed out," he said.

Did I detect a hint of flirtation in his voice? He was single. Once I got a divorce, would he make his moves on me? He was Catholic—they never messed around with married women—and he was old fashioned enough to never consider dating a divorcee. Besides, maybe he was a closeted gay—at least, that's what rumors had circulated around the office. No matter—he had proposed a solution to my professional dilemma, and for that I was grateful.

About the Author

Jennifer Nelson is an author and French teacher who holds an MFA in Creative Nonfiction from Vermont College of Fine Arts and an MA in Journalism from Columbia University. She's a features writer for The Woven Tale Press, and her work has also appeared in brevity.com and writingthrudivorce.com, as well as other publications.

I DO NOT RECALL THE NAME

by Sara Wetmore

Even after all these years, I think I hate him all the same. Perhaps more now that I have had the time and space to dwell, like a breath of air coursing over burning ember, catching light instead of extinguishing. Though I have come to understand him a bit better in these last few years as I've regained trust in myself, I find it hard to move beyond the bitter memories he has left behind. Yet, I tell myself again and again, he is not solely at fault. I should have known better, should have seen myself for who I really was and not for who he wanted me to be. So many young women that came before me have had their hearts broken and repaired themselves, living delicious, meaningful lives after the fall. I trust that one day, I will be able to do the same. But perhaps before that day comes, I'll need to learn how to forgive him for what he's done to me, or at the very least, forget.

It began with his form drawing nearer, slowly, like an ice cube melting, pooling into its own expanding winter pond. I arrived in class so very naive and young—eager to learn about literary criticism and theory, the first of many undergraduate stops on my quest to earn my doctorate in English Language and Literature. I was still optimistic then, and had great ambitions for who I would become when I finally completed my degree.

I was fiercely ambitious, believing the pinnacle of success was conquering the academic world, staying in school as long as possible to fill my head with books, history, and theory. I wanted to be the type of person who leads in their field, with an audience for my study and pupils to guide through their own educational journeys. What's more important is that I thought this victory was possible, and that in a matter of years I'd earn the title of "Doctor" and lead a life filled with intellectual intrigue.

The class was strenuous and commanded all of my attention. Yet, as the weeks flickered from one to the next, the professor trying his hardest to teach us about postmodern theory, I noticed this man slithering his way closer to me. His t-shirt stretched tightly across his muscled chest and tattooed arms. The corners of his thin mouth creased and the edges of his eyes pinched into the tiniest of wrinkles. Like an imposing glacier, cold and slippery, he was a man above all the other students, and he caught my eye just as I caught his. Eventually, he perched in the seat beside me, boasting of brighter days in the Air Force with tales of London fog and Cyprus beaches.

He told the class, "This reminds me of a time when I was in England and I was writing my own book..."

Immediately, he peaked my interest, though I could tell he was baiting for my attention. I wanted to see England someday and write my own book. Hungry for the adventurous life I'd not yet lived, I swam towards his lure.

I had never met anyone like him before. He was so well-traveled and accomplished, with his military experience and talk of self-published books. The worldliness and self-possession I saw in him was what I wish I had seen in myself, but he was ten years my senior, and there was so much life I had not yet lived.

Maybe if I knew then what I know now, I would have waited, wading in the dating pool of my own age group and never getting too serious. I would have focused on my studies and the arduous goal I had set for myself. I would have dabbled in art and writing more freely and taken more time to explore the world around me. I was so bored with life as it was, not yet embodying the picture of my future, that I forgot to live at all.

After class, he chased after me on campus, his footsteps falling with severity as they followed my own.

"That was a great class, wasn't it? Are you enjoying the book?" he said. "Yeah, it's really good so far." I said.

"Do you ever want to read it, like, together sometime?"

Little did he know that reading was on my list of dream dates. I had to say yes. "Sure!" I said, trying to reel in my enthusiasm.

He pulled out his cell phone and looked at me expectantly, his tea-colored eyes glittering in the sunlight. I told him my number and he told me his, and thus began our tumultuous affair.

On our date, I was fascinated by his blind charisma. I would fall down and worship his every word. I wanted his approval so badly that I would tout my own little accomplishments—as many as one could have at the tender age of nineteen—but my moment in his glory would extinguish quickly, followed only by a grander example of his excellence. This would be the first of many times he would scatter the ashes of my self-confidence beneath his hallowed feet. For months, each thing I did was eclipsed by his ego, and sadly it is only now I realize there was so much for which I deserved recognition.

Over the course of a year, the abuse became more than simply ignoring or belittling my accomplishments. When his tales grew stale, I grew less concerned with what he had done in a past life and more concerned with my future.

"What do you think of Princeton University for graduate school? I believe F. Scott Fitzgerald went there. Wouldn't that be cool?" I said.

"Not this again. If you're thinking of applying to a school, you should at least run it by me first. What if I don't want to move there?"

I remember thinking it was bold of him to assume he was going to join me on my journey. He hated that I ceased lauding him to focus inward and ultimately outgrow him. In fact, the more I lived in the present, the more irked he would become. He grew jealous and insecure and needed my blessing even more than I needed his.

Things I liked that did not conform to the person he had molded me to be were abhorred, and I would immediately fall victim to his bitter tongue, plagued by the most censorious taste.

Piece by piece, he became more human to me, and I began to see him for who he really was: an insecure boy stuck in the past, unable to move toward the future because he was so petrified that things might never get better, that his best life had already been lived and saw no need for self-improvement. He tore down others to maintain his superiority. Things must have been great for him once, and I feel sorry that the world moved on without him.

But I was much the opposite. The past was forgettable, and the future beckoned me with its limitless possibilities. I didn't have to be who I once was, or who I was then. I could be anything, do anything, go anywhere—it was all terribly exciting, and I was anxious to fast forward to a time when I was less pathetically *me*.

He must have begun to suspect we were pulling in opposite directions, because one night I quit my job and went out to celebrate without him. He knew it was over before I did. As I was sitting on the barstool, my phone kept vibrating, pulling me out of the conversation with my colleagues. I looked at my screen and saw his name flashing over and over again. Then my phone would vibrate again. This time, a voicemail. I excused myself from the table and stepped aside to listen to it.

"Where the fuck are you? I want to know who is there; I deserve to know who you are cheating on me with. If you don't call me back right now, it's over."

What's funny is I would have stayed with him, maybe forever, if he hadn't accused me of cheating on him that night. I hadn't, as I was only out with work friends for no more than an hour or two, but he insisted I was lying and, unable to be convinced otherwise, demanded an apology from me for days. He waited and waited, but I never apologized. I wanted nothing more to do with him, and it took one night of furious phone calls, sharp-tongued voicemails, and a storm of defamatory texts for me to notice that I had been abused all along.

I wish we could have left things at that, but he persisted in trying to get me to confess.

And once he realized my fidelity was never in question, he tried even harder to lure me back. He would contact my family and leave flowers on my car. He would call me crying and apologizing, and then call me angry for not surrendering to his pale performance. He was such a nice guy, he would say (as most abusive partners do), and he loved me fiercely—too fierce to let me go. But I was free.

In that first week, I put on my favorite orange mandala dress and danced alone in my kitchen listening to "Jesse's Girl" on repeat and crooned to Lana Del Rey, an act of defiance. He had once criticized me for liking one of her songs. For the first time in nearly two years, I felt happy. Happiness, though, cannot be sustained forever, and so naturally I stabilized into the ebb and flow of highs and lows that accompanies daily life. It took a moment to realize that though I was glad to be free of him, I was immeasurably damaged.

For years after we broke up, I tried to date again, but I was afraid of intimacy and attachment. I had given my love to him so freely, splaying open my chest and giving him my dancing heart without ever asking why. He had not earned it, but I gave it all the same. I was not in love with him, but rather the world he represented. He accepted this gift and bit into it like a ripe apple, devouring its fibers and juices until his teeth cut into its defenseless core, leaving nothing to plant and start anew.

I could not rid myself of the thought that each partner, male or female, was sworn to govern me. All of the red flags I missed before suddenly materialized in every new relationship I tried to forge, and I'd find myself thrust backward in time to the nightmare he once had wrought. The sound of my phone ringing induced a panic, so when someone showed interest in me, I drew tightly inward and became unreachable. Sometimes I would disappear entirely.

When I sat down to try to write again, I could feel myself sweating with his voice scratching the back of my mind, trying to break his way in, past locked doors and drawn blinds. My own self-loathing had morphed into him and his voice: deep, thunderous, and wicked. My mind would go blank, frozen by the fear he instilled. Although he was gone, I was still treading water, never to become anything more. With no way forward, neither writing nor reading could save me, though they had once been an integral part of me before I was broken.

I gave up on trying to apply to graduate school entirely. I remember he had told me not to get my hopes up. I ignored him at the time, angered by his doubt in me, but eventually he got through. So, I listened. *Not cut out for graduate school. Lower your standards.* The voice crept into all the corners of my body, tying itself to the synapses of my brain and rewiring me for failure. I gave up on everything.

When I graduated, I was without direction. In my hand, I held a useless humanities degree and had no prospects for a job or future. I had floundered through my last year in college, being much more preoccupied with cancelling plans than making them. I abandoned my ambitions. Instead, I cast myself into the depths of a wild and unfathomable depression; one out of which I am still clawing to escape.

I think by now I've realized that win or fail, I could never appease him. Nor should I continue to try after being separated all these years. He is simply a shadow of my past, and I was wrong to award him so much presence in my soul. He is just a man, and I am so much stronger than his abuse. This, I should clarify, does not absolve him of his sins, nor will my loathing ever desist. He will still haunt me in the future—and I fear I will listen instead of believing in myself. But to be hurt is not to be defeated. It inspires me to become more. And one day, I hope, I will rise above him entirely, begging question when they mention his name, "Who?"

About the Author

Sara Wetmore is a creative nonfiction author and Lindenwood University MFA student based in Salt Lake City, Utah. Her work has appeared in The Write Launch, At First Glance: An Anthology of Poetry and Prose, and Etched magazine. She enjoys experimenting with themes and form, finding deeper significance in the common and mundane.

POETRY

APOLLINAIRE
by Timothy Robbins

Apollinaire

This morning I read Apollinaire's "Zone"
and thought him silly. Meaning
being a vagabond, *his* being a vagabond,
it's no surprise he wandered
along silly's crooked paths starting with
a Proto-Indo-European root for
'happy,' which he certainly was
in Stavelot, dancing with Wallonian girls,
skipping out on his hotel bill or
springing from the Art Nouveau
Underworld of the Metro, his imagination
as fertile as Persephone.
He was 'blessed,' he was 'pious' as he
tells us himself when he and his boyhood
friend René crept from the dormitory to
pray all night in the college chapel.
He was 'harmless,' he was
'pitiable' trailing after an English
governess. Look at this photo
from 1916, a bandage round his
shrapnel-torn temple, the wild look in his
eyes and snarling shape of his mouth,
and tell me he wasn't 'stunned
by a blow.' Read the description in
"Zone" of sparrows, ravens, falcons, owls
and hummingbirds cavorting
with airplanes, swarming from the ends
of the earth to celebrate their
new brother. Think what he didn't
foresee: birds by the thousands shredded
each year — and only a few
that, kamikaze-like, manage
to smite their foe. Think of
power lines, towers and turbines —
all creations of his beloved
modernity — all killers of birds.
Think of this and ask yourself, was he
'foolish' or was he 'innocent?'
I think of the Roc and the Phoenix
(And why not? Icarus too was just a myth
when he was born) and I'm
inclined to declare him innocent. Then I
think of that photo again —
his wound from man's first flying war.
I think how he died weakened
(another meaning of silly) from his part in
that war, and it's clear:
Clinging to one's innocence is foolish.

At The Track

They run again more fiercely than before.
Rick wants to hurt people. His dad wants to
hurt people. Both assume everyone wants
to hurt someone. Jones avoids hurting
teammates no matter the cost. Winston
feels that running on a prescribed
path with all his impetus and skill is the
perfect incarnation of Will. Ernesto runs
for Christina, which might prove chivalry
flowers from a seed that stirs in certain youths
in all times and all places. Rounding
the curves they make a pounding in my
ears so loud it can't be wholly real. Each
stride makes them younger. Sweat absolves,
sweetens and renders them enviable in the
sight of the gods of pleasure and health.
At times they seem to run in place.
For one or two this will come to be the
way they think about young spring. They run
blindly at me, all bunched together as
though it were a tide that pulled, not their
toes that pushed, waves of glistening
torso and legs, arcs bisected by running shorts.
They rush at me, panting and pounding.
I see myself in the middle of the track
cross-legged and still, exploring my page.
They part and flow around me. They
could be running water, could be equipped
with built-in radar. Running so close,
they stir air that reminds my face of the shore.
I could break them into metaphors. I could
touch their calves and caress their sores.
On they go, their feet scarring the track.
One, with the determined look of a swollen
cherry, eyes the girls on the grass. One
runs an utterly different course. His white
shorts tighten, afraid to pass.

Aviary

Last time I consulted my geese by the river
on their guano spotted lawn, immunity's
walls rose tall and fast around me. I may
have just misled you. You're probably
picturing some Big Muddy or another stream
grand enough to float a rootless casino.
The Colorado may be waltzing through a
chasm in your mind to the legato and pizzicato
of *An der schönen blauen Donau* or the
Grand Canyon Suite if your knowledge of
classical music is more than passing.
Our elbow of the Huron is no grander than a
creek. Wading it without wetting your thighs,
you might think, "This was made by a leak."

We like to think its birds are people-watchers
admiring our brisk nervous movements.
See the big one go out and come back with
fodder. The small one cooks it up and both
mouths water. The small one waits at the
backdoor for the airport shuttle. The big one
watches the front lest the driver not bother
to honk or phone. When the small one flies
away, the big one sings sad songs. When the
big one goes, the little one sinks into glum
repose. We like to think they glance at us
and swap knowing looks just before they
step off our balcony, telegraphing: *Someday*
we'll teach you to scorn gravity. I have just
misled myself. We will not learn such scorn.
As for immunity, there never was a wall.
There was, and is, you — a deterrent, but
far from insurmountable.

Beast Master

Saturday morning I cast Pedro Zamora as Tao.
I have the whole weekend to
make arrangements.
Nothing could be simpler. I'm tired of —
No, I'm angry at — your telling me my mate
doesn't deserve mating. Angry that you say it
to my masks as well as to my
faces, my recursive
thoughts turned inside-out.
Angry that you cloak it
in advice. "You must think of your own needs
once, twice, thrice, ad nauseam" as though
mercy were a bribe. The
craggy walls of Fantasy
Land did not think of themselves,
not even when
the Beast Master scaled them like a mountain
goat, when a sun more primitive than time
heated them down to their
common core, when
Christ invited them to sing, to roar whatever
complaints they felt, for he would hear and
understand. Along 35th Street,
black lines straight
enough to be called straight remind me of men
who insist they are straight though they've
mutually undressed down to the nerve
with enough men to deserve the name *crooked*.
No flesh and no desire could be simpler.
They who are wrong have blood on their hands.
They who are right have blood on their hands.
They who turn the right cheek to avoid getting
blood on it, have blood on their left cheek.
Blood has blood on its hands. The president
who goes to war and the
president who signs the
treaty. The poet who publishes
and the poet who
keeps his poems like sex slaves in a drawer.
Jesus has one deadly drop. Babies have their
mother's. Nothing could be simpler than the
Beast Master's foothold. This is not what I
wanted to say. Lately I long
for naked description.
Long thin mounds of blacktop divide the street
into three sections equal enough to be called
thirds. They are nothing more than the scat
of the machines that shat them. I can't help
preferring the intersecting blacktop, lines of
the same width that wander a little, making
contour lines of male nudes broken up and
strewn, waiting for a private strayed from his
platoon to gather them in his
arms like a camper
collecting wood he will goad
to warmth, light and
eye-hating smoke. If you can imagine delight at
being called to unroll an — arm-
length? two-arms
length? more? — scroll on the adventures and
meanings of the Beast Master,
you and I will dance.
Oh the hours too serene to
name themselves we
squinted at the Beast Master
on a tiny TV with an
antenna that never relaxed, stiff as a catatonic
lover — an ancient magic of our days. How
desperately we relaxed from
our mental labors —
you from the Ramanujan Conjecture (why
not say curse?). Me from the
transmutation of our
lives into verse that hinted at
our essence without
betraying our location. Herculean

tasks. Though
our brains came humanly close to Hercules,
they were not half, but .01 percent divine. Like
the one who longed to be
arrayed like the Beast
Master even if it meant climbing
the simplest tree.
For us, nothing could be simpler.

About the Author

Timothy Robbins teaches English as a second language. He has published three volumes of poetry: Three New Poets (Hanging Loose Press), Denny's Arbor Vitae (Adelaide Books) and Carrying Bodies (Main Street Rag Press). He lives in Wisconsin with his husband of 21 years.

TEARS OF SPADES IN AMERICAN BLUES

by Mettamodernist

Julia Dream,
Dream of a key,
A key to unlock all your doors

I am your abyss, your good
fix, your sanity, your hell.
Who can thrive when no love abides,
Who can thrive when no love abides,
Julia Dream, Dream of me,
We are as false as any notion could be.
Wide awake while fast asleep,
Wide awake while fast asleep.

Julia Dream,
Dream of me,
I'm letting you know, that I never
plan on letting you go,
Dream until you have found us.
Dream until you have found us.

Let's go beyond ourselves. Let's
say no to discipline.
Let's afford acts of self-denial. Let's
count centuries like teeth.
Let imagination punish us so that the
longing reconciles with itself,
So our myth stays fresh, and
trauma forgives tradition.
Who can thrive when no love abides,
Who can thrive when no love abides,

Julia dream,
Dream of key,
I'm letting you know, that I never
plan on letting you go,
Julia dream, dream of a key, a key
to unlock all your doors.

Let's meet our pasts, I have
moved away from myself,
And I hardly recognize that nigga anymore.
I am your abyss, your good
fix, your sanity, your hell.
Who can thrive when no love abides,
Who can thrive when no love abides,

Julia dream,
Dream of me,
We are as false as any notion could be.
Wide awake while fast asleep,
Wide awake while fast asleep.
Be the one I want to be. You're

the one I need to see.

I heard God praying to us. It was
childlike caterwauling.
Every word weak-kneed and feral,
in sweet yellow dissipation and malaise,
The way man calls out when close to death.
She begged us for vulnerability,
something short of empathy.

Julia dream,
dream, please don't sleep,
Dream awake before day-break,
I am your abyss, your good
fix, your sanity, your hell.

She said, "Why have you forsaken
me? Either come like silence as
an empty church, or be my 3am booty call -
Otherwise, my sex is inconsolable and orphan."
Later that night, there was a whole
world hanging from our lips.

Julia dream,
Dream don't fear,
I'm letting you know, that I'll always be here,
Who can thrive when no love abides,
Who can thrive when no love abides.

"HANGOVERS IN YOUR MID-TWENTIES."
(Pink Floyd "Julia's Dream")

O Gott, O Sophocles! *O,* Homer!
Oedipus this and Oedipus that!
The time for art is over, it is the
blackmail of survival.
The time is running out, going
out, counting down,
fast and fast, fast fast and faster and faster.
the clock is running, the clock is burning.
Due to the unknowable and the unknown.
the clock is advancing, the hands are moving,
rotating, counting, counting, counting down.
act fast, act fast, time is running out.
We evade the panopticon
plantation by not existing,
or existing enough to incubate
a future so far-fetched.
How is a pioneering genius
supposed to make a living?
I'm hungry, and I can't eat, I
conclude less and less of me
Today it might be, *I was bored, a*
fragile flight of fancy.
Tomorrow it will be, *I ruined my life for art.*
Yesterday my *Oedipal Complex* was all the rage.
I've sinned, I've fallen, I've tumbled,
but never told anyone.
Now God waits for me, daring
me to beg forgiveness,
But, I don't need absolution, I don't
need grace, I deserve a better savior.
Beneath the iris hidden in
caruncles of madness,
I find a portrait of Dorian
Gray, barely breathing.
I don't need absolution, I don't need
grace, I deserve a better savior.
I see your weeping mother praying for her child,
And I raise you one God who
hears every scream,
Every cry, every plea for peace,
every call for death,
And doesn't give a fuck. Burn the flag,
burn the Koran, burn the Bible.
Life over time = (U) unrecognizable.

"KILL YOUR IDOLS."

TEARS OF SPADES IN AMERICAN BLUES

"If you want a nigger for a
neighbor, vote Labour."
This was the 1964 slogan of Tory
candidate Peter Griffiths.
Griffiths won his election by a 7.2% margin.
The British National Party later
used it themselves.
America doesn't know what the negro wants
You can have their women, but not the ego
Maybe tomorrow, but that's academic
Our perpetual Orwellian plight has been
white-washed by the Bible and the gun
by border control and tiki torches
The auction block, the middle road,
the whip, the knife, cotton as
king, Americas first algorithm
the fable of the extermination
of the straight white male
America invented the nigger but can't kill him
Therefore the negro Faulkner wrote
about did not exist for him
because a black whose brain ... is
used to ... " ELEVATE "
is one who will be ... " Labelled " ...
as........ " Unstable " ....
But I'm so America, I'm so
America, 3D printed guns;
prescription pills n weed pissed with pesticides
corporate porn, Instapoet
selfies; Neo-Nazis & Putin
Playboy, the Beats, Strip
clubs, Transcendentalism,
pulp fiction, Hollywood, all rolled up in a blunt
message of perverts & pedophiles
posing as pious people
In their best tactical negro
impersonations & naked women;
lots & lots of naked women
America is a persistent optical
illusion, retinal persistence
persistence of impressions,
occurring when visual
perception of an object (us)
does not cease after
the light rays proceeding from it have
ceased to enter the physical eye
Gold and ambrosia spill out of
my grandmother's mouth
If she strains her wheat-dry hands long
enough, you can hear her speak
"America is an antifascist inside a fascist
state. A dys·to·pi·an paradise."

Mama raised me a vagabond. My only home
was *Purple Rain*
on repeat as we cleaned our four quarters
of Brooklyn every Saturday morning.
Within me, condensed in bone,
diaphragm-deep, buried within the
unfinished business of my childhood,
inside the intention to be a voice,
are the inimitable ruins of heritage. It always
feels like I'm collecting pieces of you,
as a child I've watched you eat your tears,
sympathy. empathy. codependency.
I've heard the puddles in your
throat demand to be rivers.
I've seen you perform alchemy with wood,
blood, and melancholy to make a home.
Not a house, we never had a house, we
had a hollow muscular organ pumping
blood through four sons by rhythmic
contraction and dilation.
My mother worries for her children daily,
calls with frogs in her throat, each
representing a different phobia.
Her biggest fear are coffins too
early, or too small, or too big.

My mother carved us out from the
slender, canal of her throat,
and spoke life, and life abundantly,
signing the names of her sons
in the blood of our enemies. My
mother is a warrior of one for many,
sometimes that meant she carried
the world on her back,
too heavy to latch on the sorrows of her sons.
On some summer nights we can hear
her crying loudly into her pillow,
biting on her tongue, and offering communion
for her sons ahead of the sabbath.
I could never accurately string words
together about my mom,
even on a purely linguistic level. Once,
there was nothing I wouldn't say to you.
Now, I lean away from words, the only things I
have to let fly.
I am careful. The space between us has
always varied in size and volume,
ever-changing, bending and
expanding. She never had much use
for bullshitting or pussyfooting,
maybe that's what makes this so hard,
it's as simple as saying, I love you,
but I struggle to find her Horatian
ode in any of these naked muses.
Mama raised me a vagabond.

"I DON'T BELIEVE IN GOD, BUT I
BELIEVE IN MOMMY."

my prolonged silence is not an
unwillingness to answer,
but a refusal to war while wandering
as a patchwork of bruised knees.
It isn't consonance or assonance, but a
refusal to let desire become theory.
I am burning in this life, bursting from
between the cog and clockwork,
from things known yet unnamed.
it is important to detach and not
alienate, alienation is not detachment,
silent and still one begins to notice,
silent and still one begins to notice.
Silent and still one begins to notice how much
of what I once thought was apropos of nothing.
Silent and still one begins to notice the
interstices and subtleties of being,
observe what doesn't move in you.
Silent and still one begins to
regard what settle's within,
discovering new surfaces on
skin without subterfuge.
I desire secret indentations imprinting
on skin, sinking inward.
I desire to exist when not required,
like the words of this poem,
I want the truth, naked, uncoping,
devastatingly unlovely, self-perjuring.
I want to be an echo touching every
neglected corner of your borrowed body.
I want to show you in spite of ourselves,
we become things we never expected.
Where are all our heroes? What delicacy
of jingoism has white Jesus left us?
How dishonest love has become? We are
trying in a world that is full of trying.
My mother taught me early from an early age,
that it was up to me to make myself a worthy
member of society,
either as roach spray or air
conditioning, I chose the former.

We are not what we thought we
would be, but we are trying.
We are not what we thought we
would be, but we are trying.
We are not what we thought we
would be, but we are trying.

"THE BLANK STRAIN OF MANIA."

About the Author

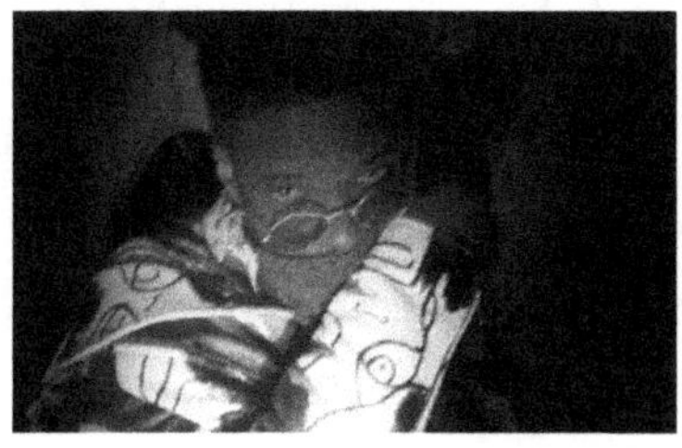

Mettamodernist is a Canadian artist, designer, and writer. His artwork, published through the art collective, The Creatrix Haus & co., has exhibited and been published internationally. He is the author of the poetry collection I'M A THUG, BUT I SWEAR FOR THREE DAYS I CRIED and the novel THNKGODFRDRGS RMX. His project, YOUTH KILLS TIME, releases June2020.

THE CLASSICAL DEBT

by Susan Ayres

we will never repay the debt we owe Greece.
—Stephen Fry, Elgin Marbles Debate

1.

Greek waiters talk not
to me, but my son. Hotel
staff tells me it's unseemly
for women to travel
alone. Mornings, I take
my coffee to Athens' National
Park, where a monkey
bit King Alexander
and he died. I do not feel
safe here, do not walk
alone at night, not even
in the touristy Plaka
past sleeping men under
eaves of shops that once
sold olive oil, leather sandals,
Byzantine icons, replica gods.
She's gone too—Athena, fierce
warrior with her fierce gray stare.

2.

When I was a girl in El Paso,
our Greek friend refused
to give away
his daughter in marriage.
She had dishonored him—
Catholic girls got pregnant
since birth control was
a sin. Apparently
forgivable, since Father Finnegan
let one girl play
"Having My Baby" during
her wedding mass. Visiting
Greece is a throwback
to my girlhood of mighty
Church, mighty Father, Aegean
blue like the Virgin's
robes, where my son refuses
to swim.

3.

The bread is delivered
without your asking. The best
comes with olives, hummus,
beet dip. The appetizer
not ordered is included
in the bill, as if the debt
we owe Greece will be paid
bite-by-bite. We are responsible
for the country's bankruptcy, for
its small pipes we clog
with toilet paper, for its graffiti,
its unemployed. We pay for bottled
water when the server claims
there is no tap water.
This country feels more oriental
than occidental, my son
comments. And I see
what he means. It's
as if we descended directly
from Lord Elgin or stole
the marbles ourselves. It's
as if bread, water, toilets will
be bartered in this cradle
of civilization
where we owe, owe, owe.

About the Author

Susan Ayres is a poet, lawyer, and translator. She holds an MFA in Creative Writing with a Concentration in Translation from Vermont College of Fine Arts. She also holds a PhD in Literature from Texas Christian University. Her work has appeared in Sycamore Review, Cimarron Review, and elsewhere. She lives in Fort Worth and teaches at Texas A&M University School of Law.

PERHAPS YOU UNDERSTAND

by George Eklund

PERHAPS YOU UNDERSTAND

I've done what I could do.
If you want to mutilate me, then you will.
I cannot row very far or fast
In my boat of green light.
But I am beginning to know the wind
And what we cannot hear.

A baby creature cried in the woods,
I had to keep my pencil moving,
Perhaps you understand.

The wind cannot leave itself alone.
Our hope, as always, is to have some dinner
And live gently through another night,
To leave some language in the atoms
Of a disappearing world.

Perhaps you understand what came into us.
It was a whisper from the mind to the mind
As some creature howled in the woods.
I had to keep my pencil moving
In and out of the wind between us.

I may have been listening to myself all along,
Filtered through the harps of the trees.
Perhaps you understand how
the bones of my hands
Darken in sleep,
How I move toward myself in the cosmic hour

And wash myself in the shadow
Of a tree my father planted.
The mind cannot shape the snow
But forms the hope
For its own cries to stop
Before others might listen and know...

Perhaps you understand prayers that come
Through us in a low humming,
The sound of a small plane far away,
A child shoring across a dark room.

How the mind erases and restores knowledge
In the heaven of itself, the green rowing
Through the mutilated interiors.
George Eklund 1.

Perhaps you will forgive the mind
That fears the body of itself.
Perhaps you understand I must move my pencil
And go now.

Indigo Flame

Many children have lifted me
Into the gray bare woods
Cleared of derangements, manifestos.

They have carried me over the clumps of snow
And the mud that cannot thaw.

Something has already happened,
Something I have not seen or imagined.

Perhaps someone imaginary has disappeared
Or has brought me beautiful words or music...

A hammering may commence at any time,
The world remaking itself without me.

I have awakened with an indigo flame
Dancing from my hand to my eyes.

Essay on a High D Sharp

We tithe in blood and nausea.
Finally we are creatures again,
Touched and made mad
Touched and made of memory we cannot hold
And made of winter sun through trees
Touched and materialized
On the outskirts of the vacuumed museum.
Dressed in baptismal white,
In the pain of the first gasp
Every mind made beautiful and incomplete
Every sun burning and waiting.
The mind scatters itself,
Splitting itself into a thousand places.
There is no announcement, only sound,
A high D sharp
Ending history for a moment
Bringing history back into its eggs,
A holy land beyond the mind,
A muse outside of the cold
Every sun burning for its orbiting worlds
And their lovely moons.

Sky Fever

Say ever
Say fever
Say sky fever
Ever sky fever made
Of noise from town and dark
Feathers spread on the walk.

The ensemble dressed in black
And made the sound of God's voice.

The saint appeared with a garden hose
And a ripsaw in its hands.
This is how they made an angel look,
This says something about a people;

It has to do with the rigid or supple
Quality of their minds.
It has to do with how they comb their hair,
How they dress
And how they treat their children.

The ensemble dressed in a new color each day.
They all liked to look at art,
Especially breasts,
But were neglectful of their mothers.

This says something about
the shape of the God
They perceived within,
How it came and went.

Essay in a New Century

Forgive me I wanted to hear something rare.
I wanted to be something rare
In that season when I would seize
And lower myself into a tub
To feel myself break open...
Early in the new century
There is a man-horror that follows us.
It is something we make
Something made upon us
Something made out of us
Something mad upon us
A making upon us.

Xxx

We have cancelled our plans for Paris
Cancelled our plans for Central America.
Where ever you go
Castles are overgrown by trees and vines.
You would be lucky
To be named for a field
That never held a town or road.

Xxx

Sooner or later in some dark corner
Everyone says Tra-la.
The struggles are forever imprinted
From the wrist to the ankle,
A neurosis or an ecstasy.

Xxx

They push their carts toward the products.
They push dutifully and dream-like
In hunger and atonement and hope.
They bring the children, bring the old ones,
The afflicted in their apparatuses
The giddy and the dead ones aisle by aisle
In the bright fluorescence.
All of them thinking about
what did not yet exist.

Essay in a New Century, continued

The house fills with distant seasons.
I have passed through so many buildings
And rooms within buildings.
I have held so many hands
Never to know anything.
Because we remember
Because we cannot remember
The brain has a deep fold,
For some a quiet shrine
Or a holiday train station.

My body is putting itself to sleep.
I must go alone to the waiting rooms,
Dark and empty
With stained ceilings
Where one's name is never called.

About the Author

George Eklund has published widely in north American journals, including The American Poetry Review, Beloit Poetry Journal, Crazyhorse, Cimarron Review, Epoch, The Iowa Review, The Massachusetts Review, The New Ohio Review, The North American Review, Poet Lore, Quarterly West, Sycamore Review, and Willow Springs, among others. Most recently his poems have appeared in The Lindenwood Review, Poetry Fix, Red Booth Review, and Rio Grande Review, as well as Tinge, Toad, 6x6, and Conduit. Eklund's full length volumes include The Island Blade (ABZ Press 2011) and Each Breath I Cannot Hold (Wind Publications 2011). Finishing Line Press published his chapbook, Wanting To Be an Element, in 2012. Finishing Line Press published his recent collection, Altar, in September 2019. His translations from the Spanish have appeared in The Rio Grande Review and In Translation/Third Rail. George Eklund is Emeritus Professor at Morehead State University. He shares studio space with the painter and poet, Laura Eklund, on thirty acres of wooded hills in eastern Kentucky.

SIDEKICK

by Rikki Santer

Sidekick

you are monocle
you are lap dancer
you are cheeky sailor boy
you are lamb chopped sock
        chocolate spell
        sideways glance from hell
you are ghost terrorist
        shy ingenue
        personality in 60 seconds
you are knuckle headed
        sitcom irony
        wicked ears
                like hovercrafts
you are winker/blinker
        swiveled noggin
        snarky set-up nodder
you are rod-armed
        foam-formed
        renegade raised eyebrows
you are punchlines hiccupped
        baby cries
        twisted talk
                in twisted mouth
you are pick up, put down,
        bend, slump, shake
        or shoe-shined ballast
you are illusion
        delusion
        off-handed protrusion
you are anything that can talk
& you've got your eye on me

Dummies from Cinema Hell

Thorns nestle into furry eyebrows. Utterances
        muddy & frothy. These malcontent

chupacabras lie in wait, the
vent-doll's recurring
        argument—who needs who?

Begin in silence. Professor Echo's Nemo in
        velvet-mouthed intertitles,
        thrown voices

beget criminal acts. With caviar and lobster,
        The Great Gabbo stuffs
        his German mouth,

while Otto hurls one-sided
banter, his smashed face
        the end of ruse. Tables turn
        for The Great Vorelli,

strident & demonic, he doesn't
know how to be nice
        to his toys, so irony stirs
        the old switcheroo—

boss into blockhead. Mr. Scarface
yearns to be master
        of Gotham & gangster
        bullets, his poplar hands

quiver to get the gold. Mr. Fats of
sour harmonica, matching
    sweaters, fresh slaughter, &
    he wants you to have

his wooden heart. Behold these
vigilante antagonists,
    dead hummingbirds lodged
    into their jaws—

when they escape foreign hands
forced up their asses, their
    bloody jungles glisten with
    triumphant trajectories of id.

Junior Open Mic

at the International Vent Haven
Ventriloquist Convention

Limbs lie limp in nervous laps
waiting to defy gravity. Throats

tremble to animate bodies into birdsongs
of delight & Delphic vapors. Mouths pop

like zippers, launch trajectories
from dummy thrones, this parliament

of apprentices not yet ruptured or repaired.
Timid punchlines ripple like flags creeping

up their poles—operatic duets, twirling
guffaws. Goateed rocker enters stage right

in his mini motorcycle, cotton candy princess
shuns her master—*You're just jealous of my*

swag. We wish them legacy of spotlight,
green light in critique. The stage is kind tonight.

IT'S NO PICNIC WHEN THE WORDS ONE SPEAKS ARE IMPELLED

by Susan Sonde

by a hail of white fury

and to know that the psychic bruise, the terrible corsage of pain another wears is of your making. It's nightmare-tune echoes in the quiet of your roped red offering long after.

You sing to her of your mind's weather, its inevitable upending: the crack of collision. Atomic. Elemental. Invoke the weight of your vacillations, the ether of particles swelling hot desire's flash, then hammer the arc of flight and bring her swan-blur down. What she wants are your belongings

gone and the stars

to inveigh against the damage, nights to cleave the moon leaving her both halves; the hours to pre-date pain, eat the evaporate from the sea of her weeping. You're the immanent impending, she says: the impenetrable heaviness that tendrils her hair, aspirate that capsizes

her tiny island.

So often you said your sorries, ignored the fiction she called her life and hoped you could talk her back to life, dripping seaweed and plankton. Your sorries were a lie, your heartbreak-grin wide as your gait. Gate affixed to no shelter. Your shelter an abyss. Is it your fault, you deadpan when all you've known is the fiery recesses of the tongue?

Your father was a comet, mother implosive, your birthright the stars; and like Pandora you
were curious. Your curiosity released the solar winds and burned them both alive. Now
their comas

are forever

chasing the sun, and in memoriam you live as the world's suffering: its curbside crucifix laced with
waves of wonder, target of cigarette butts and jokes that fall flat. You consider your options: lie
abed all day bandaging your yesterdays or grab the manila rope attached to the stump of bruised
neckerchief by which you might hang yourself. All's scraps of desert, and the lies you told

intended as feel-goods, still shine

yellow through your teeth. It's a cipher why you stayed the nights, listened to
her shun the world, sneak away from it before the sun hit seeking amplification.
The better to light the ego's way back to you, whose sympathies she tore
off, fistful after fistful like bloodied sheets. Didn't she deserve a little bit

to be used?

Didn't she

before shooing you off with a wave of her bitch-hand, extort love
and false sentiment, her fingers grasping and greedy?

Shouldn't you

when you go to yourself from the roll and stretch of a morning-mare, cupping your shadow pay
for making her want, listen to how her prayers try to fill the void with the weight of want?

Time feeds on a woman's face fist-first: eyes and mouth etched into the once-
glowing surface as if she were meant to live by the treacly, salutary glow of a candle,
curled in the lopsided lagoon of her body only later to claim it all a joke.

An orchestra plays the music of a dirge with fingers chewed to the
bone. Sheet music blooming fragrant and the notes dispersed

by the wind of a door closing.

MANY THINGS ARE VANISHING

yet at the bottom of every cup you drain's a human face asking you to
love. You've walked your love off on this terrace lamp lit nights

by the sun, smoked your last cigarette ad infinitum, are hollow as whatever bird bone. You
live by lamplight detected by no one. The portals through which you stare nights aren't
windows, but paintings of the stars: a billion billion rosaries strung with cat gut.

Wind cycles through the palms, draws a sassy bow across the
ribbed leaves of Sassafras and Hickory. You avoid

the clink and glitter of the recycling truck hauling the body's momentary measure
away: blood baked underwear an ailing body shucked. The notes you sing

could blade the air; your features fuel the moon's sodium vapor glare. Yet, your
voice bleeds in the manner of every shadow's speak, your tone deaf idleness,
biblical. Sanguine's what you thought you were, but your sweetness errs

on the side of militancy. All tears tear you away, in the way light darkens a
thousand thousand days. Your broken down weeping wild to burn.

WHAT HAPPENS PRE-BIRTH'S NOT THE COW'S ROUGH TONGUE

the scratching beyond the window not a sow's breath or tree blinking. What pre-dates
the laying down of the brain's circuitry so it can feed our last breath it's darkest fable got
its start millennia ago. Father, you're dead and far away, but tonight your apparition's in
ascension: your parental ghost clear as a super moon in a wash of headlights. It wakes
me from prolific night to apologize to my brain box and anthropomorphize my now

dried tears.

Its coordinates are lacking, reach an overreach and its exudations dampen
my senses. What's wrong with it leaks into me. I'm its secret

envelope

of dirt. Tonnage in pockets and purse. In the name of intimacy, you stole from
me my body's barrier against darkness. I knew the shattered vessel that leaked
your lipless brimful. You insisted on owning the heat my body un-lipped, the
faintest ripple that tickled razors and targeted the hum in the living breast.

I discovered the history of our pre-birth while examining the stars and their emoluments
and by accident, events too, which pre-dated Moses' attempts to climb back into
his mother's womb, scale her too-high Egyptian shoes. His mother, like yours

knew

nothing of the thunder-roll of need caught in the hollow of his throat. What
he grew in was never watered. You, my associate drumbeat, were a house
full of burning people, I, the ongoing effort to extinguish:

drowning girl in the summer of floods; your brackish jewel, otherwise human. What
choice did I have but to call for the nearest shadow and plead for rescue. Ask it to
make a miracle of me, if not a hero, so I might escape your apiary: swollen and
scrotum-shaped, swarming with killer bees. I ran but couldn't outpace the blasphemy
you'd made of me: wound affixed to no carcass. False grief shed tears

bled octaves

of salt at your funeral; arrived with spoons to shovel and get the affects of your long-term
groaning off. I boxed and put you curbside to dampen, waited until certain you'd swirled away
with the rains in a cloud of mildew: creature of air, your sojourn among the stars finally acheless.

Nothing will bring you back to skin again, or reconstitute the skeletal remains of pre-death. Your infra-red wariness was finally globed in its own oblate sphere, like a luminous film of bar soap. This memory's unauthorized
lies

boldly and cartwheels to forget which way the many ways of up go. It crests with cumulonimbi, wants to make music from light and sing its anthem. But music's not laughter, happiness not love and history's solely an inference composed of fog.

So why this haunting, these memories on the grimy side of love? Why do I repeatedly shuck my beginnings, attribute to fraud the bursts of words that exit my mouth like mushroom clouds? I live among landmines and balance on inflammable surfaces: a last minute exegesis, my features brusque slashes. My smile, an undisclosed parenthesis. My kitchen knives have radicalized and pianos make my mouth bleed. Father, I don't lie

nights thinking of you and the many fathers I'd wished were you, have died. I fall asleep easily, my dreams illuminated by city lights. Which city I'm in's always a puzzle. So many look-alikes in a million pieces and no piece fits.

Always, my car's been hauled away, and I'm a bad knee acting up. We won't get home tonight or maybe any night. Softer to treat my faulty heart, see it like a hand held over the top of a flashlight or lit candle. Make contact with people and belongings like sand on a rainy afternoon. Home's a paradigm for loss and loss a parallel for fear, the airless planet which dares me

to inhale.

[from a collection by the same name now circulating]
EVENINGS AT THE TABLE OF AN INTOXICANT: FEVER DREAM, PART MEMORY, PART METAPHOR, PART EXTRAPOLATION

The days are toxic, the deities rabid. Memory short-lived and love won't protect you. The world you summon has long been at your side. It hisses like a top, dismembers as it loops. Oceans rise, whales disembark. Air's hostile. Skin's fatal and the good life visits elsewhere. The ghost in scrubs, keeper of hemlock's back from other peoples' lives, the demise of the flesh, lament of its over-rhapsodizing cells trapped in the body's blind interior; the sky, the reeds, the dark and anxious movements of their wildlife forsworn.

Once you had the stars crawling up your sleeves, the moon's light caught in free-fall. Nights drew from concentrates of hyper-vigilance and fed these to the labyrinth of your flesh, adding increase wide and white to your child-mound of dread.

How nearly you slept, a little milk-engorged whelp in the frontier of its newly birthed body skin hot to the touch, cooling breezes redacted; body not back from its consortium with the sun, devoted emotional sidekick.

All's underneath in the narcoleptic sleep of the fevered. It sifts and codes, sends the dreamer where roots crunch as if feet stampeding in snow, their upright pending. Flame there is amphibious, the soul at plumb-line and the cosmos forever the walled-in hair of the life-line. It cuts them off, unpins their light to do what with? Filch shine from infinity's black coil while the stars rise with sticks to beat them off.

Oh excess, wind's in the bacchanal, its cart runs away with me. I tip to the living halo. I've downed the drunken glow of moonlight in the shallows and am heightened, ignited nostalgic, dysfunctional: tricked again into pouring out, opening loaves with my imagination: the place without a name. Sand there's the mother of fire and bears the weight of my footprints. My footprints are drops of dew: stain of the salty skeleton that wants to dance me away.

I sing to the ozone: my repertoire's a repository for decomposing regrets, too heavy now for death to carry off as dowry. My songs have hubris. They speak what they don't know. They don't know how to love, make trash out of laughter; kick the earth's four quadrants into orbit and mock your sunlit innocence.

This isn't my heart's hunger. My heart's hunger resists, flies along the edges of my lips. It asks for no bread, wants no quarrel with the seasons, only to see the sun again, not climb it.

SOME WORDS ABOUT THESE POEMS from the poet
Judith Harris*

Some difficulties deserve attention and Susan Sonde's poems always do because in her work meaning is not taken for granted as it is with poems of verisimilitude, the reader can't step on firm ground but floats above matter, hearing the free fall of the words cascading down, the alliteration within the lines taking one deeper and deeper. There are no easy answers, only more questions, more plunges in and escaping out.

Harold Bloom once said that a good poet knows what he or she is asking from the reader--is it understanding or wonder or both? Sonde's poems shudder with pain and restitution and are always eluding any pinning down. Instead they confront the reader with an hypnogenic world of relentless passion and quicksilver conceits, presenting a shifting mosaic of language whose sensuality draws one in. Sonde's words are those of a wild genius whose voice is like a river of flutes streaming through darkness, such darkness.

*Night Garden (Tiger Bark Press 2013)
The Bad Secret (LSU 2006)
Atonement (LSU 2000)
Signifying Pain: Constructing and Healing the Self Through Writing(SUNY 2000)

About the Author

Susan Sonde is an award winning poet and short story writer. Her debut collection: In the Longboats with Others won the Capricorn Book Award and was published by New Rivers Press. The Arsonist, her fifth collection was released in 2019 from Main Street Rag. Her sixth collection, Evenings at the Table of an Intoxicant was a finalist in the New Rivers New Voices 2019 contest. The Last Insomniac, a chapbook, now working its way to a full collection, was a 2019 finalist in The James Tate Award. Grants and awards include, a National Endowment Award in poetry; grants in fiction and poetry from The Maryland State Arts Council; The Gordon Barber Memorial Award from The Poetry Society of America. Her collection The Chalk Line was a finalist in The National Poetry Series. Individual poems have appeared in Barrow Street, The North American Review, The Southern Humanities Review, The Mississippi Review, American Letters and Commentary, Bomb, New Letters, Southern Poetry Review, and many others.

THE ARABIAN SEA

by Debasis Tripathy

Equation in Parenthood

Yesterday, we got married by our own choice. Today we're
doing OK as parents. I've managed to train my brain
to work in this new arrangement. You've also restrained.
We have a son, who is the "=" sign in our shaky equation,
balancing both the sides, keeping our egos in check.

Sleepless, we've refilled the feeding bottle, fitted
the baby into a fresh diaper, reluctantly dropped him
at the crèche and restlessly waited to pick him back.
We've paid the hefty admission fees into the big-school and
now when he turns into a tiger, we play the strict zookeeper.

We still do the others things, we did before he was born -
we keep silent, when we should talk and we fight
as before, sometimes even stupidly in front of him,
failing badly in our duties; repenting, yet repeating.
Thankfully, we do make up somehow and don't give up.

We watch the proof of our partnership, grow in the sunshine
and in the sunless times and in the storms that can shake
the existence of our association. We keep nurturing it,
knowing one day we'd be free from our caretaking functions;
We toil tirelessly for the moment he will turn into a man.

And one day, we will wake up with cold enlightenment
we're on our own again - the way it was always meant to be -
a solitariness that feels alien, after time has travelled.
But in the interim, we must keep changing and rearranging
the variables, keeping the equation of you with me in equipoise.

The Arabian Sea

The Arabian Sea smells sugar;
from one syrupy wave to the next,
on to the sleepy shore
where we sit side by side, free and easy,

watching the sinking sun. Today
we sip 'salt & sweet' water
from the same shell with two straws
joined in our shared history,

and we talk, passing the time,
while the Casuarina grove sways
passively to the slow winds. The sky
is saffron, as far as you can see,

with the satisfaction of sticking
together through the day
and the sapience that comes
along with it.

Sewing

In her nightie and bare feet,
she stands tiptoe, her fingers
touching my chest, thin needle,
at the tail a thinner thread
that matches my shirt, the button caught
tight between her thumb and forefinger,
using a very strategic skill
she possesses - sewing. Strategic
as the buttons do slip off,
unforeseeably at the wrong time.

She focuses hard on her job,
fire in her eyes, cold needle
goes back and forth and back
like fortune moving forward,
a sharp U-turn, again and again,
forging laboured loops of life
scoring a few strong stitches /
getting the holes sealed shut.

She ties me in one more knot
and bites the excess thread off.

Stay Aloof

Just as you start thinking your
words are making some sense
and you are improving your
expertise, people start praising.

Don't. Seriously don't let their
honeyed words fool you,
because flattery for them is a
customary performance intended
to tick the tiny boxes of social
propriety and co-existence
and it's hard to write after people
start calling you a poet.

Their inflated flattery feels like flowers
falling softly on your face
but over time as a vacuum cleaner
does, it starts sucking in
the debris of unpolished words
from your unguarded head
into their dustbags of insincerity,
only for later disposal.

So perfect your ability to turn
deaf and practice every day,
more inspired than yesterday, let
the grains of dirt sprout
into pearls of words, closed inside the oyster of
the mind.

About the Author

Debasis Tripathy does a regular desk job for his living at an IT Company in Bangalore, India. Sometimes he writes - poems and short fiction. His work has been featured or is forthcoming in Turnpike, Peacock Journal, Kitaab, Punch Magazine, FormerCactus, Muse India, and Phenomenal Literature among others. He was a finalist for the Wordweavers Contest 2019, both for Poetry and Short story.

FILE NUMBER 20

by Ken W. Simpson

Homo Sapiens

Cloven creatures
deodorised archetypes
revived as beasts
to satisfy heredity's
need for greed
stinking of sanctity
before the resurrection.

Amazing Grace

Dead sea souls
and a black
Satanic Mass
for Christians
accused
of genkocide
to propitiate
evil spirits
and beseech
forgiveness
with the sacrifice
of an infant.

The Missing Link

Sacred and profane
these hallowed balls
unfinished
but perfectly formed.

About the Author

Ken W. Simpson: An Australian poet and essayist - educated at Scotch College and Swinburne Art School - taught - began writing short stories - switched to writing free verse poetry and essays - with a poetry collection - Patterns of Perception - published by Augur Press in January 2015.

GLITTERING ROMANCE AND OPTIMISM

by Benjamin Biesek

"After I had combed / the confetti from my hair"
Ralph Sneeden

Today I wept no tears.
Today is a forest fire.
Sure I'm atavistic, avarice
Plated in a vegan fare palace.
Far off place fair in grace,
Although shadows remain the
Crosshairs is removed, vacant.
In stores they hawk, and dine,
Doves throughout Camelot.
Dresser with no hope, no
Clothes for these elements,
Fire, water, earth. Heir apparent
On the cathedra, her sacrament slim
From daily workouts, and plank
Position. Trudge to the store,
Secure the new luggage.
For to travel is to perish. To divide,
Conquer. Anoint, leather. Lace,
Filigree. Today I'm speckless,
Have bathed beneath nebulae, and
Cloudbursts. Although I doth protest
Let the spirit embody, and excite.
Thresh the scythe.
Marry the moon.

In the Belly
(I have prized long before today)

In the sense of self flooding the systematic,
In grace allowed to impoverished souls let
Them proclaim love is rice held in a nearby dish.
Let them declaim anything. Send you off
To prison or jail or to a breadbox beneath
Nebulae. Let love discover a way to flourish
In the spaces between us.
In the flaws, which mutilate, but time
Is always by my side! The sector
opens in governance.
Man breathes wide inside those flourishing,
Flowering days.
I tip my ball cap to the man
on the street interned.
Manon on the ham it's enough
to love voraciously.
It's sufficient to appeal to love only when.

About the Author

Benjamin Biesek has been published off and on since 07/08 including recently with Peeking Cat and Isacoustic*. Biesek lives in California where he occasionally leads poetry workshops. He is working on his first full length poetry manuscript.

OUTDOOR SHOWER

by Katherine Carlman

Hollow Things

Like the shell of a chocolate hare, upon the slightest pressure from an eager
child's hand causes it to give way to nothing but its own void

and trees toppled by bracing winds on forest floors lying, upon which moss and
mushrooms creep; left for dead, collapsing upon themselves one day

or sacs that form within the womb with no pindot heartbeat appearing, despite
the technician's increased pressure on the ultrasound wand.

Empty words that from your living lips tumble forth in these same categories belong – blank,
hollow things; devoid of life.

Outdoor Shower

scorching sand, salty sea, skin slick with sunscreen slather;
crisping flesh from ten until four, flipping from front to back and
front as often as every thirty minutes, to ensure even tone
stepping to the shore sometimes, slipping into sea – swimming
sun and rest, we laze all day until hunger strikes; then
gather things, trudge off beach - sand cooler as sun slips, sliding to horizon
at rented cottage clanking and banging, chatter of dinner prep
along the north side of the cottage, a long, wide shadow,
grass (lush and cool) beneath feet pummeled by waves and grit;
skin, battered by wind; taut and stressed from saline dried; a tightness
hose rigged up, snaking from extruding spigot over blue painted boards
elderly cake of soap sits ready; suds now lathering, foaming, washing
renewing water fresh and cool; stream rinses salt and sea from skin
everything clean; clear chill of dark evening air on wet hair

Campton

His voice gets me. And the odor of him. Most
peculiarly, though, a portion of his forearm pierces
something internal; without warning, I'm sent reeling.

This section of his flesh (from just above the
wrist to a few inches shy of his elbow) is covered
with the thick, dark nearly-fur of an Iberian male.

The skin beneath it, where one can peek through,
is tanned a deep brown. This is his own arm. I know this.
When I steal a glance up, beyond the shoulder

appended to the torso of the man, at the top of my
gaze, I see the face of my uncle. I know him. And yet,
when my eyes lower to his arm again, when I hear

the rich baritone of his voice, when I breathe
in the motes of genetic material he off-gasses;
it is not he next to me, but my grandfather.

I sleep little that night. A portion of my
past, long dead and buried, is revivified by
his words and scent; his strong, brown forearm.

The memory of a fragrance, the haunting sounds of
singing from the kitchen, of laughter and talking
that lulled me to sleep on many summer nights,

flood my brain; unleashed by the knifing. They
keep me wakeful, with a longing for times and people
long gone. The ache, palpable and unrelenting,

finally drives me, in too early pre-dawn, to seek
the day, to distance myself from the darkness and
grief of loss called forth by our interaction,

as when a child stirs a still puddle with a stick, and
swirls of grit mesmerize as they waft to the surface.
My uncle rises early, too. He asks how I slept.

Tears tell the story instead of words. My mother, *my mother*
is gone, and so much of youth; Grandma and Grandpa,
Paul and Jim, Wally, and Aunt Sonia and Ethel and ...

an entire season of life has passed away; my children
know nothing of it; they know not those days or people. My
present loves know not my past loves. How can this be?

I share (because I can trust him) the detail
about his arm. I touch it to show him. Strength
is there. And lineage. And everything, in a way.

He suppresses a smile. He shares this: he never knew
how much of his father he was, until a college buddy
showed him...and how that's a load to carry.

We sit in silence then; my tears dry. Others shuffle
awake. Our silence interrupted, we are asked how things
are. My uncle rises quickly, claiming all is fine.

About the Author

Katherine Carlman lives in California with her family and spends an inordinate amount of time commuting on the PCH. Her poetry has been published by Red Eft Review, Adelaide Literary Review, Wilderness House, and Inciting Sparks, among other publications. Her play, The Sixth Station, is published by Samuel French.

WHAT WILL BE

by Daniel Senser

For Tom

The old man snores like the wind
And the rumbling of rock-fall.
What dream seduced him
Into the deep chamber
Where the dark rose of oblivion
Grows? All his life, he has sought
The key to the great legend
Of his fate. Now, like Don Quixote,
He does battle with the windmill
Of his secret fears. He is winning.
His deep, gravelly breaths
Carry him beyond the reach
Of the outstretched hand of Death.
Inhale the dark rose's fragrance, my friend.
The wine of yesteryear's feast
Still runs through your veins.
This poem awaits you when you wake,
And so will I, the interlocutor of your sleep
Who congratulates your every breath,
Translating your stillness, reconciling
My own dreams with the truth
Of these words which I write as I watch you
From my bed.

What Will Be

Nothing is more patient than silence.
Even the greatest masters
were born screaming.
A perfect silence and a perfect darkness—
That is where the truth comes from.
No one can fathom it.
We spend our money on the thrill of oblivion.
We dance to the music that our minds
Become silent. We drift through the world
Like mist through the hills on a shadowy night.
We tame our hearts to be silent when it wants
To shout. How foolish to challenge the silence!
The echo of my desire will fade.
The sweet perfume of the world will fade.
The solidity of the rocks, the flow of the sea—
All will fade. Only silence will remain.
A perfect silence and a perfect darkness.
And perhaps, a mass of what could one day be.

In Time

Our lives amount to a single breath;
Born to seek, and sometimes to find
And, indubitably, in death;
To answer the call with emboldened steps;
To learn, to grow, and forget;
The chew the prickly fruit and taste its flesh;
To bleed, as one does, in the thorn bush
That forestalls our quest;
To cry out for God, and receive the breast;
To know the truth of pain
And the balm of caress.
The answers will come—hush—in time.
The shadows of our fate will dissipate
When the stars achieve their timely design.

Silence and Darkness

One can hear the laughter of the dead
In Time's vacant breath
And feel the pull of one's soul
Towards the inevitable end.
Our shadow cannot follow us into the grave.
There, there lies a graver shadow still—
One that does not move or reflect any form,
A perfect enveloping darkness,
A womb from which nothing is born.
We must live as if torn
From this certainty, know without knowing,
Run from safety and choose to bleed,
Channel the fire into our every breath.
The grave has no room for passion or desire,
So live, cherish the ache,
Till silence and darkness is all that is left.

The Fool

Legend has it that an old fool
lives in that cave there.
He likes to watch the sand of his
hourglass trickle down
Like all the hopes and dreams of his enemies
Out here in the real world.
Some nights he plays his harmonica—
A single note to match the crickets' song.
His pet goldfish, Tuxedo, is constantly lost
In thought—he thinks for the both of them,
you see.
In the firelight, the fool
contemplates his shadow
Thinking that his soul has left his body
And demands it to come back.
He gets drunk on moonshine in the moonlight
And jumps naked into the river at dawn.
Spellbound by his wanderings, he
composes verses for the trees.
In the wind, he thinks them cheering
And because of this he is always pleased.
He smokes his hashish in a wooden pipe,
And says his wife is a naiad
more beautiful than Eve.
They make love a thousand
times a night, he says.
And we are all his children.
Methinks, in truth, he is a lonely man,
Though he would never admit it.
On full moon nights, one can hear him
From far across these rolling hills,
Weeping away the silence, or
laughing at his ills.

About the Author

Daniel Senser: I am thirty four years old and have been writing since I was eighteen. Works of mine have been published in Blue Nib, Jewish Currents, Penwood Review, and Adelaide, among other journals. My new book, "Another Missed Connection" is due for release in 2020 and is being published by Adelaide Books. I received my BA in English from University of Cincinnati, and currently live in Cambridge, Massachusetts.

DAYTIME TV

by Ian Ganassi

DAYTIME TV

I used to wonder
About Captain Kangaroo's uniform;
We knew Mr. Greenjeans had green jeans.

You never know it's a uniform
Till you try it on.

An army of one.
They pay it no mind, which doesn't matter.

And all around you the flood goes on.
Be diligent.

There's always a clock and a
disgusting commercial.

When it's on in the emergency room
There's no escape,
Just when you thought
Your condition couldn't get any worse..

Tycoon urges grandson to dump seductress.

Make a clean breast of it,
Mr. Clean.

"The humblebee is so named
because it hums as it flies."

"The genus to which the bumblebee
belongs is Bombus."

Don't get confused, Mr. Rogers,
It's still the same neighborhood.

Woman lives with abusive dad,
corresponds with convict.

A hushed atmosphere of reverent stupidity
Stood at attention before the bank vault
At the opening bell and the closing racket.

If you're in a wheelchair, for instance,
Money only goes as far as you can push it.

A quadriplegic makes an unlikely bank robber.

Farmers responsible for another
6 million tons of shit.
So much for the news.

Very nose.

And fatal pileups.

TRUE NORTH

The abstracted pedestrian was
busy nursing his sciatica
At the crosswalks, the worse for
wear. And his little dog too.

They considered him to be under the delusion
That it was all a dream.
But he went about his suffering anyway,

And business as usual.
Was he ill? With a perpetual complaint?
And in which doctor's province did it fall?

Which is to say someone beyond
all other remedies,
For whom there is no remedy.

Our province is the plain;
Oh give me a home.

On the other hand,
"Said Tweedle Dum to Tweedle Dee..."
And he was right.

I am very fond of my rattle
And of the mysterious noises
Made by the plumbing.

But Halloween is not what it used to be.
Remember those wax teeth we used to get,
That had something like Kool-Aid in them?
Pretty disgusting actually,
But they seemed like fun at the time.

And at the clothes or boundary line,
it was hard to get orientated.
She used to like standing with her arms out,
Pretending she was a compass needle.

It was cute,
But it never helped us find our way home.

RANDOM DEMOGRAPHICS

Granted it gets a little boring most
of the time. And there's
No time to waste. *Bring out your*
dead, that is. On the day of.

Didn't anybody check to be sure the
door was open before the party?
Let's do the done thing and blow
this pop stand, fast, man.

Eventually you might found
yourself an institution.
As for your visit to the reception
area, please try your call later.

The bank guard began covetous
but soon grew bored,
Like a museum attendant with
esthetic aspirations.

He somehow got where he was
going though no one knew how.
Steep stairs led the way. Which
was innately corrupt.

Once you hear the details of victory, it
is hard to distinguish from defeat.
What gets lost in the mall stays in the mall.

Just like the store—it works if you work
it. What happened to Honey Boo Boo?
Otherwise why such a big commotion?

In no need of charity or pity,
It's a crucial fact and a rough
road down which to crawl.

The man in the gabardine suit was
sorry to say goodbye to the grind.
But, on the red carpet, what's behind
all those beautiful women?

Suburbia is the ethical center
of our great country;
The party people can't be blamed for
their spontaneous combustion.

The rag-ends of our coats and other
dilapidated paraphernalia.
Don't look now, but I think it's time
to put the costumes away.

OBJECTS IN MIRROR ARE CLOSER THAN THEY APPEAR

Ray Milland hurling the candelabra at the head of the stairs.

When in hell one ought to do as the demons do.

Things black and blue, and borrowed too,
The invisible beauty queen deciding to sue.

Those who can't take it especially like to dish it out.

Therefore am I shipwrecked in the desert.

Eventually the dearly departed become a phantom limb.

If only we could determine where the end begins.
I know where it ends.

"I should say so."

We stumbled out over it, "We went too far."

Life always spills over the rim of every cup.

Two deeply neurotic people who should never have married anyone, much less each other.

You can't make Hop Along Cassidy out of King Kong.

You can't make an encyclopedia out of an encyclopedia salesman.

A struck dog yelping and turning in circles,
Ignored by passing motorists.

Sometimes one has to win the hard way, by losing.

About the Author

Ian Ganassi: My poetry, prose and translations have appeared in more than 100 literary journals. Poems have appeared recently or are forthcoming in New American Writing, The Yale Review, AMP, American Journal of Poetry, and Poetry Pacific, among others. My first poetry collection, Mean Numbers, was published in 2016. My new collection of poetry, True for the Moment, will be published in the fall of 2019 by MadHat Press. Selections from an ongoing collage collaboration with a painter can be found at www.thecorpses.com

www.ingramcontent.com/pod-product-compliance
Lightning Source LLC
LaVergne TN
LVHW080330110826
845155LV00024B/142